Sea Island Seasons

A Collection of Favorite Recipes

Published By
Beaufort County Open Land Trust

Post Office Box 75
Beaufort, South Carolina 29901
1980

2

Copyright 1980
Beaufort County Open Land Trust
Box 75
Beaufort, South Carolina 29901

Suggested retail price $15.95

First printing May 1980   10,000 books
Second printing March 1981   15,000 books
Third printing July 1983   10,000 books
Fourth printing October 1987   5,000 books
Fifth printing July 1989   10,000 books
Sixth printing August 1995   5,000 books
Seventh printing January 1998   5,000 books
Eighth printing April 2001   5,000 books

International Standard Book Number 0-9647460-1-8

Printed in the USA by

WIMMER
The Wimmer Companies
Memphis
1-800-548-2537

Sea Island Seasons Committee

EDITORS

Mrs. John M. Trask, Jr.   Mrs. Hugh O. Pearson, Jr.

COOKBOOK COMMITTEE

Mrs. Richard Bateson
Mrs. Jack Chaplin
Mrs. Morris Cooke
Mrs. Marvin H. Dukes
Mrs. William Elliott
Mrs. Charles Friedman
Mrs. John W. Gray
Mrs. Kenneth Olson
Mrs. Edward G. Herendeen
Mrs. John K. Hollins
Mrs. John S. Hopkins
Mrs. William J. Kennedy

Mrs. L. Brent Kuhnle
Mrs. Julian S. Levin
Mr. John K. Murphy
Mr. Kenneth Olson
Mrs. Catherine W. Pratt
Mrs. Richard G. Price
Mrs. Mack Sanders
Mrs. Sam Stafford, III
Mrs. John P. Staggs
Mrs. Neil W. Trask, Jr.
Nancy Ricker Rhett
Voluntary Action Center

Cover Design and Illustrations

by
Nancy Ricker Rhett

HONEYSUCKLE

Greetings from the author of *A Sea Island Lady* . . .

This cookbook, *Sea Island Seasons*, will surely be welcomed by everyone who appreciates the important part good eating plays in the art of good living. How fitting that it is originating in Beaufort, with all its natural resources and skills for the creating of great dishes.

What a splendid gift the book will make for serious cooks in every region of the world. And with it goes the added incentive of knowing that in giving it you will be benefiting not only the recipient, but also the environs and vistas of old Beaufort, by helping to support the Beaufort County Open Land Trust.

That whole magic seacoast is a priceless inheritance. A return to Beaufort is a fond dream always, and now more than ever, as a reminder of many things, including the enduring truth of our responsibility to preserve and further the best of our heritage.

I send my best to our beloved Beaufort, with its vistas safely preserved, thanks to the Open Land Trust, so we can all continue to see what lies beyond them, a view to the farthest reaches of the universe, on a fine sea-island day.

Francis Griswold

Francis Griswold

TABLE OF CONTENTS

MAGNOLIA

Because historic Beaufort is an agricultural and coastal community, our culinary talents are particularly attuned to and directed by Mother Nature. Each season reflects a distinct mood of its own.

Autumn is a time of brilliant sunsets and pyracantha. Along with the first chill in the air there is an aroma of pickling and candied apples. The big pleasure boats pass by, going south again. It is time for lunch-box cookies and nourishing soups. Drumfish and trout are biting, and the creeks abound with crab. Roses are deepening their hues, and a subtle bloom develops on the marsh grass.

As Beaufort's winter deepens, the hunting season enters into full swing, and we feast on dove, venison, quail, and duck. Wild rice or grits usually accompany the game. Oyster roasts are a popular form of entertaining. Camellias and narcissi burst into bloom and herald the beginning of the holiday season. Then come smilax and fresh pine, cookies, fruit cake and country hams. Homes are permeated with the low-country tastes and fragrances of Christmas.

Spring arrives early and the air becomes sweet with yellow jessamine. These are days for walking through the woods and discovering masses of brilliant wisteria cascading down the trunks of pines. Purple finches and pine warblers dart among the azaleas, dogwood, yellow daffodils and redbud. Magnolias bask in their glory as each grandiflora triumphantly opens its blooms. Now the farmers are harvesting string beans and squash. Shad are biting, and Yemassee caviar once again is available. St. Helena's Episcopal Church and the Historic Beaufort Foundation present their tours of old homes and plantations. The Beaufort County Open Land Trust entertains visiting groups with delightful luncheons. The second Sunday after Easter a magnificent service is held at Old Sheldon Church where, among ancient tabby ruins and enormous towering oaks, we worship and picnic together.

Summer is tomato season. It's okra, sweet corn, cucumber and shrimp-pie time. Honeysuckle fills the air and blackberries and wild plums abound. The hand-turned freezer on the porch is filled with rich peach ice cream. Figs are ripe. Zinnias, oleanders and crepe myrtle defy the long, hot days with their determined blooms. Palmetto and yucca trees are bathed in sunshine. The river becomes the center of activity with waterskiing, sailing and swimming. The living is easy.

Beaufort is an ideal place to live or visit any time of the year. The new waterfront park and the continuing restoration of old houses are evidence of the town's pride in its past and faith in its future. But it is the ever-present friendliness and graciousness of the inhabitants of these sea islands which make Beaufort so very special—no matter what the season.

Priscilla Jones Dukes

Open Land Trust Luncheon

When prearranged for visiting tour groups, a delectable luncheon is served by the Open Land Trust in a member's gracious home and with lovely table settings of china, silver and flowers provided by other members—truly the epitome of Southern hospitality.

Tomato Juice   Sherry
Hot Chicken Salad*
Congealed Cranberry Salad*
Carolina Trifle*   Coffee or Iced Tea

Summer Luncheon

Hot days do come, but with cooling drinks, appropriate fare to accompany them, and talk of vacations past and future, they slip by almost unnoticed.

Sangria*
Iced Curry Soup with Apricot Cream*
Poached Fish with Hollandaise Sauce*
Tomato Aspic*   Doris's Biscuits*
Lemon Sponge Cake*   Iced Tea with Mint

Twilight Hours on the River

"Boating, simply boating" . . . nothing is grander in Beaufort than watching the sunset on a boat of any kind . . . being very still while the sky dominates the earth.

Peach Daiquiri   Herbed Cheese*

Tzatsiki (Cold Yogurt and Cucumber Soup)*

Crab Salad in Tomatoes*

Fresh Kosher Dill Pickle*   Deviled Eggs

Lemon Bread*   Fudge Brownie Delight*

Picnic on the Beach

Bring a lawn chair or blanket. We'll build a fire and watch the tide come in.

Nivernais Soup*   Sliced Marinated Beef*

Oatmeal Bread*

Mayonnaise*   Mustard Sauce*

Cold Curried Rice*

Raw Carrots, Celery and Cucumbers

Bread and Butter Pickle*

S'mores   Bessie Bell's Cookies*   Lemonade

Spring Formal Dinner Party

As nature reawakens, so does our desire to share this most delightful of seasons.

It's the perfect time to invite our fondest and dearest—to the year's perfect dinner party.

Escargot*

Vichyssoise*

Lamb en Crouté*

Baked Cherry Tomatoes*

Lemon Zucchini*

Parsleyed Potatoes

Cold Orange Soufflé*

Coffee

Tea

Tea time is talk time, and a time to take the edge off healthy appetites with any number of tempting delicacies.

Russian Tea*   Coffee

Shrimp Paste Sandwiches*

Cheese-Olive Sandwiches*

Coconut Pound Cake*

Cheese Hot Bits*

Three Layer Cookies*   Date Pastry*

Oyster Roast

Wrapped in warm jackets, we stand around an open fire. The steaming oysters are piled on long tables.

Oysters   Boiled Shrimp

Hot Butter   Cocktail Sauce

Saltines

Brunswick Stew*

German Slaw*   Brownies*   Coffee

Thanksgiving

Whether it's over the meadow and through the woods or to the condominium, we go to be with those we love and to count our blessings.

Paté*

Apple Soup*

Sautéed Doves in Wine with White Grapes*

Wild Rice*

Stuffed Yellow Squash*

Scalloped Oysters*

Beaten Biscuits*

Date Pudding*   Cranberry Sherbet*

Coffee

Nancy Ricker Rhett

Christmas Eve

The "can't stop smiling time" is upon us. Warmth and magic fill even the darkest corners. The church bells proudly announce "it is the night of our dear Saviour's birth."

Liptauer Cheese*

Country Ham*

Crab Meat Maison*

Baked Fruit Casserole*

Laurie's Yeast Rolls*

Garden Salad*   Trifle*   Coffee

Supper by the Fire

In Beaufort we wait long for cold winter nights, and when they arrive it is all the more fun to gather close to a blazing fire with good food and good friends.

Hot Spiced Wine*

French Oignon Soup*

Ham Biscuits   Spinach Salad*   Pecan Pie*

YELLOW JESSAMINE

Beverages

MOTHER'S EGG NOG

3 dozen eggs, separated
2½ cups sugar, divided
1 quart brandy

1 pint rum
1 quart thin cream

Cream egg yolks with 1½ cups sugar. Add brandy, rum and cream. Fold in egg whites beaten stiff with 1 cup sugar. Makes 28 5-ounce servings.

Mrs. Francis P. Jenkins (Virginia)

HOLIDAY EGGNOG

6 eggs, separated
½ cup white sugar
½ cup brown sugar
1 cup bourbon
1 cup brandy

2 cups light rum
1 pint whipping cream
1 quart half and half
1 quart milk

Beat egg yolks with sugar until well blended. Slowly add bourbon to yolks while continuing to beat. Add remaining liquor and mix well. Wash and dry beaters. Beat egg whites until stiff. Then beat whipping cream until stiff. Mix, alternating liquor with other ingredients. Chill until *VERY* cold. Stir before serving. Makes 3½ quarts.

Dale Hryharrow Friedman

EGG NOG

6 eggs, separated
½ cup sugar
1 pint whipping cream

4 jiggers bourbon
1 quart vanilla ice cream (optional)

Beat yolks. Add ¼ cup sugar and beat. Add bourbon slowly while beating. Stir this mixture occasionally while egg whites are being beaten. Beat whites stiff, add ¼ cup sugar and beat. Whip cream until fluffy. Combine egg yolk mixture, egg whites and whipped cream. Scoop 1 quart vanilla ice cream into serving bowl and pour above mixture over ice cream. Ice cream helps keep nog cold. Yields 16 cups.

Mrs. Doadie Johnson

COFFEE PUNCH

2 quarts coffee, sweetened
1 half-gallon vanilla ice cream
1 half-gallon vanilla ice milk

3 28-ounce bottles ginger ale
Small chunk of ice

Have all ingredients cold. Mix together the coffee, ice cream and ice milk. Add the ginger ale. Place ice in punch bowl and pour punch over it. Serves approximately 30 people.

Mrs. Brantley Harvey, Jr. (Helen)

FISH HOUSE PUNCH

1 quart lemon juice, strained
    through cheese cloth
2 cups granulated sugar,
    dissolved in just enough
    water to make syrup

6 ounces peach brandy
1 quart rum
2 quarts Cognac
1 50-pound block of ice

Mix ingredients in order listed. Add ice. Cover with a cloth and allow to blend for 6 or 7 hours. Do not add additional water as water from melting ice will dilute. Makes 80 5-ounce glasses of punch.

Mrs. Edward Herendeen (Marguerite)

FROZEN PUNCH

½ cup loose tea
12 cups water, divided
5 cups sugar
2 12-ounce cans frozen orange
    juice, thawed

2 12-ounce cans frozen lemonade,
    thawed
2 12-ounce cans frozen pineapple
    juice, thawed
1 quart ginger ale

Brew tea in 6 cups water. Add 5 cups of sugar and 6 cups of warm water. Dilute juices according to instructions on can. Mix juices and tea thoroughly. Place in appropriate containers for freezing. Freeze until mushy then stir every 20 minutes. Do this several times. This can be frozen for an indefinite time. When ready to serve, add 1 quart ginger ale to 1 quart punch. Serves 50 punch cups.

Mrs. D. J. Burch, Jr. (Virginia)

MARTHA'S VINEYARD PUNCH

1 6-ounce can frozen orange
    juice
1 6-ounce can frozen lemonade

1 6-ounce can limeade
4 cups very cold water
1 28-ounce bottle ginger ale

Mix orange juice, lemonade, limeade and water. Put in punch bowl with ice. Add ginger ale. Yields 14 6-ounce servings.

Mrs. Edward Herendeen (Marguerite)

SPRING PUNCH

2 1-pint 2-ounce cans
    unsweetened pineapple
    juice, chilled
1 6-ounce can frozen lemon
    concentrate, chilled, not
    frozen

1 12-ounce can frozen orange juice
    concentrate, chilled, not frozen
3 cups brandy
Ice cubes or ice mold
1 quart club soda, or preferably dry
    champagne

Mix and serve very cold. Makes 24 5-ounce servings.

Mrs. Sam Stafford III (Nancy)

SUMMERTIME SLUSH

4 cups sugar
8 cups water
2 bananas, peeled
2 oranges, peeled and
    sectioned

1 cup lemon juice
1 48-ounce can unsweetened
    grapefruit juice
1 26-ounce bottle gin
Tonic water

Mix sugar and water bringing to a rolling boil. Boil for 20 minutes. Cool thoroughly. In blender, liquefy bananas, oranges with lemon juice. Add blended fruit, grapefruit juice and gin to cooled syrup. Freeze at least 24 hours (mixture will only turn slushy since it contains alcohol). Serve by placing 2 heaping tablespoons in 6-8 ounce glass and fill with tonic water. Yields approximately 100 glasses.

Mrs. G. G. Cumming (Carol)

WHISKEY SOUR PUNCH

2 6-ounce cans frozen
   lemonade
2 24-ounce cans orange juice
2 18-ounce cans pineapple
   juice

1 fifth whiskey
2 28-ounce bottles ginger ale

Mix and serve over ice. Serves 24.

Mrs. C. A. Larsen, Jr. (Eleanor)

HOT SPICED WINE

1 quart dry red wine
4 cloves
1 lemon peel, julienned

½ cup to ⅔ cup sugar
½ stick cinnamon
1 tablespoon lemon juice

In a heavy pot combine all ingredients. Let mixture boil for 1 minute. Reduce heat and serve warm. Yields eight 4-ounce servings.

Mrs. George G. Trask (Connie)

THIRD & ELM PRESS WASSAIL
Great on a cold winter's evening.

Juice of 2 lemons
4 cups frozen orange juice
3 cinnamon sticks
2 tablespoons cloves, whole
2 tablespoons ground allspice
1 tablespoon nutmeg, grated

1 cup sugar
2 quarts apple cider
3 cups rum
Apple rings and halved cherries for
   garnish

Mix and bring to a boil the first 7 ingredients. Simmer for 10 minutes, then strain. Meanwhile bring cider to a boil. Add strained ingredients and rum. Serve hot in a punch bowl with garnishes. Makes 36 5-ounce servings.

Mrs. Sam Stafford III (Nancy)

ORANGE WASSAIL

1 cup sugar	3 quarts orange juice
1 cup water	1 quart cranberry juice cocktail
12 cloves, whole	3 oranges
2 2-inch pieces stick cinnamon	

Combine sugar, water and spices in saucepan. Simmer 10 minutes. Remove cloves and cinnamon. Add orange juice and cranberry juice cocktail. Heat. Pour into heatproof punch bowl. Float baked oranges on punch. To prepare baked oranges, stud 3 oranges with cloves. Place in baking dish and bake at 325 degrees for 3 hours. Makes about 34 punch cup servings.

Mrs. Bruce Whitney (Mary Olive)

SANGRIA

½ cup sugar	1 orange, thinly sliced
1 cup water, cold	12 to 16 ice cubes
1 lime, thinly sliced	1 25-ounce bottle red wine

Combine sugar and water in a small pan and place over moderate heat. Stir constantly until sugar is dissolved. When syrup just reaches boiling point, remove from heat and add lime and orange slices. Allow the fruit to marinate at least 4 hours at room temperature. Place the ice cubes in a pitcher and add 6 slices of the marinated fruit and ½ cup of the syrup. Fill the pitcher with red wine. Serve. Makes 1 quart.

Mrs. J. E. McTeer, Jr. (Gail)

EMERT'S PUNCH

1 pint grain alcohol	2 quarts ginger ale
1 gallon frozen lemon-lime punch, defrosted to ice crystal stage	

Mix above in large punch bowl. Serve over ice. Approximately fifty 4-ounce servings.

Mrs. O. Stanley Smith (Connie)

BRANDY ALEXANDER

3 ounces brandy
3 ounces Créme de Cacao

Blender of vanilla ice cream (about
½ gallon)

Mix above in blender. Serves 6. Nice in summer in place of dessert.

Mrs. R. C. Harris, Jr. (Rena)

BRANDY GIMLET

2 ounces brandy
1 teaspoon sugar
1 ounce lime juice

Cracked ice
1 slice of lime

Mix first 3 ingredients. Shake well with cracked ice. Strain into chilled glass. Serve with a slice of lime.

Mrs. Sam Stafford III (Nancy)

MULLED GRAPE JUICE

1 stick cinnamon
12 cloves
1 quart grape juice
½ cup sugar

1 pint water
Juice of 2 lemons
1 lemon rind

Place spices in loosely tied muslin bag. Add grape juice, sugar and water. Slowly heat until steam rises. Stir well and let stand 10 minutes. Add juice of lemons and rind of lemon. Bring to boiling point. Remove muslin bag and lemon rind. Serve as winter beverage. Yields 8 to 10 cups.

Mrs. D. J. Burch, Jr. (Virginia)

SAVORY TOMATO JUICE

1 peck tomatoes (8 pounds)
4 large onions
1 bunch celery
2 green sweet peppers

¼ cup salt
¼ cup sugar
½ teaspoon pepper

Cut up vegetables and simmer, covered until very soft (about 45 minutes). Strain with Foley Food Mill (or use blender for thick juice) and add seasonings. Pour into sterilized jars, seal and process. Pressure cooker: 5 pounds for 10 minutes. Hot water: boil 30 minutes. Yields 6 quarts.

Sarah Lou Olson

RUSSIAN TEA

2 cups water
3 tablespoons loose tea
½ teaspoon cloves
½ teaspoon cinnamon
2 cups sugar

1 cup water
Juice of 3 oranges
Juice of 3 lemons
10 cups water

Boil 2 cups water and steep tea for 5 minutes. Strain. Mix spices, sugar and 1 cup water together and bring to a boil. Add tea water to spice mixture. Add juice of oranges and lemons and 10 cups of water. May be served hot or cold. It is better if made 24 hours before using. Makes 24 5-ounce servings.

Mrs. Joe Anthony (Betty)

RUSSIAN INSTANT TEA

2¼ cups Tang
½ cup instant tea
1½ cups sugar

1 teaspoon cinnamon
½ teaspoon cloves

Mix and store in jar with lid. To serve: 2 teaspoons to 1 cup hot water.

Mrs. Morgan Randel (Julia)

SPICED TEA

8 cups water
4 tea bags
2 cups sugar
1 cup orange juice
2 tablespoons cloves, whole

2 tablespoons allspice, whole
2 cups pineapple juice, unsweetened
2 tablespoons lemon juice

Boil water and remove from stove. Add tea bags, cover and steep 5 minutes. Remove tea bags. Add all other ingredients to tea. Place allspice and cloves in tea ball or cheese cloth bag so it can easily be removed. Let simmer for 15 minutes or more to get taste desired. Makes 16 5-ounce servings.

Mrs. Edwin Pike, Jr. (Mary Jane)

Appetizers

BEEF TENDERLOIN
Great for Cocktail Parties

Beef tenderloin
1 cup red wine

1 cup soy sauce
1 cup olive oil

Marinate beef tenderloin in wine, soy sauce, and olive oil for 2 days turning several times. Remove from marinade and cook uncovered in 500 degree oven for 40 minutes only. If using for cocktail party, allow 4 to 5 people per pound.

Mrs. Barney Rickenbacker (Florence)

CANTONESE SPARERIBS

1 rack loin back spareribs
1 inch ginger root, grated or
1 teaspoon powdered
ginger
½ cup soy sauce

½ cup sugar
½ cup catsup
2 ounces sherry
1 clove garlic, crushed

For buffet, slice between ribs. For cocktails, have butcher slice between rib, then crack across to make finger sized pieces. Place rib pieces in zip-lock bag. Blend other ingredients and pour over ribs. Marinate overnight. Place ribs in roasting pan with sauce. Bake in 325 degree oven for 1 hour. Check and if not crisp, bake 15 minutes longer. Watch because they burn easily. One rack of ribs serves six for dinner. Use 3 or 4 racks for cocktail party for 40.

Mrs. Jonathan O. Seaman (Mary)

BARBECUED MEAT BALLS

2 pounds ground chuck
2 teaspoons salt
¼ teaspoon pepper
Oil to brown meat balls
¾ cup catsup

3 tablespoons brown sugar
3 tablespoons vinegar
3 teaspoons Worcestershire sauce
3 teaspoons prepared mustard

Roll meat, salt and pepper into small bite-size balls. You should have 75-80 balls. Brown balls in oil in skillet. Place in chafing dish or other container which has been kept hot. Combine remaining ingredients and pour over the balls. Simmer very slowly until ready to serve. Keep hot while serving. This will serve 30-40 people. The same sauce can be used for small sausages.

Mrs. Louis de Geofroy (Fontaine)

COCKTAIL MEATBALLS

3 pounds ground chuck
¾ clove garlic, crushed
1½ medium onions, finely
   chopped
½ teaspoon oregano
½ teaspoon savory
½ teaspoon paprika
1 tablespoon salt
1½ cups seasoned
   breadcrumbs
1½ tablespoons prepared
   mustard

3 dashes Tabasco sauce
1 tablespoon Worcestershire sauce
Flour
6 slices bacon, cooked and cut into
   small pieces
1½ cups strong coffee
¾ cup Burgundy
1½ teaspoons salt (taste first)
1½ teaspoons sugar
2¼ tablespoons flour
½ cup cold water

Combine first 11 ingredients and form into bite size balls. Spread out and dust very lightly with flour. Turn to coat. Sauté meat balls in bacon fat until lightly browned. Add coffee, Burgundy, salt and sugar. Simmer 15 minutes. Return bacon to pan. Stir in the flour which has been mixed with cold water and cook until sauce thickens. May be refrigerated or frozen. To serve, return to room temperature and heat until hot throughout. Shallow pan in oven is best. Yields 175 meatballs.

Mrs. Hugh Pearson (Marie)

STUFFED GRAPE LEAVES
Dolmathes

1 pound extra lean ground beef
¾ cup long grain rice
1 teaspoon salt
Pepper to taste
1½ tablespoons chopped mint
1 tablespoon chopped parsley
1 small onion, finely chopped
2 tablespoons catsup

2 tablespoons lemon juice
2 tablespoons water
1 1-pound jar grape leaves
2 tablespoons butter
3 tablespoons lemon juice
1 10¾ ounce can chicken broth
5½ ounces water

Mix together beef, rice, salt, pepper, mint, parsley, onion, catsup, 2 table-spoons lemon juice and 2 tablespoons water. Rinse and drain grape leaves. Trim excess stems of grape leaves. Place 1 teaspoon of beef mixture at stem of leaf, vein side up. Fold sides into center and roll up carefully towards tip. In dutch oven, cover bottom with unfilled grape leaves, and then place dolmathes, stuffed grape leaves, snugly together in layers. Make sure the seam side is turned down. Weight dolmathes with heavy flat plate. Mix butter, 3 tablespoons lemon juice, chicken broth, and 5½ ounces of water. Heat until butter melts and pour over dolmathes, making sure plate is barely covered. Add more water if necessary to cover plate. Simmer 45-60 minutes or until rice is tender. Add more water during cooking if necessary. Remove dolmathes to heated platter. Reserve cooking liquid for egg-lemon sauce. Serve with yogurt or egg-lemon sauce. Yields 35-40 dolmathes.

EGG-LEMON SAUCE:

3 eggs
1 tablespoon cornstarch
¼ cup water

Juice of 1 lemon
Hot dolmathes broth

Blend eggs, cornstarch and water in blender. Add lemon juice. *Slowly* pour 1 cup broth into mixture keeping blender running on stir cycle. Next pour a second cup of broth slowly into blender. Then pour blender mixture into remaining dolmathes' broth and return to heat *stirring constantly* until it thickens. Pour over dolmathes and serve.

Mrs. Stratton Demosthenes (Chris)

ESCARGOTS Á L'AIL

2 dozen snails
2 dozen snail shells
2 cups butter, softened
6 cloves garlic, chopped

½ cup parsley, chopped
½ tablespoon salt
½ tablespoon ground black pepper

Put 1 snail in each shell. Mix well butter, garlic and parsley. Add salt and pepper. Put 1 teaspoon of this mixture in each snail shell. Divide snails between 4 snail platters. Put in 450 degree oven and bake about 8 minutes or until bubbly. Serve with French crusty bread and red wine. Serves 4.

Mrs. Merle F. Ormond (Monique)

GRENOUILLES (FROG'S LEGS PARISIENNE)
Lovely cocktail funfood.

4 dozen frog's legs, canned or
    frozen
½ cup flour

1 cup butter, melted
6 cloves garlic, chopped
1 cup parsley, chopped

Defrost, wipe and pat dry all frog's legs. Sprinkle flour over the frog's legs. Sauté in butter with garlic until tender. Serve on hot platter. Sprinkle with parsley.

Mrs. Merle F. Ormond (Monique)

CURRIED SHERRY PATÉ

6-ounces cream cheese
1 cup Cheddar cheese, grated
½ teaspoon curry powder
½ teaspoon garlic powder
¼ teaspoon salt

4 teaspoons cocktail sherry
9-ounces chutney
½ bunch green onions, finely
    chopped (include tops)

Blend cheeses, curry powder, garlic powder, salt and sherry thoroughly. Shape into a flat topped round and place on a serving plate. Before serving, cover with chutney and onions.

Mrs. Jack A. Boulger (Lorrain)

PATÉ

3 tablespoons Cognac
2 tablespoons gelatin
1 pound calf's liver, chopped
1 pound ground pork
½ pound veal cutlet or chop,
  chopped
4 ounces bacon fat
1 large onion, chopped
1 garlic clove, crushed
Pinch of thyme
¼ teaspoon allspice

1 egg
1 tablespoon flour
1 tablespoon butter
¼ cup dry white wine
2 teaspoons salt
Pepper
½ pound sliced bacon
3 small truffles
2 bay leaves
2 cloves

Dissolve the gelatin in the Cognac. Chop liver, veal, bacon fat and onion. Mix calf's liver, ground pork, veal cutlet and bacon fat together. Add onion, garlic, thyme, allspice, egg, flour, butter, white wine, salt and pepper. Mix ingredients well and add gelatin mixture. Line a bread tin with sliced bacon. Pour one half of paté mixture into the mold. Place truffles on top. Pour in remaining paté mixture. Fold bacon on top. Place bay leaves and cloves on top of bacon. Seal the tin with aluminum foil. Bake in 350 degree oven in pan of boiling water for 1½ hours. Leave paté in oven another 30 minutes with heat turned off. Remove foil and press while cooling with another tin containing a weight of about 3 pounds. When cold, place in refrigerator with the weight on overnight. Must be made 3 days before serving and will keep in refrigerator for 2 weeks. Serve on bed of lettuce with cornichons.

Mrs. C. A. Larsen, Jr. (Eleanor)

CRAB DIP

3 cups crabmeat
3 8-ounce packages cream
  cheese
½ cup Miracle Whip
2 teaspoons powdered sugar

2 teaspoons powdered mustard
¼ cup sherry or white wine
Dash of garlic juice
Seasoning salt to taste
Onion salt to taste

Blend all ingredients. Heat in double boiler and turn into casserole dish. Bake for 20 minutes in 375 degree oven.

Mrs. John Strong (Ethel)

CRAB APPETIZER

1 pound backfin-lump
   crabmeat
2 cups mayonnaise
½ teaspoon Accent

1 tablespoon horseradish
Tabasco sauce to taste
½ cup sharp cheese, grated
½ jar capers, divided

Mix crabmeat, mayonnaise, Accent, capers, horseradish and Tabasco sauce in pie plate. Top with grated sharp cheese and capers. Bake at 350 degrees for 30 minutes. Serve with crackers or Melba toast. Can freeze for 4 to 5 days.

Mrs. Mary L. McDowell

CRAB-CHEESE ROLLS

4 tablespoons butter
½ pound Velveeta cheese
1 pound crabmeat, cut in
   pieces

2 loaves Pepperidge Farm
   thin-sliced white bread
Butter, melted

Melt in double boiler butter, cheese and crabmeat. Remove crust of bread. Roll very thin with a rolling pin. Spread with mixture. Roll up and freeze. When ready to serve, cut each roll in half and spread with melted butter. Defrost and bake at 300 degrees for 10 to 15 minutes. Makes 60 to 80 rolls.

Mrs. C. A. Larsen, Jr. (Eleanor)

CRABMEAT-SPINACH CANAPES

1 medium bunch green onions
   and tops, chopped
4 tablespoons butter
2 10-ounce packages frozen
   chopped spinach, barely
   cooked and drained
8 ounces fresh crabmeat, finely
   cut

3 ounces Parmesan cheese, grated
¼ teaspoon garlic powder
Salt and pepper to taste
Few drops Tabasco sauce
Fresh parsley, chopped (optional)

Sauté the green onion in butter until tender. Add the remaining ingredients. Combine thoroughly. Heat through and serve immediately with crackers or corn chips. Keep warm in chafing dish. This recipe may be frozen. Recipe may be doubled. Serves 12 to 15.

Mrs. Bayard Sawyer (Janet)

OYSTERS ROCKEFELLER

1 tablespoon anise seeds
1 cup water
1 10-ounce package chopped
    frozen spinach, thawed
1 bunch fresh parsley, chopped
1 bunch fresh green onions,
    chopped
10 fresh celery leaves
1 2-ounce tube of anchovy paste

4 dashes of Tabasco sauce
¼ teaspoon thyme
Salt and pepper to taste
1 cup butter, melted
1 cup bread crumbs
1 box rock salt
3 dozen oyster shell halves
¾ cup grated Parmesan cheese
3 dozen oysters

Boil anise seeds in water for 10 minutes. Strain and discard seeds. Combine spinach, parsley, celery, green onions, anchovy paste, Tabasco, thyme, salt and pepper. Put in blender with butter, anise water and bread crumbs. Fill large broiler pan with rock salt. Place oysters in half shell on top of salt. Run under broiler without sauce. When oysters curl, pour off oyster juice. Then cover each oyster with Rockefeller sauce, sprinkle Parmesan cheese over sauce and put back under broiler and broil until slightly brown. Serve on shells on plates. Serves 8 as hors d'oeuvres. Sauce freezes well.

Mrs. Joe H. Benton (Marjorie)

OYSTERS CASINO

48 oysters on half shell
Rock salt
1 cup butter
⅓ cup shallots or scallions,
    finely chopped, include
    green tops
¼ cup chives, finely chopped

⅓ cup celery, finely chopped
½ cup parsley, finely chopped
Juice of 1 lemon
48 small squares bacon, partially
    chopped
48 pimento strips

Loosen oysters in half shell. Layer rock salt in 4 pie tins. Arrange 12 oysters in each pie tin. Place in 450 degree oven until edge of oysters begin to curl. Drain water from oysters carefully and replace shells on rock salt. Cream butter, shallots or scallions, chives, celery, parsley and lemon juice. Place a little of the creamed mixture on top of oysters. Place a strip of bacon and pimento on top of each oyster. Return oysters to oven and bake until bacon is browned—5-8 minutes.

The Editors

"ANGELS ON HORSEBACK"

Oysters, drained and unwashed
Cayenne pepper, few grains
Strips of lean bacon

Small toast triangles
Lemon quarters
Parsley or chives, finely minced

Set a cake rack on a cookie sheet. Sprinkle oysters lightly with cayenne. Precook bacon until fat is rendered. While hot, cut bacon into short strips. Roll the strips of bacon around the oysters and secure them with toothpicks. Place "Angels" onto the rack in cookie sheet. Preheat broiler. Broil "Angels" 5 inches from heat until bacon is crisp. Turn and broil them on the other side. Have small triangles of toast arranged on a serving platter. Place "Angel" on each triangle. Dip edge of lemon quarter in parsley. Serve with the "Angels on Horseback." Serve hot.

Mrs. Carl Dorr (Cecile)

PICKLED OYSTERS

1 quart oysters
2 pods of red pepper, sliced
Few flakes of whole mace

Dash allspice
Salt to taste
½ cup vinegar

Cook oysters in their juice a little longer than when the edges curl. Remove oysters and add pepper pods, mace, allspice, and salt to liquid. Add vinegar. Let boil once and remove to cool. Add cooked oysters and place in crock in refrigerator. Do at least 24 hours before serving. Keeps 2-3 weeks.

Mrs. Francis P. Jenkins (Virginia)

SHRIMP PASTE

5 pounds raw shrimp
2 teaspoons salt
1 large Bermuda onion, peeled
and quartered

1 pint Miracle Whip salad dressing
Juice of 1 lemon
Salt and pepper to taste

Boil shrimp for 5 minutes in a covered pot, using just enough salted water to cover. Large shrimp may require an extra few minutes cooking time. Drain shrimp and peel. Put shrimp and onion through meat grinder, using coarse blade. Mix well with salad dressing, lemon juice, salt and pepper. May be used on crackers or made into sandwiches.

Mrs. J. E. McTeer (Lucille)

SHRIMP TOAST

½ pound raw shrimp, shelled,
deveined and minced
4 water chestnuts, minced
1 egg, lightly beaten
1 tablespoon cornstarch
1 teaspoon salt

1 teaspoon sugar
½ teaspoon white wine
6 thin slices bread
Oil for frying
Parsley for garnish

Mix shrimp and water chestnuts with egg, cornstarch, salt, sugar and wine. Trim crust from bread slices and cut each into 4 triangles. Spread each piece with about 1 teaspoon of shrimp mixture. Heat oil to 350 degrees. Lower bread into oil with shrimp side down. After 1 minute, turn over and fry for a few more seconds or until bread is golden brown. Drain on paper towel. Can be frozen and reheated in 325 degree oven for about 25 minutes. Garnish with parsley in center. Yields 24 pieces.

Mrs. Robert N. Hughs (Ria)

PICKLED SHRIMP

1 quart shrimp, shelled and
   cooked
2 cups onions, sliced
1 2¼-ounce bottle capers and
   juice
4 tablespoons fresh lemon juice
1½ teaspoons salt

Dash of Tabasco sauce
1 teaspoon sugar
1 cup oil
1 cup vinegar
¾ cup water
Bay leaves
2½ teaspoons celery seeds

Layer shrimp, onions and capers in jar. Mix all remaining ingredients and pour over shrimp mixture. Add more salt and lemon juice if needed. Marinate in refrigerator overnight before serving. Serves 12.

Mrs. Roscoe Mitchell (Virginia)

SHRIMP BALL

1 pound boiled shrimp, finely
   chopped
8 ounces cream cheese,
   softened
1 small onion, finely minced
1 clove garlic, finely minced

Dash of Worcestershire sauce
Dried parsley flakes
Fresh lemon juice to taste
Red pepper flakes and hot sauce to
   taste

Mix all ingredients except parsley flakes and roll into a ball. Press a few parsley flakes over ball. Chill at least 4 hours or until firm.

Mrs. Lorene Talbert (Shirley)

BLEU CHEESE CRISPS

¼ cup butter, softened
1 teaspoon onion, grated
¾ cup crumbled bleu cheese

½ cup Cheddar cheese, grated
¾ cup flour, sifted

Mix all ingredients well. Shape into small balls and place on ungreased baking sheet. Press with fork to form small wafers. Chill 2 hours. Bake in 450 degree preheated oven for 10 minutes or until golden brown. Makes 3 dozen 1-inch wafers.

Mrs. Arthur S. Jenkins (Frances)

CHEESE PUFFS

1 large loaf French bread
½ cup butter
1 3-ounce package cream
   cheese
¼ cup Mozzarella cheese
¼ cup sharp Cheddar cheese,
   grated

⅛ cup Swiss cheese, grated
½ teaspoon dry mustard
⅛ teaspoon cayenne pepper
Salt to taste
2 egg whites

Trim off crusts on bread and cut bread in 1-inch cubes. In saucepan combine butter and all cheeses over moderate heat until blended. Add mustard, cayenne pepper and salt. Beat egg whites until stiff and fold into cheese mixture. Spear bread and coat in cheese mixture. Freeze immediately. When ready to use, preheat oven to 400 degrees and bake on an ungreased cookie sheet for about 10 minutes. Serve hot.

Mrs. S. N. Clark, Jr. (Carolyn)

CHEESE HOT BITS

1 cup flour
2 cups New York cheese,
   grated
½ cup butter

¼ teaspoon salt
½ teaspoon cayenne pepper
1 cup pecans, chopped

Cream flour, cheese, butter, salt and cayenne pepper with hand. Add nuts and cream until they are well mixed. Roll in logs. Wrap in wax paper. Chill overnight. Slice thin and bake on ungreased pan for 10 to 15 minutes in 325 degree oven. Do not brown. Sprinkle salt on wafers when they are first taken from the oven. May be frozen.

Mrs. Gunnar Erickson (Marjorie)

CHEESE CRACKERS

20 ounces sharp cheese, grated
1 cup butter
2 cups flour

2 cups Rice Krispies
½ teaspoon Tabasco sauce
½ teaspoon Worcestershire sauce

With hands mix all ingredients well. Form small balls about the size of large olives. Place on cookie sheet and press down with a fork. Bake at 375 degrees for about 15 minutes or until brown on the bottom.

Mrs. Joab M. Dowling (Tut)

"DIFFERENT" CHEESE RING

1 pound sharp Cheddar
   cheese, grated
1 cup pecans, chopped
¾ cup mayonnaise

1 medium onion, grated
1 clove garlic, pressed
½ teaspoon Tabasco sauce
1 cup strawberry preserves

Combine all ingredients except preserves. Mix well. Chill and then mold into a ring. Chill again and when ready to serve, fill the center with strawberry preserves. Serve with crackers.

Mrs. Paul Trask (Marjorie)

BRANDY CHEESE BALLS

1 pound sharp Cheddar
   cheese, grated
½ pound Roquefort cheese,
   crumbled
1 pound cream cheese
1 onion, grated
6 tablespoons Worcestershire
   sauce

¼ cup brandy
2 teaspoons Tabasco sauce
½ teaspoon celery salt
2 dashes garlic powder (optional)
1 cup nuts, chopped
1 cup parsley, chopped

Let all cheeses reach room temperature. Put cheese, onion, Worcestershire sauce, brandy, Tabasco sauce, celery salt and garlic salt in a large bowl of mixmaster. Cream thoroughly. Chill several hours. Shape into balls, wrap, refrigerate or freeze. Before serving, roll in chopped nuts and/or parsley. These balls will become soft, so do not take out of refrigerator too long before serving. Recipe may be halved. Make another batch instead of doubling, as you will have too much to beat smoothly.

Mrs. Pete Spragins (Joyce)

HERBED CHEESE

2 tablespoons *fresh* herbs,
minced (Use whatever you
have fresh, but chives,
parsley, thyme and savory
are a good mixture.)
½ pound feta cheese

½ pound cream cheese
Heavy cream
Fresh ground black pepper
Dash of cayenne
1 large clove garlic, pressed

Blend the feta and cream cheese in a food processor or blender until creamy. Remove to serving bowl and add a little heavy cream if texture seems too thick. It will thicken slightly when chilled. Add herbs. Add peppers and garlic to taste. Chill for at least an hour. Will keep tightly covered in refrigerator for about 1 week. Serve with crackers. Serves 6-8.

Dale Hryharrow Friedman

LIPTAUER CHEESE

8 ounces cottage cheese
4 ounces Cheddar cheese,
grated
4 tablespoons butter
2 tablespoons chives, chopped
1 tablespoon beer

1 tablespoon onion, finely chopped
1 teaspoon Dijon mustard
1 teaspoon Hungarian sweet
paprika
2 ounces anchovy filets, mashed
Salt to taste

In a bowl combine cottage cheese, Cheddar cheese, butter and blend well. Add chives, beer, onion, mustard, paprika, anchovy filets and salt. When all is mixed thoroughly, pack cheese into small crock and refrigerate. Serve at room temperature with dark bread. Keeps for about 2 weeks. Yields 2¼ cups.

Mrs. George G. Trask (Connie)

MOCK BOURSIN

2 tablespoons butter, softened
1 or 2 cloves garlic, minced
8 ounces whipped cream
cheese

1 tablespoon chives, chopped
2 teaspoons dill weed, chopped
1 teaspoon parsley, chopped
Salt and pepper to taste

Mix butter and garlic. Add all remaining ingredients. Serve on crackers. May be frozen.

Mrs. Royal Luther (Helen)

FRITTATA

¼ cup frozen chopped spinach, thawed and well drained
½ cup feta cheese, crumbled
2 cups large curd cottage cheese
½ cup Parmesan cheese, grated

6 eggs, beaten
½ teaspoon salt
5 tablespoons bread crumbs
Parmesan cheese
Bread crumbs

Mix spinach, feta cheese, cottage cheese, Parmesan cheese, eggs, salt and bread crumbs. Grease 8-inch square pan and sprinkle bottom of pan with small amount of Parmesan cheese and bread crumbs. Spread cheese, egg-spinach mixture over crumb and cheese lined pan. Sprinkle top generously with Parmesan cheese and bread crumbs. Bake at 450 degrees for 15 minutes. Reduce heat to 400 degrees and bake for 15 minutes. Cool and cut into squares. Freezes nicely.

Mrs. Marshall B. Garth (Martha)

BACON AND CHEESE CANAPÉS

1 pound lean bacon
8 ounces sharp Cheddar cheese

1 cup mayonnaise
1 party loaf rye or pumpernickel

Fry bacon very crisp and break into small pieces. Shred cheese and combine with bacon. Add mayonnaise. Put in refrigerator until an hour before the party. Spread mixture on bread slices and return to refrigerator. When ready to serve, put into 350 degree oven for about 10 minutes or until cheese melts.

Mrs. Donald Shepard (Kiki)

CHEESE-OLIVE SANDWICH SPREAD

1 3-ounce package cream cheese, softened
¼ cup crumbled bleu cheese, at room temperature

2 tablespoons mayonnaise
¾ cup ripe olives, coarsely chopped
¼ cup celery, minced

Combine cream cheese, bleu cheese and mayonnaise in a medium bowl; mix until smooth. Stir in olives and celery. Yields about 1 cup.

Mrs. John Hardy (Sue)

SWISS SANDWICH PUFFS

½ cup mayonnaise
¼ cup chopped onion
2 tablespoons parsley, snipped

1 loaf tiny rye slices, 32 slices
8 slices Swiss cheese

Combine mayonnaise, onion and parsley. Spread on rye slices. Top each with ¼ slice cheese. Broil 2 to 3 minutes.

Mrs. Edward N. Sutton (Jean)

MONTE CARLO SANDWICH

1 egg
2 tablespoons milk
2 slices white bread
1 tablespoon butter

1 slice chicken or turkey breast
1 slice baked ham
1 slice brick or Swiss cheese

Mix egg and milk. Butter both sides of bread. Put chicken, ham and cheese slices between bread slices. Toothpick if necessary. Dip sandwich in egg and milk mixture. Cook sandwich in greased frying pan until golden brown. Serves 1.

Mrs. Joel Patrick (Mary)

INDIVIDUAL PIZZAS

1 pound hot bulk sausage
1 teaspoon sage
1 teaspoon salt
3 tablespoons onion, chopped
1 tablespoon oregano
1 8-ounce can tomato sauce

1 6-ounce can tomato paste
1½ cups sharp cheese, grated
½ cup Parmesan cheese
2 10-ounce cans biscuits
Additional grated cheese, as
   needed

Fry sausage and drain off fat. Take up excess with paper towels. Mix sage, salt, onion, oregano, sausage, tomato sauce, tomato paste, sharp cheese and Parmesan cheese together in bowl. Separate each biscuit into thirds. Roll into rounds. Place on lightly greased cookie sheet. Place heaping teaspoon of mixture on each round. Sprinkle with additional cheese. Bake at 400 degrees for 10 minutes or until hot and bubbly. Serve hot. Can be frozen before baking. Place entire cookie sheet in the freezer. When pizzas are frozen, remove and store in plastic bag in the freezer until needed. Increase baking time a few minutes. Yields 60.

Ms. Jane D. Fender

MUSHROOM FILLING FOR TARTS

1 pound mushrooms, thinly
   sliced
1 tablespoon shallots or spring
   onions, finely chopped
1 teaspoon salt

9 tablespoons butter
6 tablespoons flour
1 cup milk
1 cup cream
6 tablespoons dry sherry

Sauté mushrooms and shallots or spring onions in 3 tablespoons butter in covered pan for 15 minutes. Stir occasionally to prevent sticking. Add salt. If there is still juice left at the end of 15 minutes, remove cover and let moisture cook out. Melt 6 tablespoons butter and add the flour. Bring milk and cream to the boiling point and add quickly to the butter mixture beating with a whisk to prevent lumping. Bring to boiling point and cook for 1-2 minutes. Add mushrooms. Add sherry and reheat but do not cook after adding sherry. This may be done the day ahead and reheated in a double boiler before spooning into the tart shells. Place a spoonful into each tart shell. Heat in 400 degree oven until hot. Watch oven carefully as they burn easily.

PASTRY FOR TARTS:
1½ cups unsifted flour
1 cup butter

½ cup sour cream

Place flour in bowl and cut chilled butter in with a pastry cutter until mixture resembles cornmeal. Stir in sour cream. Mix until dough holds together, wrap in wax paper, and leave in refrigerator overnight. Roll dough very thin and cut with a 2½ inch biscuit cutter. Place in 1½ inch tart pans. Prick dough. Bake in 450 degree oven until done—about 8-10 minutes. These may be frozen until ready to use.

Mrs. John C. Bull (Coralee)

HOT MUSHROOM TURNOVERS

9 ounces cream cheese	1½ cups flour
½ cup butter	

Allow cream cheese and butter to get to room temperature. Mix cream cheese and butter. Add flour and work until smooth. Chill at least 30 minutes.

3 tablespoons butter	½ teaspoon salt
1 large onion, chopped	2 tablespoons flour
½ pound mushrooms, chopped	¼ cup sour cream
¼ teaspoon thyme	Pepper to taste

Melt butter. Add onion and lightly brown. Add mushrooms and cook for 3 minutes. Add thyme and salt and sprinkle with flour. Stir in sour cream and pepper to taste. Roll out pastry and cut in circles. Place 1 teaspoon of filling on each circle. Fold over and seal edges with fork. Prick crust. Freezes well. Bake 15 to 20 minutes in 450 degree oven. Yields 2 dozen.

Mrs. William G. Clark III (Gray)

ARTICHOKE-MUSHROOM SPREAD

½ cup butter	8 ounces Parmesan cheese, grated
3 tablespoons flour	2 tablespoons butter
1 cup light cream	1 quart fresh mushrooms, chopped
Tabasco to taste	2 8-ounce cans artichoke hearts,
Worcestershire sauce to taste	drained and chopped
Salt and pepper to taste	

Make a cream sauce of the first 3 ingredients. Season with Tabasco, Worcestershire sauce, salt and pepper. Add cheese and stir until it melts. This seems thick but after adding mushrooms and artichokes it is thinner. Combine with remaining ingredients and serve with crackers as a spread or with patty shells from chafing dish. Should be made several hours before serving to allow flavors to meld. Serves 20.

Mrs. B. L. Credle (Shirley)

ARTICHOKE HEARTS

4 tablespoons butter
2 ounces bleu cheese

2 14-ounce cans artichoke hearts,
well drained

Melt butter and cheese together over low heat. Cut artichokes into bite size pieces. Add to cheese mixture. Serve in chafing dish. Serves 12.

Mrs. Richard Stearns (Dorothy)

HOT CHIPPED BEEF APPETIZER

1 3-ounce package cream
   cheese
1 8-ounce carton sour cream
1 4-ounce package chipped
   beef
¼ cup green peppers, finely
   chopped

1 tablespoon onion, finely chopped
¼ teaspoon garlic powder
½ cup pecans, chopped
1 tablespoon butter
Crackers

Blend together cream cheese and sour cream until smooth. Cut or tear chipped beef into small pieces and add to creamed mixture. Add green peppers, onion, and garlic powder. Mix thoroughly and spread mixture in a lightly buttered 9-inch pie plate. Brown pecans in butter for 3 minutes and sprinkle on top. Heat appetizer in 300 degree oven for 15-20 minutes until bubbly. Serve hot spread on crackers.

Mrs. Nick Nichols (Laura)

EGG ROLLS

½ pound beef or pork, ground
1 teaspoon ground ginger
1 teaspoon salt
3 teaspoons onion, chopped
2 teaspoons wine or Saki

2 teaspoons soy sauce
2 teaspoons cornstarch
Oil for frying
8 egg roll skins

Mix all ingredients together except skins. Separate into 8 portions equally and roll into skins. Fold tightly, wet and seal. Fry in hot oil until brown. Serve with hot sweet sauce and hot mustard sauce.

Mrs. MacDonald Dixon (Phyllis)

CAUCASIAN CAVIAR

1 large eggplant
1 large onion, finely chopped
1 green pepper, finely chopped
¼ cup plus 2 tablespoons
  cooking oil

1 6-ounce can tomato paste
1 clove garlic, finely chopped
Salt and pepper

Bake eggplant, skin and mash. Sauté onions and green pepper until soft in ¼ cup oil. Add tomato paste and 2 tablespoons oil. Simmer 5 minutes. Add eggplant, garlic, salt and pepper to taste. Simmer 30 minutes. Remove from heat, cool, then chill. Serve with crackers. Makes about 2 cups. Freezes well.

Mrs. Albert Ahrenholz (Roma)

CHILI CON QUECÉ

2 medium onions, finely
  chopped
1 or 2 cloves of garlic, sliced
¼ cup butter, melted
2 tablespoons flour

1 28-ounce can tomatoes, drained
1 4-ounce can green chilies,
  chopped
2 pound box of Velveeta cheese,
  grated

In a Dutch oven fry onion and garlic in butter. Remove garlic. Add flour, tomatoes, chilies and cheese. Stir until cheese is melted. Serve warm with dip size corn chips.

Mrs. Lowell Keene (Linda)

JALAPEÑO COCKTAIL PIE

1 pie shell, unbaked
4 ounces sharp Cheddar
  cheese, grated
3 or 4 jalapeño peppers

3 ounces Mozzarella cheese
3 ounces sharp Cheddar cheese,
  grated
1 egg, beaten

Cover pie shell with Cheddar cheese. Mince jalapeño peppers and spread on next layer. Cover with Mozzarella and 3 ounces Cheddar cheese. On top of this drip on egg with fingers. Bake at 350 degrees for about 30 minutes. Let set for 10 minutes before cutting. Makes 16 slices.

Mrs. George Tucker (Martha)

MEXICAN BEAN DIP

1 pound country sausage (mild,
    regular, or hot flavor
    according to taste)
½ teaspoon garlic powder
1 medium onion, chopped

1 16-ounce can refried beans or
    pinto beans
8 ounces Cheddar cheese, grated
1 4-ounce can jalapeño slices
    (recipe does not require entire
    can)

Brown sausage, garlic and onion in skillet or until sausage is crumbly. Drain fat. Add beans. Mix ingredients well. Reheat. Place mixture in casserole dish. Sprinkle with Cheddar cheese. Arrange 5 or 6 jalapeño slices over top. Jalapeño slices are very hot and the amount will vary to taste. Place in oven. Broil until cheese is browned or about 2 to 3 minutes. Serve with tortilla chips.

Mrs. Neil Trask III (Donna)

HERB CURRY DIP

1 cup mayonnaise
½ cup sour cream
1 teaspoon finé herbes, crushed
¼ teaspoon salt
⅛ teaspoon curry powder
1 tablespoon parsley, finely
    chopped

1 tablespoon onion, grated
1½ teaspoons lemon juice
½ teaspoon Worcestershire sauce
2 teaspoons capers, drained

Mix mayonnaise, sour cream, herbs, salt, curry powder, parsley, onion, lemon juice, Worcestershire sauce and capers. Refrigerate at least 4 hours. Makes 1½ cups. Serve as dip with raw vegetables.

Mrs. Hugh Pearson (Marie)

AVOCADO DIP FOR RAW VEGETABLES

½ clove of garlic,
    pressed
1 large avocado
¼ teaspoon salt
¼ teaspoon Tabasco sauce

1 teaspoon lemon juice
2 teaspoons onion, minced
¼ cup homemade mayonnaise,
    made with lemon juice

Combine garlic with avocado. Mash until smooth. Add salt, Tabasco sauce, lemon juice and onion, Mix well and put in bowl. Cover with thin layer of mayonnaise sealing sides. Just before serving mix mayonnaise with dip. To keep leftovers, seal again with more of the mayonnaise. Store for at least 4 hours before serving. May be kept overnight. Yields about ¾ cup.

The Editors

COREOPSIS

Soups

MRS. RHODES' ICED CURRY SOUP WITH APRICOT CREAM

2 medium onions, chopped
3 celery ribs, chopped
½ cup butter
2 tablespoons flour
1 tablespoon imported curry
    powder

2 apples, peeled, cored and
    chopped
2 quarts chicken stock
1 bay leaf

APRICOT CREAM:
1 cup port
½ cup apricot purée
2 teaspoons curry powder

½ cup heavy cream, slightly
    whipped

Sauté vegetables in butter until soft. Add flour and curry powder. Stir well and cook for several minutes. Transfer the mixture to blender or food processor bowl. Add apples and 1 cup of the stock. Blend until smooth. Combine puréed mixture with remaining stock in a 3-quart saucepan. Heat until well blended. Add bay leaf and chill. Reduce port by half. Add apricot purée, curry powder and cook over gentle heat for 5 minutes. Cool and stir and cook over gentle heat for 5 minutes. Cool and stir in cream. Stir in apricot cream when serving or pass separately. The apricot cream makes a lovely sauce for cold meats. Serves 8.

Mrs. Sam Stafford, III (Nancy)

CREAM OF CURRY SOUP

1 quart chicken broth
2 tablespoons curry powder
4 egg yolks

1 cup heavy cream
Salt and pepper

Bring chicken broth and curry powder to a slow boil and cook 10 minutes. Mix the egg yolks with cream, salt and pepper and add to the boiling chicken broth, stirring all together until the boiling point is reached. Cool. Set in refrigerator. Serve throughly chilled in cups. Serves 8.

Mrs. Jack Snow (Gulia)

POTAGE SENAGLESE

1 small onion, chopped
1 small apple, chopped
3 cups clear chicken broth
1 10½-ounce can green pea
    soup

1 cup milk
Small piece of butter
2 teaspoons curry powder
Salt and pepper

Put onion and apple in blender with chicken broth and undiluted green pea soup. Add milk. Beat until thoroughly blended. Add butter, salt, pepper and curry powder. Heat. Serves 4 to 6.

Mrs. S. N. Clark, Jr. (Carolyn)

APPLE SOUP

2 10½ ounce cans consommé
1 onion, quartered
1 cooking apple, quartered

2 tablespoons Scotch whiskey
½ pint light cream

Simmer consommé with apple and onion for 20 minutes. Strain. Add whiskey and cream to broth. Serve very hot or well chilled. Serves 2 to 3.

Mrs. George G. Trask (Connie)

CHICKEN CUSTARD

1 cup very strong chicken
    broth

1 cup half and half
3 egg yolks, well beaten

Scald together the chicken broth and cream. Pour the scalded mixture over the egg yolks and cook in double boiler, stirring constantly until slightly thickened. Season to taste and serve ice cold in cups. Serves 2.

Mrs. Jack Snow (Gulia)

CHEESE SOUP

½ cup butter
1 cup flour
½ teaspoon salt
1½ pints milk
7 ounces Cheddar cheese
¼ cup celery, finely diced

¼ cup onions, finely sliced
¼ cup green pepper, finely
    chopped
¼ cup carrots, finely chopped
1 pint chicken stock
Paprika to color

Melt butter and blend in flour. Add salt and milk. Whisk until thickened. Add cheese to butter mixture. Parboil all vegetables in chicken stock. Combine all ingredients. Bring to a boil, stirring constantly. Serves 8.

Mrs. John E.Bryan (Gladys)

THE BELGIANS CALL IT DRONKEMAN'S SOEP

2 large onions, thinly sliced
2 tablespoons butter
½ cup white wine
2 cups consommé or chicken
stock

Salt and cayenne pepper
Finés herbes
4 slices French bread
4-6 ounces Camembert cheese

Sauté onions in butter until tender. Add wine, stock and seasonings. Simmer for 20 minutes. Pour into ramekins before serving. Top with slices of bread spread with Camembert cheese, and place under broiler. When cheese turns gold, soup is ready. Serves 4.

Mrs. Richard G. Price, Jr. (Mary Jo)

BARLEY AND BEEF-BALL SOUP

1 pound lean beef, ground
2 tablespoons oil
1 large onion, diced
2 stalks celery, sliced
½ cup tomato sauce

¾ cup pearl barley
2 quarts water
½ cup chopped parsley
Salt and pepper

Mold beef into small balls and brown in oil. Put meatballs into soup pot and add onion, celery, tomato sauce, barley, water, parsley, salt and pepper. Simmer until barley is tender, about 1 to 1½ hours. Correct seasonings and serve with garlic toast.

Mrs. John Hryharrow (Dee)

BRUNSWICK STEW

2 quarts water
2 large hen or 2 large fryers,
cut up
5 28-ounce cans tomatoes,
mashed
4 tablespoons bacon drippings

2 teaspoons smoke salt
1 teaspoon red crushed pepper
4 16-ounce cans tiny butterbeans
½ cup butter
4 16-ounce cans white cream style
corn

Cook chicken in water until tender. Reserve chicken stock. Remove chicken from bones and cut in large pieces. Put tomatoes and chicken stock in a large pot. Add all the seasonings and simmer with lid off for 1 hour. Add chicken, butterbeans, butter and cook slowly for ½ hour. Add corn and cook 30 minutes, stirring often as stew will stick.
Serve with slaw and cornbread. Serves 12.

Mrs. William W. Elliott (Martha)

FRENCH VEGETABLE SOUP

3 quarts water
6 medium summer squash
½ head cabbage
3 or 4 large tomatoes
1 quart green or wax beans
1 pint lima beans

2 cloves garlic, mashed
½ to ¾ pound sharp cheese
1 tablespoon basil
2 teaspoons salt
½ teaspoon pepper

Grind in meat grinder or food processor squash, cabbage, tomatoes, beans and limas. Put in large kettle, heat to boil and simmer for 1 hour. Add remaining ingredients, ladle into hot bowls and serve. Makes 6 quarts.

Mrs. M. W. Clapp (Polly)

VEGETABLE SOUP I

3 cups water
2½ teaspoons salt
1 cup potatoes, diced
1 cup carrots, diced
1 cup green peas

1 cup cauliflower pieces
1 cup broccoli flowerets
3 cups milk
2 tablespoons flour
⅛ teaspoon pepper

In large saucepan place water and salt. Bring to a boil. Add carrots and potatoes; simmer, covered, for 10 minutes. Add peas, cauliflower and broccoli; simmer, covered, for 10 minutes. Blend flour with small amount of milk until smooth. Add to vegetables with remaining milk and pepper. Simmer 5 minutes. Serves 6 to 8.

Mrs. Gerado Heiss (Jo)

VEGETABLE SOUP II

4 pounds soup bone cut from
   shank of beef
12 center cut marrow bones
Water
1 carrot, thinly sliced
1 Irish potato, finely diced
6 okra pods, thinly sliced
8 medium tomatoes, chopped

6 Kentucky wonder beans, thinly
   sliced
1 medium squash, finely diced
1 teaspoon sugar
3 ears corn, cut from ear
2 stalks celery, finely chopped
1 medium onion, finely chopped
Salt and pepper

Wash soup and marrow bones and soak in cold water. Place on stove in that water and bring to a boil. Simmer for 2 hours only. Add carrots, potato, okra, tomatoes, beans, squash, and sugar and cook for an additional 2 hours, no longer. Add corn, celery, onion, salt and pepper. Cook 20 minutes. This can be served immediately, stored in refrigerator or frozen.

Mrs. John C. Bull (Coralee)

VEGETABLE SOUP NIVERNAIS FOR FOOD PROCESSOR

½ cup butter
1 cup carrots, sliced
1 cup turnips, sliced
1 cup leeks, sliced

1 cup potatoes, sliced
1 tablespoon salt
4 cups chicken stock or water
1 cup heavy cream or half and half

GARNISH: (optional):
2 tablespoons butter
1 small turnip, diced

1 carrot, diced
1 stalk celery, diced

Melt butter in heavy pot. With slicing disc in place, slice carrots, turnips, leeks, and potatoes. Add sliced vegetables and salt to pot. Cover tightly and cook over low heat 20 minutes. With chopping blade in place, chop the vegetables again and return to pot. Add chicken stock or water and bring to a boil. Simmer 20 minutes. With chopping blade in place, finely dice turnip, carrot, and celery for garnish. Mix 2 tablespoons butter, add chopped vegetables and brown quickly. Add to soup. Add cream and correct seasonings. Serve hot or cold. May be frozen. If frozen, don't add cream until ready to serve.

The Editors

CREAM OF AVOCADO SOUP

3 ripe avocados, peeled and cut up
3 cups vichyssoise
2 cups light cream
1 cup chicken broth

¼ cup lemon juice, divided
½ avocado, sliced for garnish
Bacon bits
Parsley

Put half of avocados in container of blender or food processor. Add 2 cups of vichyssoise, 1 cup cream, ½ of the chicken broth and 2 tablespoons of lemon juice. Blend until smooth. Pour into a bowl and blend the remaining ingredients. Chill at least 4 hours and serve with avocado slices on top. Garnish with bacon bits or parsley. Serves 4 or 5.

Mrs. Sam Stafford III (Nancy)

CUBAN BLACK BEAN SOUP

1 pound black beans
8 cups water
2 tablespoons salt
1 cup onion, minced
1 cup green pepper, minced
¾ cup celery, minced
¾ cup carrots, minced
6 tablespoons olive oil

5 cloves garlic, minced
½ tablespoon cumin
1 tablespoon white vinegar
1 teaspoon Maggi's seasoning
Salt
Pepper
Raw onions, minced
Egg yolks, hard boiled and sieved

Soak beans, rinsed and picked over, in water to cover. Drain and add to water with salt. Bring to boil and simmer until beans are just soft. Sauté onion, pepper, celery and carrots in oil until onions are brown. Add garlic, cumin, vinegar and Maggi's seasoning. Cook and stir for 3 minutes. Drain a little water from the beans. Add water to vegetables and cook slowly, covered for 30 minutes. Combine with beans, adding more water if needed. Reheat and adjust seasonings with salt and pepper. Simmer for 30 minutes or longer. Pass bowls of minced raw onions, soaked in olive oil and vinegar if desired, and sieved egg yolks. This is a highly seasoned soup that can be served as a main meal over rice. Serves 8 to 10.

Dale Hryharrow Friedman

FRENCH OIGNON SOUP

2 pounds oignons, thinly sliced
3 tablespoons butter
1 teaspoon sugar
3 tablespoons flour
2 quarts brown stock, boiling

½ cup white wine
1 teaspoon salt
6 slices fresh bread, toasted
3 tablespoons Swiss cheese, grated

Cook oignons slowly in butter. Add the sugar and cook until browned lightly. Sprinkle flour and cook for 3 minutes. Add the brown stock plus the white wine. Add the seasonings. Simmer for 30 minutes. Pour in individual soup tureens. Put toast in each container. Sprinkle grated cheese on bread. Put under the broiler for 3 minutes and serve at once. Serves 6.

Mrs. Merle F. Ormond (Monique)

GAZPACHO I

4 tomatoes, peeled
½ cucumber, peeled
1 medium onion, peeled and
    quartered
1 stalk of celery, cut in 2-inch
    pieces
1 clove of garlic

1 teaspoon salt
¼ teaspoon pepper
½ teaspoon Worcestershire sauce
¼ cup wine vinegar
½ cup olive oil
Cucumbers and sour cream for
    garnish

Blend all ingredients in blender or food processor. Place covered in refrigerator for at least 4 hours. Serve in chilled bowls, garnished with thinly sliced cucumbers and sour cream. Will keep 4 or 5 days in refrigerator. Serves 4.

Mrs. Robert Sams (Mary)

GAZPACHO II

1 clove garlic, peeled and
    mashed
4 to 5 ripe tomatoes, cut in
    eighths
½ green pepper, seeded and
    sliced
½ small onion, peeled and
    sliced

1 cucumber, peeled and cut
1 5¼-ounce can mixed vegetable
    juice
1 teaspoon salt
2 tablespoons olive oil
3 tablespoons wine vinegar
¼ teaspoon Worcestershire sauce
Cucumber slices, garnish

Place all ingredients in container of a blender. Cover and blend on high speed for 5 to 10 seconds. Place container in refrigerator until thoroughly chilled. Blend briefly before serving. Garnish with a thin slice of cucumber. Serves 4 to 6.

Mrs. Frank Mears (Jeanne)

COLD SQUASH SOUP

1 medium onion, chopped
2 tablespoons butter or
    margarine
1 pound yellow crookneck
    squash, sliced

1½ cups chicken stock
½ cup sour cream
Salt and pepper to taste

Sauté onion in butter. Add squash and cook in 1 cup of chicken stock about 15 minutes or until soft. Puree in blender. Transfer to bowl. Stir in ½ cup of the chicken stock and sour cream. Season to taste. Chill thoroughly and serve garnished with chopped fresh dill. Serves 4.

Mrs. James B. Stout (Kinne)

JAMAICAN SQUASH SOUP

2 pounds winter squash (Turk's Turban, Butternut, Hubbard or Acorn), peeled and cubed
1 pound tomatoes, peeled and diced
½ cup rice, uncooked
1 large clove garlic, crushed
2 bay leaves
¼ teaspoon marjoram leaves
¼ teaspoon dried thyme leaves
1 cup scallions, chopped
1 tablespoon steak sauce
1 dash ground allspice
1 teaspoon sugar
2 teaspoons salt
½ teaspoon black pepper
3 10½-ounce cans beef consommé
5 cups water
4 tablespoons parsley, chopped

Place all ingredients except parsley in large kettle or Dutch oven. Heat to boiling, stir, reduce heat and let simmer 45 to 60 minutes, or until vegetables and rice are very tender. Ladle into soup bowls and sprinkle with parsley. Makes about 3 quarts. Serves 8 to 10.

Mrs. Harold O. Danielson (Mary)

ZUCCHINI SOUP

3 cups zucchini, diced
2 strips bacon, coarsely cut
2 cups chicken stock
1 small onion, chopped
1 small garlic clove
½ teaspoon basil
2 tablespoons parsley, chopped
¼ teaspoon salt
¼ teaspoon pepper
Seasoning salt
Parmesan cheese or sour cream

Cook all ingredients together until tender. Put in blender and liquefy. Sprinkle top with Parmesan cheese or sour cream. Serve hot or cold. Serves 3-4.

Mrs. Annette S. Tuthill

COLD ZUCCHINI AND BUTTERMILK SOUP

3 tablespoons butter
2 cups onions, coarsely chopped
4 cups zucchini, unpeeled and sliced
2 cups chicken stock
2 teaspoons Cavender's Greek seasoning
¾ cup buttermilk
Parsley or sour cream

Sauté onions in butter until soft. Add zucchini and chicken stock to skillet and cook on low until zucchini is soft. Cool. Add Greek seasoning and buttermilk. Put in blender and blend on middle speed for 10 to 15 seconds. Refrigerate until thoroughly chilled. Garnish with parsley or sour cream. Serves 4 to 6.

Mrs. Hugh O. Pearson, Jr. (Nancy)

MUSHROOM BOUILLON

3 cups water
1 pound fresh mushrooms,
  chopped
1 small onion, diced
1 small carrot, diced
1 stalk celery, minced
6 sprigs parsley

¼ teaspoon each of tarragon and
  thyme
3 10½-ounce cans beef or chicken
  consomme
Salt and black pepper to taste
4-6 tablespoons sherry

Simmer the vegetables with the herbs in water, covered, for 1 hour. Strain the broth, discarding the vegetables. Add the consomme. Simmer 10 minutes more to blend flavors. Season with salt and pepper. Serve in bouillon cups, adding a tablespoon of sherry to each. Serves 4 to 6.

Mrs. Hugh O. Pearson, Jr. (Nancy)

OKRA SOUP

1 beef bone
2 quarts water
Bay leaves
1 large onion, chopped
2 pounds fresh okra, finely
  chopped

2 16-ounce cans tomatoes, mashed
1 teaspoon sugar
Salt and pepper

Cook meat in water with bay leaves and onion for 1 hour. Add okra and cook another hour. Add tomatoes, salt, pepper and sugar and cook for another 2 or 3 hours. Season to taste and add more water if desired. Stir often. Serves 12.

Mrs. G. P. Apperson, Jr. (Frances)

SPLIT PEA SOUP

2 1-inch thick beef shanks
2 quarts water
1 12-ounce package dried split
  peas
1 cup potatoes, diced

1 cup carrots, thinly sliced
1 cup yellow squash, thinly sliced
1 medium onion, finely chopped
Salt
Thyme

Boil beef shanks in water until tender. Remove bone and gristle. Chop meat. Add all the ingredients to water. Add salt and thyme to taste. Cook about 1½ hours or until peas are tender. Add more water if necessary. Serves 4 to 6.

Mrs. DeAlton Ridings (Jane)

SOUPE DE TOMATES

1 2-pound can peeled tomatoes
 or 2 pounds fresh (ripe)
 tomatoes, sieved
2 medium onions, peeled and
 quartered
3 medium potatoes, peeled and
 quartered
1 garlic clove

2 teaspoons parsley, chopped
1 shallot, chopped
2 teaspoons salt
Pepper
¼ cup heavy cream or milk
2 teaspoons butter
Water or milk, optional

Put tomatoes and onions into a heavy saucepan with all remaining ingredients except for butter and heavy cream. Barely cover with water. Bring to a boil and simmer with lid on for 30 to 45 minutes. With a potato masher, mash vegetables but leave some lumps. Add water or milk if too thick. Bring again to a boil. Turn heat off. Add butter and cream. Serves 6.

Mrs. C. A. Larsen, Jr. (Eleanor)

COLD FRESH TOMATO SOUP

12 large tomatoes, ripe
2 small onions, grated
2 teaspoons salt
1 teaspoon black pepper

1 tablespoon sugar
1 teaspoon dried basil
Sour cream

Drop tomatoes into boiling water for 1 minute. Remove and peel. Mash or grind tomatoes through a medium grinder. Add onions. Stir in salt, black pepper, sugar and dried basil. Chill thoroughly. Taste for seasoning. Add more of the seasoning if necessary. Garnish with a spoonful of sour cream. Serves 8 to 12.

Mrs. Charles P. Graham (Jean)

COLD TOMATO SOUP

3 cups tomato juice
2 tablespoons tomato paste or
 chopped tomatoes
4 tablespoons scallions,
 chopped
2 tablespoons lemon juice

½ teaspoon curry powder
½ lemon rind, grated
Salt and pepper to taste
Thyme to taste
1 cup sour cream
Sugar

Mix first 8 ingredients. Chill. Before serving add sugar to taste and sour cream, well blended. Serves 4 to 6.

Mrs. Robert L. Huffines III (Douglas)

CUCUMBER SOUP

3 medium cucumbers
1 medium onion, peeled and
   chopped
1 10¾ ounce can cream of
   chicken soup

1 8-ounce carton sour cream
1 teaspoon basil
1 teaspoon dill
½ teaspoon seasoning salt
Chives, chopped

Peel, quarter and scrape seeds from cucumbers. Cut in large pieces and put in blender with onion and soup. When mixed, add sour cream and seasonings. Blend again. Chill and serve with chives sprinkled on top. Serves 6.

Mrs. Ernest S. Collins (Sue)

TZATSIKI (GREEK COLD YOGURT AND CUCUMBER SOUP)

3 cups yogurt
2 cloves garlic, crushed
4 medium cucumbers, coarsely
   grated

1 tablespoon olive oil
Juice of ½ lemon
Salt to taste
Chopped mint or dill

Mix together all ingredients except mint or dill. Seal with plastic wrap and chill for 8 hours or overnight. Stir and spoon into chilled bowls. Sprinkle with mint or dill. Serves 8.

Mrs. Charles P. Graham (Jean)

VICHYSSOISE

1 onion, cut in 1-inch pieces
2 leeks, white only, cut in
   1-inch pieces
4 tablespoons butter
3 medium potatoes, chopped
1 cup water

2 14½-ounce cans chicken broth
¼ teaspoon salt
Dash of white pepper
½ cup whipping cream
Fresh chives

Melt butter and slowly cook leeks and onions for 5 to 10 minutes, but do not brown. Add potatoes to onions and leeks. Add water, chicken broth, salt and white pepper, Bring to a boil. Reduce heat and simmer slowly for 40 minutes. Cool and purée in blender or food processor. Refrigerate overnight. Stir cream in before serving. Sprinkle with fresh chives. Serves 6.

Mrs. John M. Trask, Jr. (Caroline)

GINNY'S CLAM CHOWDER

4 slices bacon, chopped
2 medium onions, chopped
2 stalks celery, chopped
2 carrots, chopped
1 green pepper, chopped
1 clove garlic, minced
1 teaspoon paprika
1 sachet bag (bouquet garni) or
    ¼ teaspoon thyme, ¼
    teaspoon rosemary and 1
    bay leaf
3 dozen or 1 quart clams,
    minced or ground; reserve
    liquor

3 medium potatoes, cubed
1 cup tomatoes, chopped
½ cup tomato sauce
3 cups clam liquor, strained
    through 2 layers cheesecloth
1 quart milk
1 teaspoon salt
¼ to ½ teaspoon freshly ground
    pepper
3 tablespoons flour
3 tablespoons butter
2 tablespoons butter for each bowl
2 tablespoons parsley for each
    bowl

Sauté the following in a deep kettle until golden brown: bacon, onions, celery, carrots and green peppers. Add garlic and paprika. Sauté briefly. Add bouquet garni or equivalent and stir. Add clams, potatoes, tomatoes and tomato sauce. Cover with just enough water or broth to cook the clams and potatoes. Simmer on lowest temperature for 30 minutes. Add clam liquor, milk, salt and pepper. Stir well. Thicken with a paste of flour and butter. Cover the kettle and simmer 1 hour stirring occasionally. Garnish each serving with 2 tablespoons each of parsley and butter. Serve piping hot with crackers, spoonbread or cornsticks. If freezing for future use, it is suggested that you omit the potatoes until second cooking. Serves 8 to 10.

Ms. Ginny Lentz Hucks

CLAM CHOWDER

½ pound salt pork, diced
4 medium onions, chopped
1 small clove garlic, chopped
4 large stems celery, chopped
1 large bell pepper, chopped

1 large potato, peeled and cubed
2 28-ounce cans tomatoes
2 7½-ounce cans clams, minced
2 8-ounce bottles clam juice

In deep kettle, sauté salt pork until crisp. Sauté onions, garlic, celery and bell pepper in salt pork. Add tomatoes and potatoes. Simmer uncovered over very low heat for 30 minutes. Add clams and clam juice to soup mixture and simmer uncovered 10 minutes. Add salt and pepper to taste. Serve with saltine crackers or hot cornbread. Serves 6.

Mrs. Harold Hendricks (Sue)

TIDALHOLM SEAFOOD CHOWDER

¼ cup oysters, diced, reserve
   liquor
1 cup small shrimp, peeled
4 tablespoons butter
1 quart of whole milk
½ cup crabmeat
1½ cups fish, cooked and diced
½ cup water chestnuts, thinly
   sliced, including liquid

1 cup whole kernel corn, including
   liquid
1 cup white potatoes, cooked,
   diced, including liquid
1 pint of half and half
Salt and pepper to taste
Parsley to taste

Sauté oysters and shrimp in butter for 3 or 4 minutes. Add oyster liquor and milk. Turn heat to low. Add crabmeat and fish. At this point, recipe may be frozen successfully. Add water chestnuts, corn, potatoes, salt, pepper and parsley and cook very slowly for 10 minutes. Stir often. Then add the half and half and cook for 2 more minutes, very carefully stirring. Too much heat will cause milk to curdle. Serves 4 to 6.

Mrs. O. Stanley Smith (Connie)

OYSTER BISQUE

1 quart oysters; drain and
   reserve liquor
2 cloves garlic, pressed
4 tablespoons butter
2 to 3 tablespoons butter
2 tablespoons green onions,
   finely minced
2 tablespoons celery with
   leaves, finely minced
2 tablespoons parsley, finely
   minced

2 tablespoons bell pepper, finely
   minced
Paprika
2 tablespoons butter
2 tablespoons flour
2 cups milk, heated
1 cup heavy cream
2 drops Tabasco
Salt and pepper

Pureé the oysters with the steel blade of food processor for 10 seconds. Heat oysters and garlic in butter until edges curl. Don't overcook. Set aside. In another pan, sauté onions, celery, parsley and bell pepper in 2 to 3 tablespoons butter until wilted. Add paprika and set aside. Make a roux with flour and remaining butter. Remove from stove and add all at once milk, cream and oyster liquor. Return to heat and cook, stirring, to the boiling point. Add the oyster and vegetable mixtures. Season with Tabasco. Add salt and pepper to taste. Heat on low heat but do not boil. Serves 6.

Mrs. John M. Trask (Flora)

GRANNY'S SEAFOOD CHOWDER

¼ cup butter
¼ cup onion, minced
2 leeks, thinly sliced
2 cups chicken stock
3 carrots, sliced
1 heart of celery, diced
½ pound haddock, cubed

1 teaspoon salt
¼ teaspoon pepper
½ teaspoon bay leaves, crumbled
½ teaspoon thyme
1 cup crabmeat, flaked
1 7½-ounce can clams with liquid
3 cups milk

In a large pot, melt butter, add onion and leeks. Sauté until limp and translucent. Add chicken stock, celery, carrots and haddock together with seasonings. Cover and simmer for about 30 minutes. Add the crabmeat, clams with liquid, milk and light cream. Heat to boiling and serve with crusty rolls. Serves 8.

Mrs. Charles Reeves (Carol)

COLD DILL AND SHRIMP SOUP

¼ teaspoon powdered mustard
1 quart buttermilk
1 cup celery, thinly sliced
6 radishes, thinly sliced
4 or 5 green onions, chopped

1 pound shrimp, cooked,
   peeled, and chopped
Fresh dill to taste
Salt and pepper to taste

Mix mustard with part of the buttermilk. Combine with all other ingredients. Let chill for 4 to 6 hours before serving. Serves 4.

Dale Hryharrow Friedman

SHE-CRAB SOUP

2 tablespoons butter
2 tablespoons flour
1 quart rich milk
2 cups crabmeat plus roe
Worcestershire sauce to taste
Salt, to taste
½ teaspoon white pepper

½ teaspoon mace
½ teaspoon onion powder
¼ teaspoon garlic powder
⅓ cup or more, sherry
1 cup cream, whipped
Parsley, garnish

Melt butter in a bain de marie or double boiler and blend with flour until smooth. Add milk and whisk until smooth. Next add crab, roe, Worcestershire sauce, salt, pepper, mace, onion powder and garlic powder. Cook over very low heat for 30 minutes. Add sherry. Serve in bowls topped with unsweetened whipped cream and parsley. Serves 4-6.

Mrs. Sam Stafford, III (Nancy)

CHEROKEE ROSE

Cheese and Eggs

BASIC CRÊPE

1 cup milk
¼ cup butter
1 cup flour

1 teaspoon salt
1 teaspoon baking powder
3 eggs, beaten

Heat milk and butter together over low heat until butter is melted. Cool. Sift flour, salt and baking powder. Add eggs to cooled butter and milk, then beat in dry ingredients. Refrigerate for 30 minutes. Cook crêpes, fill, and serve.

Mrs. Carl Fricke (Betty)

CRAB FILLING FOR CRÊPES

2 tablespoons onion, finely
    chopped
4 tablespoons butter
4 tablespoons flour
1½ cups milk
3 tablespoons sherry
½ cup chicken stock
Salt and pepper

1 egg yolk
3 tablespoons cream
2 cups crabmeat
½ cup mushrooms, chopped and
    cooked
2 teaspoons chives, chopped
4 tablespoons whipped cream
Pinch of nutmeg

Sauté onion in butter, stir in flour, add milk, sherry and chicken stock. Season to taste with salt and pepper. Cook, stirring until thickened. Beat egg yolk with cream. Simmer but do not boil until thickened. Reserve ½ cup sauce. Add crabmeat, mushrooms, and chives to remaining sauce. Heat. Fill crêpes, roll, and tuck ends under. Place in a lightly greased baking dish. Mix whipped cream and nutmeg with reserved sauce; mask crêpes with sauce and glaze them under the broiler. Fills twelve 6 inch crêpes.

Mrs. Morris Cooke (Georgie)

ADÉLE'S OMELET

3 eggs, separated
¼ cup heavy cream
Salt and pepper

2 tablespoons butter, melted
4 ounces sour cream
4 ounces peach chutney

Whisk egg yolks with cream. Whip egg whites until stiff with a pinch of salt. Fold egg whites in egg yolk mixture. Add pepper and cook in an omelet pan with melted butter. Fill omelet with sour cream and chutney. Fold and serve immediately. Serves 2.

Mrs. Sam Stafford, III (Nancy)

MUSHROOM FILLING FOR OMELET

6 large mushrooms, sliced
3 medium green onions, thinly
   sliced, tops and all
2 tablespoons butter

1½ tablespoons sour cream
1 tablespoon white wine
Salt and pepper

Sauté mushrooms and onions in butter only until mushrooms start to change color. Add sour cream, wine, salt and pepper. As soon as mixture is hot remove from heat and spoon onto omelet. Fold over and serve. Serves 2.

Mrs. Hugh O. Pearson, Jr. (Nancy)

SPANISH OMELET

BASIC OMELET:
4 eggs, separated
2 tablespoons flour
2 tablespoons butter

¾ cup milk
Salt and pepper

SPANISH OMELET SAUCE:
2 slices bacon
1 small onion, chopped
2 stalks celery, chopped

1 green pepper, chopped
1 16-ounce can tomatoes
Salt and pepper

Omelet:
Add flour, butter, salt, pepper and milk to beaten egg yolks. Fold in stiffly beaten egg whites. Pour in greased iron frying pan or omelet pan and cook on top of stove over moderate heat for a few minutes. Cook in 400 degree oven until done.

Sauce:
Fry bacon. Remove from frying pan. Cook onion, celery, and green pepper in bacon drippings until tender. Add tomatoes, crumbled bacon and salt and pepper. Cook until it thickens. Pour half of sauce in middle of basic omelet. Fold omelet over and pour remainder of sauce on top. Serves 4.

Mrs. S. N. Clark, Jr. (Carolyn)

PIPERADE
Excellent luncheon or appetizer dish.

6 tablespoons olive oil
½ pound onions, quartered and
    sliced
2 green peppers, chopped
½ hot red pepper or 6 shakes
    Tabasco

1 pound fresh tomatoes, diced
3 garlic cloves, chopped
Salt and pepper
6 eggs, beaten
2 tablespoons fresh basil or ½
    teaspoon dried basil

Use skillet that can go in oven. Heat olive oil and add onions. Cook onions a few minutes and add green and red peppers. Then add tomatoes, garlic, salt and pepper. Cover and cook over low heat 15 minutes. Pour eggs over mixture. Sprinkle chopped basil over egg-tomato mixture. Do not cover but place in 400 degree oven until eggs have set, about 15 or 20 minutes. Serves 6 to 8.

Mrs. John Trask, Jr. (Caroline)

MOCK CHEESE SOUFFLÉ

8 slices white bread, trimmed
    and cut into 1-inch squares
1 pound bacon, fried very crisp
    and crumbled
½ pound sharp Cheddar
    cheese, grated

6 eggs, beaten
3 cups milk
⅔ teaspoon salt

Lightly grease 8-inch by 12-inch casserole. Layer bread on the bottom and cover evenly with bacon and cheese. In mixing bowl, beat eggs, milk, and salt and pour over bread, bacon and cheese. Cover and refrigerate overnight. Preheat oven to 325 degrees. Uncover casserole and bake 45 minutes or until firm. (Bake 15 minutes longer for high altitudes.) Cut in squares to serve. Serves 6 to 8.

Mrs. Calhoun Thomas, Jr. (Debi)

NEVER-FALL CHEESE SOUFFLÉ

2 eggs, beaten
1¼ cups milk
Dash nutmeg, salt and pepper
2 cups sharp Cheddar cheese,
    coarsely grated

6 saltine crackers, coarsely
    crushed

Combine eggs with milk and seasonings. Add cheese and saltine crackers. Put in lightly greased 1 quart casserole. Bake in 375 degree oven for 40-45 minutes. Serve with crisp bacon and toast. Serves 3.

Mrs. E. B. Mitchell (Peggy)

CHEESE SOUFFLÉ

4 tablespoons Parmesan
    cheese
¼ cup butter
¼ cup flour
1½ cups milk, hot

½ teaspoon salt
½ teaspoon dry mustard
½ pound of Swiss cheese, grated
5 eggs, separated

Butter a 2-quart soufflé dish and sprinkle sides and bottom with Parmesan cheese. Set aside. Melt butter in top of double boiler. Stir in flour and add hot milk. Beat with wire whisk until thick and smooth. Add seasonings and Swiss cheese. Beat until cheese has melted. Remove from heat and add egg yolks one at a time. Add a pinch of salt to egg whites and beat until stiff. Fold into cheese sauce. Pour into soufflé dish and bake 35 to 45 minutes at 325 degrees or until a golden color.

Mrs. Harold Trask (Margaret)

BREAKFAST SAUSAGE CASSEROLE

1 pound sausage
1¼ cups Cheddar cheese, grated
6 eggs
¼ teaspoon dry mustard

Salt and pepper to taste
1 cup bread crumbs
2 cups milk

Fry sausage until it crumbles. Drain. Beat eggs with mustard, salt and pepper. Add milk and set aside. Mix sausage, bread crumbs and cheese. Place half in a shallow casserole and pour half of the milk-egg mixture over it. Repeat with the remainder. Place in refrigerator overnight. Cook 45 minutes at 350 degrees. Serves 6.

Mrs. C. L. Eaddy (Frances)

WELSH RAREBIT

1 tablespoon butter
1 teaspoon cornstarch
¼ teaspoon dry mustard
¼ teaspoon salt

Few grains red pepper
½ cup thin cream
½ pound Cheddar cheese, diced

Melt butter, add cornstarch, mustard, salt and pepper and stir until well mixed. Add cream gradually while stirring and cook 2 minutes. Add cheese and stir until melted in double boiler. Season and serve on toast. Rarebit should be smooth and creamy. If stringy, add egg slightly beaten. Serves 4.

Mrs. Neil Trask, Jr. (Rebecca)

SHRIMP OR CRAB QUICHE

3 tablespoons onion, minced
3 teaspoons butter
8 ounces crab or shrimp,
  cooked
3 tablespoons vermouth or
  white wine

3 eggs
1 cup cream
1 teaspoon salt
1 teaspoon pepper
½ cup Swiss cheese, grated
1 9-inch pie shell, unbaked

In a small saucepan, sauté onions in butter, add shrimp or crab and mash. Heat until boiling and add vermouth. Pour into pie shell. In a bowl, beat eggs and add cream, salt and pepper. Pour in pie shell and top with Swiss cheese. Bake at 350 degrees for 30 minutes.

Mrs. Ed Wise (Carol)

SHRIMP QUICHE

1 pie shell, unbaked
1 pound shrimp, cooked and
  cleaned
¼ pound fresh mushrooms,
  sliced
1 medium onion, chopped
3 tablespoons oil
1 4-ounce jar of pimentos,
  drained
1 cup Swiss cheese, grated and
  divided

5 eggs, lightly beaten
1 cup milk
1 cup heavy cream
1 teaspoon salt
⅛ teaspoon black pepper
Dash of cayenne
Dash of nutmeg
¼ cup sour cream

Sauté shrimp, mushrooms, and onions in the oil about 5 to 6 minutes. Spread mixture in bottom of pie shell and arrange pimento on top. Sprinkle half of Swiss cheese over this. Beat eggs, milk, cream and seasonings, and pour over pie. Bake at 400 degrees 10 minutes, then at 325 degrees for approximately 25 minutes until set. Combine remaining Swiss cheese with the sour cream. Spread over top and place under broiler until lightly browned (a minute or two). You may need to cover the crust edges as they brown quickly. Serves 6.

Mrs. Gary Fordham (Joan)

QUICHE AUX ÉPINARDS (SPINACH QUICHE)

2 8-inch or 9-inch pie shells, partially cooked
3 eggs
1½ cups cream
1¼ cups chopped spinach or 10-ounce package frozen, chopped spinach
1½ tablespoons butter
¼ teaspoon salt
Pinch of pepper
Small pinch of nutmeg
2 tablespoons butter
2 tablespoons green onion, finely minced
½ cup Swiss cheese, grated
1 or 2 tablespoons butter

Beat eggs and cream in mixing bowl to blend. Cook frozen spinach as follows: Melt 1½ tablespoons butter in skillet or saucepan. Stir in chopped spinach and seasonings. Cover and cook very slowly for a few minutes or until spinach has thawed and released its juices. Uncover, raise heat, and stir several minutes or until moisture has evaporated. Sauté onions in 2 tablespoons butter. Add the spinach and taste carefully for seasoning. Gradually stir the spinach mixture into the eggs and cream. Pour into pastry shells, sprinkle with cheese, dot with butter, and bake for 25 to 30 minutes in preheated 350 degree oven. Each pie serves 6.

Mrs. James Cook (Cynthia)

SPINACH QUICHE

1 pie shell
1 egg white, beaten
1 10-ounce package frozen spinach, thawed
½ pound fresh mushrooms, sliced
2 tablespoons butter
¼ teaspoon sweet basil
½ teaspoon salt
¼ teaspoon white pepper
5 whole eggs, beaten
1½ cups light cream
1 teaspoon seasoned salt

Bake pie shell, which has been rolled to fit square 8-inch by 8-inch or oblong 6-inch by 10-inch casserole dish brushed with beaten egg white, at 350 degrees for 10 minutes. Set aside. Sauté mushrooms 4 minutes in butter. Add basil, salt and pepper to thawed spinach that has been cooked and squeezed very dry. Set aside to cool. Mix eggs, cream and seasoned salt. Put spinach and mushrooms into pie shell. Pour eggs and cream over all. Bake 30 minutes at 350 degrees. Quiche is done when silver knife inserted in center comes out clean. Serves 6 or makes 50 bite size pieces.

Mrs. Madeleine Pollitzer

CHICKEN QUICHE

1 pie shell, partially baked
1½ teaspoons salt
⅛ teaspoon white pepper
2 large chicken breasts,
   deboned and cut in 1-inch
   squares
1 large tomato, chopped and
   drained
1 large onion, sliced into
   separate rings

3 eggs
1½ cups half and half
¾ cup of natural cheeses (Swiss
   and Muenster), grated
¼ cup Parmesan cheese, grated
Pinch of ground nutmeg
1 teaspoon butter

Sprinkle chicken with salt and pepper. Put butter into skillet and heat over a moderately high heat. Add chicken and sauté slowly for 5 to 6 minutes, turning occasionally. When chicken is done remove and add onion rings. Cook until nearly tender. Add tomato. Partially cover and cook 7 minutes or until the moisture evaporates. Beat eggs in a bowl with milk, cream, cheeses, nutmeg and salt. Arrange the chicken, tomato and onion rings in layers on the bottom of the pie shell. Pour the egg mixture over it. Dot with pieces of butter. Bake at 375 degrees for 30 to 40 minutes or until a knife inserted in the filling comes out clean. Serves 6.

Miss Donna Mobley

QUICHE LORRAINE

1 9-inch pie shell, partially
   baked
4 slices bacon, cooked and
   crumbled
1 cup Swiss cheese, grated
1 medium onion, chopped
1½ tablespoons butter

4 eggs
½ teaspoon salt
⅛ teaspoon nutmeg
Dash of cayenne pepper
1 tablespoon flour
2 cups light cream

Sprinkle bacon over bottom of pie shell. Sprinkle cheese over bacon. Sauté onion in butter. Beat eggs with flour, salt, nutmeg and cayenne. Add cream, onions and butter. Pour into pie shell and bake 40 minutes at 350 degrees or until custard is set and browned.

Mrs. Morris D. Cooke (Georgie)

Pasta

FRESH PASTA

Tighten pasta machine onto the edge of work table. Use the following ingredients according to the number of servings needed:

3 TO 4 SERVINGS:

2 eggs   ¼ teaspoon salt
1½ cups flour

5 TO 6 SERVINGS:

3 eggs   ⅓ teaspoon salt
2¼ cups flour

6 TO 8 SERVINGS:

4 eggs   ½ teaspoon salt
3 cups flour

Make a mountain on counter of flour and salt. Break eggs into a well in the center, blend into the flour. Keep working with fingers until blended. Don't attempt to knead, just make the dough. Pinch off pieces about the size of a small lemon. Knead each piece on the mildest setting 2 to 3 times, then send it through the next 5 settings 1 time each. Each run should begin with the dough folded in half. Cut into desired size on cutting rollers and cook in boiling water with a tablespoon oil for 3 to 4 minutes until *al denté*. Serve with desired sauce.

Mrs. Sam Stafford III (Nancy)

CLAM SAUCE FOR LINGUINE

½ cup butter   1 10-ounce can chopped clams
½ cup olive oil   with juice
7-10 cloves garlic, mashed   1 large bunch parsley, stems
½ cup beer   removed and chopped
Salt and pepper to taste   Parmesan cheese, freshly grated

Melt butter; add oil and garlic. Stir and sauté for 1 minute. Add beer and clams, salt and pepper and simmer for about 10 minutes. You can turn off heat at this point and let it sit until nearly time to serve. Ten minutes before serving reheat over medium heat and add parsley. Serve with hot linguine or vermicelli. Sprinkle liberally with cheese. Don't substitute ingredients. Serves 4.

Dale Hryharrow Friedman

WHITE CLAM SAUCE FOR LINGUINE

1 tablespoon butter
2 cloves garlic, minced
1 tablespoon flour
2 tablespoons parsley, minced

3 6½-ounce cans minced
    clams, or
2 10-ounce cans baby clams
Salt and white pepper to taste

Heat butter and gently sauté garlic for 1 minute. Blend in flour. Add remaining ingredients, bring to simmer for 5 minutes, stirring often. Do not boil. Serve over hot cooked linguine or vermicelli. Serves 4.

Mrs. Jack Treanor (Ann)

FETTUCINE WITH PESTO SAUCE

8 ounces fettucine or medium
    noodles, cooked, drained
    and hot
3 cloves garlic, chopped
3 tablespoons fresh basil,
    chopped
¼ cup parsley, chopped

½ cup Parmesan cheese, grated
1 tablespoon pignalio nuts (pine
    nuts) or walnuts, chopped
⅓ cup olive oil
¼ cup butter
Additional Parmesan cheese,
    grated

Combine all ingredients, except noodles, butter and additional Parmesan cheese in blender. Whisk until smooth. Pour hot cooked noodles into a bowl and add pesto sauce and butter. Toss quickly to coat all noodles. Serve with additional grated Parmesan cheese. Serves 6.

Mrs. Joseph A. Sedlak (Ruth)

SPAGHETTI CARBONARA

1 large onion, chopped
2 tablespoons bacon grease
2 eggs, beaten
½ cup Parmesan cheese
2 tablespoons chopped parsley

Salt and pepper
8 ounces spaghetti, cooked
½ pound bacon, fried and
    crumbled

Sauté onion in bacon grease. Mix together eggs, cheese, parsley, salt and pepper. Mix hot spaghetti with egg mixture. Add bacon and onions. Serve immediately.

Mrs. John Hryharrow (Dee)

BAKED STUFFED SHELLS ITALIANO

1 12-ounce box jumbo shells
3 pounds Ricotta cheese or
    small curd cottage cheese
3 eggs, beaten slightly
1 teaspoon salt
½ teaspoon black pepper

⅓ cup parsley, chopped
¼ cup Parmesan or Romano
    cheese, grated
6 ounces Mozzarella cheese, grated
3-4 cups spaghetti sauce with meat

Cook shells according to instructions on box. Drain and cool separately on paper towels. Combine the ricotta, eggs, salt, pepper, parsley and Parmesan cheese. Mix well until blended. Fill each shell with 2 tablespoons of cheese mixture. Arrange shells in baking pan, making 1 layer of shells. Cover with spaghetti sauce and sprinkle with Mozzarella cheese. Bake at 350 degrees for 1 hour. Use plenty of spaghetti sauce so the shells won't be dry.
Mrs. Dominick Peschi (Betsy)

VERMICELLI CASSEROLE

½ pound sliced bacon, fried
    crisp
1 pound vermicelli noodles
3 cups cottage cheese
3 cups sour cream
2 cloves garlic, crushed
2 onions, minced

2 tablespoons Worcestershire
    sauce
Dash liquid hot pepper seasoning
2 tablespoons salt
3 tablespoons horseradish
¼ cup Parmesan cheese

Crumble bacon. Cook noodles until *al denté*. Drain well. Mix all remaining ingredients except the Parmesan cheese in a large bowl. Add noodles and bacon and toss with 2 forks until well mixed. Turn into deep 3½-quart casserole. Cover and bake for 30 to 40 minutes in a 350 degree oven. Remove cover and sprinkle with Parmesan cheese. Broil until golden. Serves 12.
Mrs. Gunnar Erickson (Marjorie)

GERMAN NOODLES

4 ounces flat noodles,
    uncooked
5 tablespoons butter or
    margarine

2 large onions, sliced
Salt and pepper (peppermill grind),
    to taste
⅓ cup Parmesan cheese, grated

Cook and drain noodles according to directions on package. Melt butter in large heavy frying pan. Add onions and stir fry until onions are transparent. Add cooked noodles, salt and pepper. Stir until mixed. Stir in Parmesan cheese. Stir until cheese browns slightly in bottom of pan. Serves 4.
Mrs. F. J. Lepionka (May)

SPAGHETTI WITH SHRIMP

¼ cup olive oil
½ cup onions, chopped
6 ounces tomato paste
¾ cup Rosé wine
1 teaspoon salt
8 ounces spaghetti, cooked

3 quarts salted boiling water
1 pound shrimp, unshelled
1 teaspoon salt
½ pound Mozzarella cheese, thinly
   sliced

In a saucepan put olive oil over low flame. When hot add onions and cook until tender but not brown. Then add tomato paste, wine, and salt. Mix thoroughly, cover, and cook over low heat for at least 20 minutes, stirring occasionally. Meanwhile, cook spaghetti in boiling salted water until tender. Drain. Place shrimp in a saucepan and sprinkle with 1 teaspoon salt. Cover and cook over low flame until shrimp are pink, about 5 minutes, stirring occasionally. Drain, remove shells, and devein. In a 2 quart casserole, arrange a layer of spaghetti, then cover with a layer of shrimp, then a layer of sauce. Cover with thin slices of Mozzarella cheese. Repeat layers until all ingredients are used, finishing with cheese. Bake in 350 degree oven for 20 minutes and serve piping hot. Serves 4-6.

Mrs. L. E. Lovette (Louise)

SPAGHETTI

½ cup Wesson oil
3 garlic cloves, chopped or
   garlic powder
3 Bermuda onions, finely
   chopped
1 cup celery, finely chopped
1 green pepper, finely chopped
2 pounds ground round
2 28-ounce cans tomatoes
3 6-ounce cans tomato paste

12 ounces water
8 ounces chopped mushrooms
1 6-ounce can black olives, chopped
½ tablespoon sugar
Dash of cayenne pepper
1 bay leaf
1 tablespoon thyme
1 teaspoon parsley flakes
½ teaspoon sage

Brown garlic, onions, celery and green pepper in oil. Pour into big cooking pot. Brown beef in very little fat, or none. Put into pot. Add tomatoes, tomato paste, and water. Add remaining ingredients. Simmer the mixture for 3 hours or until thick. Serves 10.

Mrs. William C. Pitt, Jr. (Alta)

GOLDENROD

Seafood

CRABMEAT LOUIS

1 pound crabmeat
½ cup mayonnaise
¼ cup chili sauce
1 tablespoon lemon juice
3 tablespoons spring onions, finely chopped
1 teaspoon Worcestershire sauce
2 tablespoons sweet pickles
3 tablespoons bell pepper, finely chopped
¼ teaspoon celery salt
1 tablespoon horseradish
¼ teaspoon pepper
¼ teaspoon salt
Avocado, garnish
Hard boiled eggs, garnish

Place crabmeat on lettuce. Make a sauce of remaining ingredients and serve over crabmeat. Garnish with sliced avocado and quartered hard boiled eggs. Serves 4.

Mrs. F. William Scheper, III (Jean)

CRAB CAKES

1 egg
2 tablespoons mayonnaise
½ teaspoon pepper
⅛ teaspoon cayenne or dry mustard
⅛ teaspoon Tabasco sauce
½ teaspoon salt
1 pound lump crabmeat
1½ tablespoons Ritz cracker crumbs
3 tablespoons parsley, chopped
Cooking oil
Lemon wedges
Tartar sauce

Mix egg, mayonnaise, pepper, mustard, Tabasco, and salt until it forms a smooth paste. Fold carefully into crabmeat. Form into cakes, roll in cracker crumbs, and sprinkle with parsley. Place on waxed paper in refrigerator for 1 hour. Cook in enough oil to cover half of crab cakes. Drain on paper towels. Serve with lemon wedges and tartar sauce. Serves 4.

Mrs. Meyer Schein (Lois)

GRANNY GRAHAM'S DEVILLED CRAB

1 pound lump crabmeat
1 teaspoon salt
¼ teaspoon pepper
2 tablespoons mayonnaise
3 tablespoons Durkees dressing
1 teaspoon Worcestershire
   sauce

¼ teaspoon Tabasco
4 slices white bread, dried in oven,
   crushed and divided
2 tablespoons butter, melted
2 eggs, beaten
Mace
Paprika

In a large bowl place crabmeat, salt, pepper, mayonnaise, Durkees, Worcestershire, Tabasco and mix gently with two forks. Add three-fourths of toasted crumbs, butter and eggs. Add dash of mace, adjust seasonings and mix. Put into lightly greased shallow casserole or crab shells. Sprinkle top with remaining bread crumbs and paprika. Bake in preheated 450 degree oven for 10-12 minutes or until crab is bubbly or slightly brown on top. Serves 4-6.

Mrs. John M. Trask (Flora)

DEVILLED CRAB II

1 pound crabmeat
2 eggs, beaten
2 teaspoons onion, grated
1 cup mayonnaise

1 tablespoon Worcestershire sauce
Dash Tabasco sauce
Bread crumbs
Butter

Mix first 6 ingredients together. Put into crab shells. Top with bread crumbs. Dot with butter. Bake at 350 degrees for 15-20 minutes. Serves 4-6.

Mrs. R. R. Mellette, Jr. (Beverly)

DEVILLED CRAB III

2 tablespoons onion, chopped
2 tablespoons bell pepper,
   chopped
2 tablespoons celery, chopped
2 tablespoons butter, divided
½ cup dried bread crumbs

2 tablespoons mayonnaise
½ teaspoon dry mustard
1 tablespoon lemon juice
1 pound crabmeat
Salt and pepper
Butter

Sauté onions, bell pepper and celery in butter then add two-thirds of the bread crumbs and mayonnaise and mustard. Mix thoroughly. Add lemon juice, crabmeat, salt and pepper. Pat into shells, sprinkle lightly with remaining bread crumbs and dot with butter. Bake in 350 degree oven until lightly browned. Serves 4-6.

Mrs. Alfred Lengnick (Georgie)

CRABMEAT MAISON

2 tablespoons butter
1 teaspoon onion, grated
2 small tomatoes, peeled,
   seeded and chopped
1 pound lump crabmeat
¾ cup mushrooms, sautéed

Salt and pepper
⅓ cup brandy
1 cup heavy cream
1 tablespoon chives, chopped
1 tablespoon parsley, chopped

Melt butter in wide, low casserole or heavy skillet. Add onion and cook for 5 minutes over low flame. Add tomatoes to onion, and cook for 10 minutes. Put in the crabmeat and mushrooms, and add salt and freshly ground pepper. Warm brandy, ignite, and pour over crabmeat. When brandy has stopped flaming, cover casserole and cook until crabmeat is well heated. Add cream, replace cover, and continue cooking, shaking the pan from time to time until the cream begins to bubble. Add chives and parsley, mix thoroughly, and serve at once on hot buttered toast in soup plates. Serves 4-6.

Mrs. John B. Snow (Gulia)

CRAB SALAD

1 pound fresh crabmeat
8 hard-boiled eggs, chopped
1 4-ounce jar chopped
   pimentos
1 cup celery, diced

1 green pepper, diced
1 6½-ounce jar Durkee's dressing
3 tablespoons mayonnaise
2 tablespoons lemon juice

Mix all ingredients. May be served hot or cold. To serve hot, put in greased 9 x 13-inch casserole and bake 15 minutes at 425 degrees. Serves 6.

Mrs. Malcolm Goodwin (Barbara)

CRAB CASSEROLE

2 cups crabmeat
2 cups celery, finely chopped
1 cup mayonnaise
½ cup almonds
1 cup toasted bread crumbs

½ teaspoon salt
2 tablespoons lemon juice
1 teaspoon onion, grated
Crushed potato chips
½ cup grated cheese

Mix crabmeat, celery, mayonnaise, almonds, bread crumbs, salt, lemon juice, onion and place in baking dish. Cover with crushed potato chips and grated cheese. Bake in 425 degree oven for 10-15 minutes.

Mrs. Joe E. Baucom (Martha)

CRAB IMPERIAL I

1 green pepper, finely chopped
2 pimentos, finely diced
1 tablespoon English mustard
1 tablespoon salt
½ teaspoon white pepper

2 eggs
1 cup mayonnaise
3 pounds lump crabmeat
Paprika
Mayonnaise

Mix pepper and pimento. Add mustard, salt, pepper, eggs and mayonnaise and mix well. Add crabmeat and mix lightly so lumps are not broken. Divide mixture in 8-10 crab shells, heaping it lightly. Top with a light coating of mayonnaise and sprinkle with paprika. Bake in 350 degree oven for 15 minutes. Serves 8-10.
Mrs. L. E. Lovette (Louise)

FILET OF SOLE VERONIQUE

6 sole filets (or flounder)
1 teaspoon salt
¼ teaspoon white pepper
¼ teaspoon onion powder
Butter
1 cup chicken stock
½ cup dry white wine

1 bay leaf
4 whole allspice
1 cup seedless white grapes
2 tablespoons butter
½ cup cream
1 tablespoon flour

Press filets out flat. Season with salt, white pepper and onion powder, then fold in half. Place folded filets in a buttered frypan. Pour chicken stock and wine over fish. Drop in bay leaf and allspice. Cover. Cook gently for 10 to 12 minutes or until fish is done. Carefully remove filets to a heated platter and garnish with white grapes. Keep hot in slow oven. Reduce liquid in frypan over high high heat to about ½ cup. Remove bay leaf and allspice. Stir in butter and cream. Thicken with flour. Heat just to boiling point. Pour over filets and grapes. Broil a few minute to glaze sauce; do not brown. Serves 6.
Mrs. John K. Murphy (Mary)

CRABMEAT REMICK

1 pound lump crabmeat
6 buttered shells or ramekins
1 scant teaspoon dry mustard
½ teaspoon paprika
½ teaspoon celery salt

4 drops Tabasco sauce
½ cup chili sauce
1 teaspoon tarragon vinegar
1¾ cups mayonnaise
6 slices bacon, cooked

Place crabmeat in 6 shells or ramekins. Heat in 350 degree oven until hot, about 15 minutes. Blend together dry mustard, paprika, celery salt, and Tabasco sauce. Add chili sauce and tarragon vinegar, mix well and add mayonnaise. Spread this over the warmed crabmeat, top with crisp bacon slice, and glaze under broiler flame. Serves 6.
Mrs. Richard G. Price, Jr. (Mary Jo)

CRAB MORNAY

2 tablespoons butter
2 tablespoons flour
1 cup heavy cream
½ cup chicken stock
¼ teaspoon salt
Dash cayenne
½ cup Swiss cheese, grated

¼ cup Parmesan cheese
½ cup onions, chopped
½ cup green pepper, chopped
3 tablespoons butter
1 2-ounce jar chopped pimentos, drained
1 cup crabmeat

Make white sauce of butter, flour, cream, chicken stock, salt, and cayenne. Add cheese and stir until thickened and smooth. Sauté onions and green pepper in butter and add to white sauce. Fold in pimento and crab. Serve on toast points. Serves 4.

Mrs. Calhoun Thomas (Thelma)

CRAB PIE

1 9-inch baked pie shell
½ pound crabmeat
1 cup celery, chopped
2 tablespoons green pepper, chopped
2 teaspoons onion, grated

¼ teaspoon salt
1 tablespoon lemon juice
¾ cup mayonnaise
½ cup Cheddar cheese, grated
¾ cup toasted crumbs

Mix crabmeat, celery, green pepper, onion, salt, lemon juice and mayonnaise. Fill pie shell. Top with cheese and bread crumbs. Bake 15 minutes in 375 degree oven. Serves 4-6.

Mrs. W. T. Miars, Jr. (Emma)

FRIED SOFT SHELL CRABS

2 soft shell crabs
2 cups milk
2 teaspoons salt

½ teaspoon pepper
½ cup flour

Wash crab in cold water. Remove feathery substances, sand bag, and apron. Dry well. Combine milk, salt and pepper. Soak crab in seasoned milk for 15 minutes; roll in flour. Deep fat fry at 370 degrees for 6 or 7 minutes. Serve with tartar sauce.

Mrs. A. R. McAfee (Lydia)

SHRIMP-CRAB CASSEROLE

3 cups cooked rice
½ cup onion, finely chopped
½ cup green pepper, finely
  chopped
1 egg, beaten
1 pound crabmeat
½ cup mushrooms, sliced
½ cup milk

1 cup celery, finely chopped
½ teaspoon salt
1 cup tomato juice
1½ pounds shrimp, if medium or
  large, cut in half
1 cup mayonnaise
Bread crumbs
Slivered almonds

Mix first 11 ingredients together and top with bread crumbs. Bake covered 35-40 minutes at 325 degrees until shrimp are done. Place almonds on top and cook until almonds are brown—about 5 minutes. Serves 6-8.

Mrs. Stan Hurt (Gray)

SEAFOOD CASSEROLE

1 8½-ounce can artichoke
  hearts
1 pound lump crabmeat
2½ pounds shrimp, cooked
2 tablespoons butter
3 tablespoons flour
1 cup half and half
1 cup milk
½ teaspoon prepared mustard
½ teaspoon curry powder

½ teaspoon paprika
1 tablespoon Worcestershire sauce
1 tablespoon catsup
1 cup sharp Cheddar cheese,
  grated
2 tablespoons lemon juice
2 tablespoons sherry
Red pepper and salt to taste
½ cup sharp Cheddar cheese,
  grated

In a 2 quart casserole, make a layer of artichoke hearts, crabmeat, and shrimp. Make a white sauce of butter, flour, half and half and milk. Season sauce with mustard, curry powder, paprika, Worcestershire sauce, catsup, cheese, lemon juice, sherry, red pepper and salt. Top casserole with ½ cup cheese. Bake in 350 degree oven for 20 minutes. Serves 10.

Mrs. C. Blackburn Brewer (Frances)

SCAMPI

½ cup butter
½ cup salad oil
4 tablespoons parsley, chopped
2 tablespoons garlic powder
1 teaspoon salt

Dash of cayenne
4 tablespoons lemon juice
2 pounds fresh shrimp, shelled and
   deveined
Lemon wedges

In a large skillet with metal handle, or heatproof serving dish, melt butter; add oil, half of the parsley, garlic powder, salt, cayenne and lemon juice; mix well. Add shrimp, tossing gently with butter mixture; arrange in skillet in single layer. Bake in 400 degree oven for 8-10 minutes. Sprinkle with remaining parsley and garnish with lemon wedges. Serves 6-8.

Mrs. F. C. McCaleb, Jr. (Jean)

BATTER FRIED SHRIMP

1 pound shrimp, shelled
4 ounces flour, sifted
1 teaspoon baking powder
Pinch of salt
Pinch of sugar

Pepper to taste
1 egg, beaten
1 cup beer
Crisco

Shell shrimp and devein. Dry between paper towels. Mix flour, baking powder, salt, sugar, pepper, egg and beer. Dip shrimp into the batter. Drop into deep hot Crisco until golden brown. Drain on paper towels and serve hot.

Mrs. Ray Williams (Hedy)

GRILLED SHRIMP

2 pounds large shrimp,
   unshelled
1 cup salad oil
1 cup lemon juice
2 teaspoons Italian salad
   dressing mix

2 teaspoons seasoned salt
   and pepper
4 tablespoons brown sugar
2 tablespoons soy sauce
½ cup green onion, chopped

Wash shrimp thoroughly; drain on paper towels. Mix salad oil, lemon juice, salad dressing mix, salt and pepper. Place shrimp in bowl and pour in the marinade. Put in the refrigerator, and marinate 2-4 hours, stirring occasionally. Lift shrimp from marinade with slotted spoon and place on the grill about 6 inches from hot coals (if necessary, use wire basket or string shrimp on skewers). Grill for about 10 minutes, turning once and brushing with marinade. Pour remaining marinade into a saucepan. Stir in brown sugar, soy sauce, and onion. Heat to boiling. Serve as a dip for shrimp. Serves 8.

Mrs. Michael Ragsdale (Laura)

SHRIMP CREOLE I

3 pounds small shrimp, peeled
   and deveined
¼ pound salt pork
4 scallions
1 large green pepper

¼ teaspoon oregano
¼ teaspoon thyme
Salt to taste
Pepper to taste
10 medium size fresh tomatoes

Rinse shrimp and cut in half. Cut up scallions, pepper and pork in small strips. Sauté scallions, pepper, salt and pork on medium high heat. Add oregano, thyme, salt and pepper. Mash peeled tomatoes through a colander. Then add this to scallion mixture in frying pan. Stew until most of the liquid is evaporated; then add shrimp and cook only until done. Serve hot over steamed rice. Serves 6.

Mrs. W. Thomas Logan (Barbara)

SHRIMP CREOLE II

2 onions, sliced
4 stalks celery, chopped
2 tablespoons oil
1 tablespoon flour
1 teaspoon salt
2 tablespoons chili powder
1 cup water
2 cups tomatoes, mashed

1 tablespoon vinegar
1 teaspoon sugar
1¼ pounds shrimp, peeled and
   deveined
3 cups rice, cooked
1 pound breakfast bacon, fried and
   crumbled, set aside

Sauté onions and celery in oil until lightly browned. Add flour, salt and chili powder; blend. Slowly add water and cook 15 minutes over moderate heat. Add tomatoes, vinegar, sugar and shrimp. Cook 12 minutes or until well done. Serve on rice and sprinkle with bacon bits.

Mrs. R. L. Furr (Mora)

SHRIMP ROSEMARY

½ cup olive oil
2 tablespoons rosemary
¼ teaspoon oregano
6 garlic cloves

Salt and pepper to taste
2 pounds raw shrimp, unpeeled
1 cup sauterne or sherry

Heat olive oil in frying pan. Add rosemary, oregano, garlic, salt and pepper. Put shrimp in hot pan and "fry" til pink, stirring all the time. When shrimp are pink, pour wine over them, cover, and steam for 8-10 minutes. Deliciously different. Serves 4.

Mrs. Joe Benton (Marjorie)

MEDIEVAL SHRIMP

3 pounds shrimp, unpeeled
1 cup beer
6 scallions or shallots, chopped

2 cups celery, chopped—tops and
all

Place shrimp in a deep saucepan. Add beer. Strew top with scallions and celery. Cover. Simmer 6 minutes or until shrimp are pink and tender. Serve hot or cold with dill butter or sherry garlic butter.

DILL BUTTER:
¼ cup butter
½ cup beer

1 tablespoon dill weed

Heat in small saucepan. Serve in individual dishes with shrimp.

SHERRY GARLIC BUTTER:
¼ cup butter
½ cup sherry

½ teaspoon garlic salt

Heat in small saucepan. Serve in individual dishes with shrimp.

Mrs. Hugh O. Pearson (Marie)

WINE POACHED SHRIMP

1 pound raw shrimp, peeled
   and deveined
½ cup white wine
1½ cups chicken broth
¼ teaspoon basil, dill or finés
   herbes
½ teaspoon salt
½ teaspoon paprika

½ pound mushrooms
½ teaspoon celery salt
½ cup green onions, sliced
2 tablespoons cornstarch
1 tablespoon lemon juice
2 tablespoons dry sherry
1 tablespoon parsley, finely
   chopped

Rinse and drain shrimp. Place in a large skillet. Add wine, chicken broth, herbs, salt and paprika. Cover and simmer until shrimp turn pink and are tender, about 10 minutes. Add mushrooms and simmer 5 minutes. Add celery salt and onion; simmer 5 minutes. Blend cornstarch with lemon juice and sherry. Stir into sauce. Cook and stir until smooth and thickened. Add parsley. Serve with rice. Serves 4.

Mrs. Ernest Collins (Sue)

SHRIMP CURRY

½ cup butter, melted
1 large onion, chopped
1 apple, peeled and finely
    chopped
1 large tomato, chopped
2 tablespoons flour

2 teaspoons curry powder
1 pint milk
1 pint half and half
2 pounds shrimp, cooked and
    peeled

Sauté onion in butter over low heat until transparent. Add apple and tomato and cook uncovered over low heat until soft. To this add flour, curry powder, milk, and half and half. Let it cook slowly—it takes some time to thicken. Salt and pepper to taste. Add shrimp before serving. Serve over rice with condiments of coconut, chutney, chopped salted peanuts, chopped hard boiled eggs, bananas, chopped onions. Serves 8.

Mrs. Kauno Lehto (Isabel)

SHRIMP ARTICHOKE DISH

3 14-ounce cans artichoke
    hearts
¾ pound whole or sliced
    mushrooms
6 tablespoons butter or
    margarine
3 10½-ounce cans cream of
    mushroom soup
3 tablespoons Worcestershire
    sauce

¾ cup dry sherry
¾ cup Parmesan cheese
Salt and pepper
2½ pounds shrimp, cooked and
    peeled
Paprika
Yellow rice, cooked

Arrange artichoke hearts in bottom of 3 quart casserole. Save a few hearts for top of casserole. Sauté mushrooms in butter. Then mix mushrooms, mushroom soup, Worcestershire sauce, sherry, Parmesan cheese, salt, pepper and shrimp. Spoon on top of artichokes. Place remaining artichokes on top and sprinkle with paprika. Bake at 375 degrees for 30-40 minutes. Serve over yellow rice. Serves 12.

Mrs. William W. Anderson, Jr. (Sallie)

CHLOE'S SHRIMP DISH

½ cup butter or margarine
2 pounds raw shrimp, cleaned
   and deveined
1 medium onion, chopped
1 4-ounce can sliced
   mushrooms, drain and
   reserve liquid
1 8-ounce can water chestnuts,
   thinly sliced

1 10¼-ounce can cream of shrimp
   soup
1 teaspoon soy sauce
Lemon pepper to taste
Garlic salt to taste
2 tablespoons cornstarch
¼ cup sherry
Hot cooked rice

Melt butter in large skillet, add shrimp and sauté until they begin to turn pink. Add onion and sauté until soft. Add all other ingredients except cornstarch, liquid from mushrooms, and sherry. Dissolve cornstarch in mushroom liquid and add to shrimp mixture, stirring constantly. Turn heat to low and simmer for about 15 minutes. Add sherry and adjust seasonings just before serving. Serve on hot fluffy rice. Serves 6-8.

Mrs. Roger Pinckney (Chloe)

SHRIMP CASSEROLE

2 cups cooked rice
1½-2 pounds fresh shrimp,
   cooked and peeled
1 10¾-ounce can cream of
   mushroom soup
2 8-ounce cans water
   chestnuts, drained and
   chopped
8-ounces fresh mushrooms,
   sliced

1 cup celery, finely chopped
2 tablespoons fresh parsley, finely
   chopped
2 teaspoons onion, finely chopped
1 4-ounce jar pimentos, thinly
   sliced
⅓ cup Miracle Whip salad dressing
⅓ cup milk
½ teaspoon Tabasco sauce
Buttered bread crumbs

Butter a 7 by 11-inch baking dish. Put rice into baking dish and cover with shrimp. Combine soup, water chestnuts, mushrooms, celery, parsley, onion, pimentos, salad dressing, milk and Tabasco sauce. Pour soup mixture over shrimp. Top with bread crumbs and bake at 350 degrees for thirty minutes or until bubbly hot. Serves 6-8.

Mrs. Robert Hartzog (Janette)

SHRIMP LOUISE

2 cups thick white sauce
1 tablespoon Worcestershire
   sauce
½ teaspoon nutmeg
½ teaspoon ginger
Dash of paprika

3 tablespoons chili sauce
Salt and pepper to taste
¼ cup sherry
1½ pounds shrimp, cleaned and
   cooked

Combine white sauce with Worcestershire sauce, nutmeg, ginger, paprika, chili sauce, salt and pepper; mix well. Add sherry, stir in well. Add cooked shrimp; mix well. Pour into 2 quart casserole. Bake at 325 degrees for 20 minutes. Serve over rice. Serves 4-6.

Mrs. Frank Tuckwiller (Barbara)

RAMEKINS OF SHRIMP IN SOUR CREAM

1½ pounds raw shrimp, peeled
   and washed
⅓ cup butter
½ pound fresh mushrooms,
   sliced

1½ cups sour cream
Paprika, salt and pepper
2 teaspoons soy sauce
6 buttered shells or ramekins
Grated cheese

Sauté shrimp in butter briefly. Add mushrooms. Cook 8-10 minutes. Heat sour cream to boiling point, season to taste with paprika, salt, pepper and soy sauce. Add enough paprika for a rich pink tint. Add to shrimp mixture, blend well, and cook over gentle flame until sauce is thick and smooth. Divide mixture into 6 buttered ramekins. Sprinkle with grated cheese and glaze under broiler flame. Serves 6.

Mrs. Richard G. Price, Jr. (Mary Jo)

SHRIMP PIE

1 tablespoon salt
2 cups day old biscuit crumbs
   or bread crumbs
1 large green pepper, chopped
2 cups shrimp, peeled and
   coarsely cut
1 teaspoon Tabasco

4 tablespoons catsup
4 tablespoons Worcestershire
   sauce
2 tablespoons prepared mustard
4 tablespoons butter, melted
2 cups milk

Add salt, bread crumbs, and green pepper to shrimp. Make sauce of remaining ingredients and pour over shrimp mixture. Let stand 1 hour. Bake covered at 350 degrees for 40 minutes. Uncover and brown. Serves 6.

Mrs. Riley Gettys (Bruce)

PENTAGON SHRIMP

1 cup salad oil
2 cups green pepper, sliced
5 cups onions, sliced
2 cups celery, chopped
1 cup celery leaves, chopped
1 cup chili sauce
1 cup raisins
1 teaspoon thyme
1 teaspoon curry powder

1 teaspoon salt
1 teaspoon pepper
1 teaspoon cayenne
3 bay leaves
1⅔ cups almonds, blanched and
    toasted
7 cups tomatoes
5 pounds shrimp, cooked and
    peeled

Heat oil in large skillet. Add green pepper, onion, celery and celery leaves. Sauté until onion is transparent. Add remaining ingredients except shrimp. Simmer gently 1 hour stirring occasionally. Add shrimp and heat thoroughly. The sauce should be made early in the day to blend flavors. Both the sauce and the shrimp can be prepared in advance and frozen separately. Serve sauce over rice. Serves 20.

Mrs. R. C. Marshall, III (Florence)

SWEET AND SOUR SHRIMP

1 20½ ounce can pineapple
    chunks
½ cup vinegar
⅔ cup brown sugar
¼ cup soy sauce
¼ cup cornstarch

¾ teaspoon salt
1 medium onion, sliced
1 bell pepper, chopped
1 pound shrimp, peeled and
    deveined
Chinese noodles or rice

Drain pineapple, saving liquid. Combine liquid with enough water to make 1 cup in a saucepan. Add the vinegar, brown sugar, soy sauce, cornstarch and salt. Cook until sauce is thick, stirring as needed. Add onions, pepper, pineapple chunks and raw shrimp. Cover and simmer for approximately 10 minutes. Serve with Chinese noodles or rice. Serves 4.

Mrs. Frank Trimmier (Ginny)

CREOLE JAMBALAYA

2 onions, chopped
¼ cup green onions, chopped
4 tablespoons butter
1 14-ounce can tomatoes,
    drained and chopped
    (reserve juice)
1 6-ounce can tomato paste
2 ounces water
4 cloves garlic, chopped
2 stalks celery, chopped
¼ bell pepper, chopped

2 tablespoons parsley, chopped
¼ teaspoon thyme
1 bay leaf
3 cloves, chopped
2 pounds raw shrimp, peeled
1 pound bulk hot sausage, cooked
    and drained
3½ cups cooked rice
Salt, pepper, cayenne
2 cups chicken, cooked and diced
Parsley, garnish

Sauté onions in butter for 5 minutes. Add tomatoes, juice, tomato paste and water. Cook 5 minutes, stirring constantly. Add garlic, celery, bell pepper, parsley, thyme, bay leaf and cloves. Stir well. Add shrimp and sausage. Cook 30 minutes, stirring frequently. Remove bay leaf. Stir in rice. Season to taste. Gently stir in chicken. Bake in buttered casserole at 350 degrees for 30 minutes. Garnish. Serves 10.

Mrs. Albert Schaufelberger (Virginia)

DOT'S DEVILLED OYSTERS

1 quart oysters, reserve juice
5 spring onions, tops and
    bottoms, chopped
2 cloves garlic, minced
1 teaspoon thyme
1 bay leaf

3 tablespoons olive oil
3 tablespoons margarine or butter
1 tablespoon Worcestershire sauce
Salt and pepper
1 cup toasted bread crumbs
Margarine or butter

Cut each oyster in 3 pieces, drain. Sauté onions, garlic, thyme and bay leaf in iron skillet in olive oil cooking slowly. Cook oysters in separate pan in margarine for about 5 minutes. Add Worcestershire sauce, oyster juice, salt and pepper. Add to iron skillet with bread crumbs. Place in oyster shells or casserole and cover with crumbs. Put pats of margarine on top and run in oven to heat. Serve with lemon quarters. Serves 6.

Mrs. William A. Campbell, Jr. (Biz)

OYSTER CASSEROLE

4 dozen oysters, drained
2/3 cup parsley, chopped
2/3 cup green onions, chopped
1 cup cracker crumbs, finely
   rolled

½ cup butter
2 tablespoons lemon juice
½ teaspoon dry mustard
2 teaspoons Worcestershire sauce

Place oysters in shallow baking dish. Sprinkle with parsley and onion, then cracker crumbs. Melt butter; add lemon juice, mustard and Worcestershire sauce. Pour over crumbs. Bake at 450 degrees until oysters curl and crumbs are brown. Serves 4.

Mrs. Jack Bond (Elizabeth)

OYSTERS ON TOAST

2 tablespoons flour
3 tablespoons bacon drippings
1 pint oysters, reserve liquor
Salt and pepper

1 cup half and half
1 egg yolk
6 slices bacon, fried and crumbled
Buttered toast

Blend flour in with bacon drippings until well blended. Add oyster liquor and stir until smooth. Add salt and pepper to taste. Beat half and half and egg yolk and add to oyster liquor. Remove from stove and add oysters and bacon. Stir mixture constantly and cook slowly until oysters are plump. Serve on buttered crisp toast. Serves 4.

Mrs. Neil Trask, Jr. (Becky)

SCALLOPED OYSTERS

1 quart oysters, reserve liquor
Half and half
2 cups saltine cracker crumbs
1 cup butter, melted

2 teaspoons pepper
2 teaspoons salt
¼ teaspoon mace

Add oyster liquor to half and half to make 1 pint. Heat. Mix saltine cracker crumbs, butter, pepper, salt and mace. Layer the cracker crumb mixture in baking dish with oysters, beginning with crumbs and then oysters. Pour heated liquid over the top. Bake in preheated 375 degree oven for 20-30 minutes. Serves 6-8.

Mrs. Angus D. Fordham (Marjorie)

OYSTER AND CHICKEN CASSEROLE
Good with hot fruit or brandied cranberries

¼ cup butter
¼ cup flour
Oyster liquor, ¼ cup white
   wine, chicken stock
   (to equal 1½ cups)
¼ cup cream
1 teaspoon lemon juice
Salt and pepper
2½ pounds chicken breast,
   cooked and cubed

1 pound mushrooms, sautéed
2 pints oysters, drained
1 10-ounce package frozen peas
3 cups cooked wild rice
½ cup parsley, minced
½ cup crumbs, buttered and
   toasted

Melt butter and stir in flour. Add oyster liquor, white wine and chicken stock. Stir until smooth and add cream, lemon juice, salt and pepper. Combine sauce with chicken, mushrooms, oysters, peas, wild rice and parsley. Place in a 11 x 7-inch casserole and top with bread crumbs. Bake at 350 degrees for 30 minutes. Serves 10-12.

Mrs. William G. Clark, III (Gray)

SCALLOPS WITH WINE

1½ pints scallops
1 cup vermouth
7 tablespoons butter, divided
¾ pound mushrooms, sliced
¾ cup white wine

1 onion, finely chopped
1 tablespoon flour
Salt and pepper
3 egg yolks
¾ cup heavy cream

In a small saucepan, cook scallops with vermouth for 10 minutes. Sauté the mushrooms in half the butter for 5 minutes. Cook the white wine and onion together for 15 minutes in another saucepan. Heat the remaining butter and stir in the flour, cooking until it bubbles. Add wine and onions and stir until smooth. Add broth from the scallops and continue stirring until smooth and hot. Remove from heat. Add salt and pepper to taste. Beat egg yolks and cream together until well blended and add to the sauce mixture. Reheat but do not boil. Place scallops in a chafing dish or serving dish, garnish with mushrooms and pour sauce over all. Serves 6.

Mrs. C. Blackburn Brewer (Frances)

SCALLOPS PROVENÇALE

6 tablespoons olive oil
2 cloves garlic, finely chopped
1 shallot, finely chopped
1½ pounds scallops, rinsed,
   dried, quartered
1 teaspoon lemon juice

1 dash Tabasco, optional
1 large tomato, peeled and
   chopped
Salt and pepper
¼ cup parsley

Heat oil in heavy skillet. Sauté garlic and shallot until tender but not brown. Increase heat and add scallops. Sauté scallops until lightly browned and opaque—about 5 minutes. Add lemon juice, Tabasco, tomato, salt, pepper and parsley. Cook long enough to heat thoroughly. Serves 4-6.

Mrs. Nöel Seeburg (Alice)

PÉPÉ CLAM SHELLS

½ cup onion, finely chopped
½ cup celery, finely chopped
¼ cup green pepper, finely
   chopped
4 tablespoons butter
2 tablespoons all-purpose flour
1 tablespoon grated Parmesan
   cheese

¼ teaspoon salt
Dash pepper
Dash Worcestershire sauce
Dash hot pepper sauce
1 7½ ounce can minced clams
   (crab may be substituted)
¼ cup crushed Ritz crackers
Butter

In skillet sauté onion, celery, and pepper in the butter. Stir in flour, cheese, salt, pepper, Worcestershire sauce, hot pepper sauce, and clams and cook until thick and bubbly. Spoon into 4 individual shells or dishes. Top with cracker crumbs and butter. Bake at 350 degrees for 15 minutes. Serves 4.

Mrs. Claude N. Dinkins (Cathy)

CRÊPES AU SALMON

12 crêpes
1 cup sour cream, divided
½ pound smoked salmon (lox),
   thinly sliced

Coarse black pepper
12 teaspoons fresh lemon juice

Make 12 crêpes. Spread sour cream on each crêpe. Put thin strips of lox in middle of each crêpe. Grind the pepper and add lemon juice. Roll up crêpes and put in 9 x 13-inch Pyrex serving dish. Spread left over sour cream on crêpes. Place in 450 degree oven for 15 minutes before serving. Exquisite entreé. Favorite of French Embassy.

Mrs. Merle Ormond (Monique)

SALMON NUGGETS

1 16-ounce can salmon
½ cup mashed potatoes
1 tablespoon celery, finely
    minced
1 tablespoon onion, grated
1 tablespoon margarine,
    melted

¼ teaspoon salt
Dash pepper
1½ teaspoons Worcestershire
    sauce
1 egg, beaten
¼ pound sharp cheese, cubed
1 cup dry bread crumbs

Drain and flake salmon. Mix thoroughly the salmon, potatoes, celery, onion, margarine, salt, pepper, Worcestershire sauce and egg. Shape into walnut size balls. Cut cheese into ⅜" cubes. Push a cheese cube into the center of each salmon ball and reshape. Roll in the bread crumbs. Deep fat fry at 375 degrees for 3-4 minutes until golden brown. Serve hot.
Mrs. Stanley Waskiewicz (Betty)

FILLET OF SOLE OR FLOUNDER
WITH SHRIMP AND CAPER SAUCE

4½ pounds fresh fillet of sole
    or flounder, cut into
    approximately 20 serving
    pieces
Salt and pepper to taste

Paprika
Butter
Shrimp and caper sauce
10 whole shrimp, garnish

Salt and pepper fish. Arrange in 2 casseroles, overlapping pieces of fish. Cover. Bake in 350 degree oven for 35-40 minutes. Remove from oven and drain liquid from fish. Reserve liquid for sauce. Sprinkle fish in casserole with paprika and dot with butter. Spoon sauce over and around fish. Garnish with whole shrimp. Cover with foil. Place in preheated 350 degree oven for 30 minutes. Serves 8-10.

SHRIMP AND CAPER SAUCE:
½ cup butter
5 tablespoons flour
Fish liquid
3 cups or less milk
2½ pounds shrimp, peeled and
    cut into pieces

4 teaspoons Accent
½ teaspoon gumbo filé
½ teaspoon salt
⅛ teaspoon cayenne
3 tablespoons capers, washed

Melt butter in heavy saucepan and let brown. Add flour and stir until smooth. Measure liquid from fish and add enough milk to make 3 cups. Add to butter mixture and cook over low heat until sauce thickens. Add shrimp, Accent, gumbo filé, salt, cayenne and capers.
Mrs. John Strong (Ethel)

FILETS DE SOLE FROID DUGLERE
Famous recipe from "The Claridges," London

8 filets sole or flounder
1 small onion, chopped
4 tomatoes, coarsely chopped
3 teaspoons parsley
½ cup white wine
6 ounces fish stock

1 tablespoon lemon juice
Salt and white pepper
1 cup mayonnaise
1 cup whipping cream
Parsley to garnish

Place filets in baking dish with onion, tomatoes, and parsley. Add wine, fish stock, lemon juice, salt and pepper. Cover and bring to boil only and then place in 350 degree oven for 10 minutes. Remove filets very carefully to platter for chilling taking care not to remove any vegetables or stock. Reduce the stock on top to the stove to ¼ its volume. Strain the stock and remove the vegetables. Allow stock to get cold and add mayonnaise and whipping cream. Whisk until mixed. Pour over chilled filets and sprinkle with parsley. This is a lovely first course on a hot day or a delicious hors d'oeurves with toast squares.

Mrs. Barney Rickenbacker (Florence)

FILLET OF FLOUNDER, ISLAND STYLE

2 medium onions, diced
1 large tomato, peeled and
   diced
¼ cup butter
1 cup dry white wine
4 tablespoons heavy cream

1 teaspoon salt
½ teaspoon pepper
1 teaspoon thyme
1-1½ pounds fillets of flounder
1 teaspoon lemon juice

Sauté onions and tomato in butter. Add wine, cream, salt, pepper, and thyme. Season fish with additional salt and pepper and rub with lemon juice. Place fish in baking dish, add sauce, cover and bake at 350 degrees for 15 minutes. Serves 2.

Mrs. Neil Trask, Jr. (Rebecca)

STUFFED FLOUNDER OR SOLE

¼ cup onion, chopped
¼ cup butter
1 4-ounce can broiled
    mushrooms, chop, drain,
    and reserve liquid
8 ounces crabmeat
½ cup coarse saltine cracker
    crumbs
2 tablespoons snipped parsley

8 fillets of flounder or sole
3 tablespoons butter
3 tablespoons flour
¼ teaspoon salt
1 cup milk
⅓ cup white wine
¼ pound Swiss cheese, grated
Paprika
Salt and pepper

To prepare stuffing, sauté onion in ¼ cup butter until tender but not brown. Add mushrooms, crabmeat, cracker crumbs and parsley and mix thoroughly. Spread stuffing over each fillet, roll and place in buttered baking dish seam side down. Season with salt and pepper. To prepare sauce, melt 3 tablespoons butter and blend in flour and salt. Combine the mushroom liquid and milk to make 1½ cups and gradually stir into flour mixture. Stir over low heat until thick. Gradually stir in wine and cook 2 more minutes. Pour sauce over fillets and bake in 400 degree oven for 25 minutes. Sprinkle with grated cheese and paprika and bake 10 minutes or until fish flakes easily with fork. Serves 8.

Mrs. Hank Ten Eyck (Mary)

SOLE IN VERMOUTH

1 cup dry vermouth
1½ pounds sole fillets
4 egg yolks

⅔ cup butter or margarine
1 tablespoon heavy cream
Salt and pepper

Heat vermouth in a skillet. Wrap fish loosely in cheesecloth, and poach in the vermouth about 10 minutes. Put fish on a broilerproof platter. Reduce vermouth to about ⅔ cup. In top of double boiler, combine egg yolks, butter, cream, and vermouth. Cook over hot, not boiling water, stirring until thickened. Season. Pour over fish, and brown quickly under broiler. Sauce may curdle slightly, but flavor is delicious. Serves 4.

Mrs. Richard G. Price, Jr. (Mary Jo)

FILLET OF SOLE PIQUANT

2 cups dry bread crumbs or
Pepperidge Farm dressing

1 pound fillet of sole or any other
fillet of fish

SAUCE:
½ cup butter, melted
1 teaspoon prepared mustard
Juice of 1 lemon

½ teaspoon salt
⅛ teaspoon pepper
Paprika

Grease shallow baking dish and cover bottom with bread crumbs. Arrange fish over crumbs. Make a sauce with butter, mustard, lemon juice, salt and pepper. Pour over fish. Dust with paprika. Bake at 450 degrees for 20 minutes. Serves 4.

Mrs. William Satterfield (Loma)

FISH WITH WINE AND CHEESE

½ cup butter
Salt, pepper and paprika
2 pounds fillet of flounder
2 tablespoons lemon juice

1 cup white wine
2 cups sharp Cheddar cheese,
grated
½ cup Parmesan cheese

Brown butter in a shallow baking dish. Salt and pepper fish, then place it in browned butter. Sprinkle fish with lemon juice and paprika. Pour wine over fish and cook in 350 degree oven for 10 minutes. Remove from oven, baste with sauce, then cover fish with grated cheese and Parmesan cheese. Put this under the broiler until the cheese is melted and crusty (10 minutes). Serve in the sauce. Serves 4.

The Editors

FISH CASSEROLE

3 pounds halibut
¼ pound shrimp, unpeeled
Court-bouillon
6 tablespoons butter
6 tablespoons flour
2 cups milk
Salt and pepper
4 tablespoons chili sauce

2 onions, chopped
1 pound mushrooms, remove
    stems
Butter
1 cup cream
¼ cup sherry
Bread crumbs

Cook both halibut and shrimp in shells in court-bouillon until soft. Remove bones, shells and skin. Reserve cooking liquid and boil down to 1 cupful. Make white sauce of butter, flour, milk. Add seasonings and chili sauce. Pour over fish and shrimp. Sauté onions and mushroom caps and add to mixture. Add fish stock, cream, and sherry. Top with buttered bread crumbs. Put in 400° oven until bubbly and crumbs are browned. Serves 6-8.

COURT-BOUILLON

Combine 2 bay leaves, parsley, 3 tarragon leaves, 6 peppercorns, 1 onion, 1 carrot, celery tops, salt and boil in 2 quarts of water for 1 hour. Strain liquid and reserve.

Mrs. John B. Snow (Gulia)

POLYNESIAN FISH

3 pounds halibut, swordfish, or
    cod, cut ¾″ thick
⅓ cup lime juice
¼ cup butter, melted
½ teaspoon salt
¼ teaspoon pepper

Generous pinch of marjoram
½ of 10-ounce can frozen cream of
    shrimp soup
½ cup sour cream
3-4 scallions, with tops, sliced thin
½ cup tiny shrimp, cooked

Wash, pat dry and cut the fish into 6 serving size pieces. Trim. Place in an oven-proof shallow baking dish. Pour the lime juice over the top and allow to soak for a few minutes on each side. Then discard the juice. Pour the butter over the fish and sprinkle with seasonings. Broil for about 10 minutes. Baste once with the butter. Remove from heat, baste again with the pan juices. Set aside to cool slightly. Mix the soup and sour cream together and spoon on top of each piece of fish. (All this may be prepared ahead.) When ready, bake for 30 minutes in a moderately slow oven, about 325 degrees. Serve in the baking dish and garnish with scallions and tiny shrimp. Serves 6.

Mrs. Donald Fritts (Ruth)

HOW TO DRESS AND COOK COBIA

Cobia—a game fish caught in
   the Broad River during the
   months of April through
   June.

Bottled Italian salad dressing
Lemon wedges
Parsley
Charcoal briquets

Place cobia on picnic table or work space layered with newspapers. With sharp knife, cut a ring just through skin around head to tail. Skin the fish by cutting 3" strips of skin from the head to tail. When all skin has been removed, cut off head and tail. Remove entrails into pail saving roe, if desired. Clean body cavity well with brush and hose. Place fish with back up and cut 1" steaks using hack saw and knife. Wash, dry and refrigerate steaks. Cobia freezes well when wrapped in freezer paper.

Cobia is delicious when marinated for several hours or overnight in bottled Italian salad dressing. Prepare a fire in the grill using charcoal briquets. Grill steaks approximately 5 minutes on each side until fish flakes. Garnish with lemon wedges and parsley.

Mrs. Robert B. Tomlinson (Jerry)

MARINADED SMOKED FISH

12 fish filets, 1-inch thick
1 cup salt
½ cup brown sugar
½ ounce black pepper

⅛ teaspoon cayenne
½ gallon water
Hickory chips

Mix salt, brown sugar, black pepper, cayenne, and water together. Stir until salt is dissolved. Pour marinade over fish in a large bowl and weight down with a china plate. Leave overnight. Take fish out of brine and wash thoroughly in cold water. Dry each piece and place on a rack for an hour to thoroughly dry surface. Grease smoker shelves with oil. Cover drip pan with foil, fill pan with hickory chips, and place on burner. Add fish. Turn smoker on for 1 hour, then empty hickory chips and refill pan. Repeat after second and third hour. Remove pan at end of third hour, unplug smoker and leave with fish to cure for 2 more hours. Process takes a total of 5 hours.

Mrs. Mac Donald Dixon (Phyllis)

RING OF SHAD ROE

2 8-ounce cans or 1 pound
    fresh shad roe
3 slices lemon
1 tablespoon capers
2 tablespoons unflavored gelatin

1½ cups chicken broth
Watercress
Cucumber slices
Mayonnaise

Poach shad roe gently in water with lemon slices for 10 minutes. Drain and cool. Remove membrane from shad roe carefully with a fork. Put roe in a greased mold and distribute capers evenly around roe. Dissolve gelatin in heated broth and pour over roe. Refrigerate until firm. Unmold and garnish with watercress and cucumber slices. Serve with mayonnaise. Excellent as a fish course or as an appetizer with crackers. Serves 8.

Mrs. W. H. Gaither (Louise)

BONELESS SHAD

Roeshad, gutted with roe left
    within
¼ cup butter or margarine
Salt
Pepper

Lemon slices
3-4 bacon slices
1 cup water
Parsley sprigs

Wash fish and pat dry with paper towels. Rub fish well with margarine, salt and pepper. Line bottom of roaster with foil to enable easy removal of fish when done. Place fish on foil with lemon slices and bacon strips on top. Put 1 cup of water in bottom of pan. Cover roaster and cook at 250 degrees for 8 hours. Serve with lemon slices and parsley.

Mrs. William Anthony Peters, Jr. (Louise)

STUFFING FOR BAKED FISH

1 cup bread crumbs
¼ teaspoon salt
⅛ teaspoon pepper
¼ cup butter, melted

1 tablespoon parsley, chopped
1 tablespoon pickle, chopped
1 tablespoon onion, chopped

Mix all ingredients and stuff fish. Hold together with toothpicks.

Mrs. S. N. Clark, Jr. (Carolyn)

DOGWOOD

Poultry and Game

SAUTÉED DOVES IN WINE WITH WHITE GRAPES

6 doves
6 tablespoons butter
2 tablespoons onions, chopped
Salt and pepper
1 cup white wine, divided
2 tablespoons fresh parsley,
    chopped

2 tablespoons fresh tarragon (2
    teaspoons if dried)
1 cup white seedless grapes
Toast

Brown doves in butter with onions, salt and pepper. Add ½ cup white wine and simmer covered for 15 minutes or until tender. Add ½ cup white wine, parsley, and tarragon. Simmer, uncovered, for 5 minutes. Before serving, add grapes long enough to heat but not to cook. Serve on toast with sauce spooned over it. Serves 6.

Mrs. John Seymour (June)

ANDY'S DOVES

12 doves, dressed
½ cup butter
2-3 tablespoons flour
½ medium onion, chopped

8 ounces mushrooms
2 cups chicken broth
½ cup dry sherry, optional
Salt and pepper

Brown doves in butter. When browned, remove birds from browning pan and put in casserole dish. Add flour to butter left in browning pan, blend well. Brown onions and mushrooms in flour mixture. Stir in chicken broth. Add sherry, if desired. Salt and pepper to taste. Pour mixture over doves. Bake covered 1½ hours in 350 degree oven. Serves 4-6.

Mrs. John Perrill (Claire)

DOVE AU VIN

12 doves
Salt and pepper to taste
Flour
⅓ cup butter
1 cup celery, chopped

1 cup onion, chopped
1 small bell pepper, chopped
1 10½-ounce can consommé
½ cup red wine

Season doves with salt and pepper and roll in flour. In a skillet, brown doves slowly in butter until brown on both sides. Transfer to a casserole and add celery, onions, bell pepper and consommé. Cook covered in 350 degree oven for 2 hours. Add wine last 30 minutes of cooking time. Serves 6.

Mrs. C. W. Mayo, III (Miriam)

DOVES IN CASSEROLE

2 tablespoons butter
6 strips bacon
4 teaspoons peppercorns
2 large onions, chopped
Salt and pepper

20 doves
Water
1 pint sour cream
1 10¾-ounce can mushroom soup

In large skillet melt butter. Layer bacon, peppercorns and onions and season with salt and pepper. Place doves with breast side up in pan and add enough water to cover onions. Cover and steam two hours. Remove doves and strain broth. Add sour cream and mushroom soup to broth. Place doves in casserole and cover with broth. Cover casserole and bake at 350 degrees for 30 minutes. Serve over wild rice.

Mrs. W. Brantley Harvey, Jr. (Helen)

BONNY HALL SNIPE OR DOVE

8 snipe or dove
½ cup butter

1 tablespoon parsley, chopped

Dry birds thoroughly inside and out. Put in baking dish with butter and place in center of 500 degree preheated oven. When butter melts, remove from oven and transfer birds and melted butter to mixing bowl. Let cool stirring frequently until birds have become completely glazed and butter is congealed over them.

This process can be speeded up by placing bowl in a cool location. Also, the preparation can be accomplished in advance. If held for a lengthy period, refrigerate.

When ready to cook, have glazed birds at room temperature; place again in 500 degree oven and bake for 8 minutes—*no more.* Sprinkle with parsley and serve with the pan essence. Serves 4.

Mrs. Nicholas G. Penniman (Pattie)

WILD DUCK

1 large wild duck
Salt and pepper
1 onion, peeled

¼ cup red wine
½ teaspoon thyme
2 teaspoons butter

Rub inside of duck with salt and pepper. Place onion inside of duck. Lay duck on a large sheet of heavy foil and pour wine over it. Sprinkle thyme on duck and place butter on top. Wrap tightly. Cook at 325 degrees for 3 hours or until done.

Mrs. C. W. Mayo, III (Miriam)

BAKED ORANGE MARSH HENS

8 marsh hens, cleaned and
   disjointed
¼ cup butter or margarine
1 orange, sliced cross-wise and
   seeded

2 tablespoons flour
½ teaspoon salt
⅛ teaspoon cinnamon
1½ cups orange juice

In large skillet, brown birds in butter. Arrange with orange slices in 12 x 8 x 2-inch baking dish. In same skillet, blend in flour, salt and cinnamon. Gradually pour in orange juice and cook over medium heat, stirring until thickened and boiling. Pour over birds and orange slices. Bake at 375 degrees in preheated oven about 45 minutes or until tender. You may want to cover for at least half the time. Serves 4.
Mrs. Arthur Simon Jenkins (Frances)

SMOTHERED QUAIL

6 quail
6 tablespoons butter
3 tablespoons flour

2 cups chicken broth
½ cup sherry
Salt and pepper to taste

Brown quail in heavy skillet in melted butter. Remove to baking dish. Add flour to skillet and stir well. Slowly add broth, sherry, salt and pepper. Blend and pour over quail. Cover baking dish and bake at 325 degrees for 1 hour and 15 minutes. Serve with rice. Serves 6.
Mrs. F. William Scheper, III (Jean)

LOW COUNTRY STUFFED ROAST QUAIL

1½ cups Madeira
¼ cup raisins
3 whole cloves
⅔ cup cooked rice
½ cup almonds, chopped
2 teaspoons grated orange peel

Pinch of ground ginger
4 tablespoons butter, melted and
   divided
6 quail
Juice of 1 orange

Combine in saucepan Madeira, raisins and cloves, and bring to a boil and simmer for 5 minutes. Remove cloves and strain mixture. Reserve. Combine the raisins with rice, almonds, orange peel and ginger; stir in butter. Stuff the birds with mixture; truss the birds, and brush with butter. Blend the reserved Madeira with orange juice to make a basting sauce. Roast the quail in 450 degree oven for 5 minutes, lower heat to 300 degrees, baste frequently with sauce until tender (about 25 minutes). Place on a heated platter with rice and serve at once. Serves 6.
Mrs. Martin Hoogenboom (Isabel)

SMOTHERED RABBIT

1 rabbit, approximately 4
   pounds, skinned and
   dressed
1 cup self-rising flour
1 teaspoon salt

1 teaspoon black pepper
¼ teaspoon garlic powder
2 cups vegetable oil
1 teaspoon sugar
Water

Wash rabbit thoroughly. Cut into frying-size pieces. In heavy brown paper bag, mix flour, salt, pepper, and garlic powder. Drop in pieces of rabbit and shake. Heat oil in skillet or electric fryer (325 degrees). Brown rabbit on both sides, remove to casserole dish or roasting pan. Sift seasoned flour from bag into a container; add sugar. Pour off oil from skillet, leaving approximately ¼ cup in pan. Add flour, stir constantly until thoroughly browned. Add one cup of water, continue stirring. Add more water very gradually until gravy is of medium thickness. Pour gravy over rabbit and cover with foil. Bake in 325 degree oven for 1½ hours or until very tender. Serves 6.

Mrs. William Hyland (Mary)

ROASTED VENISON

3 to 4 pounds venison roast
4 slices bacon, diced
¼ teaspoon whole black
   pepper, crushed
¾ teaspoon allspice
1 large onion, diced
4 tablespoons catsup

1 tablespoon Worcestershire sauce
1 bay leaf, crushed
½ cup vinegar
½ cup water
Flour
Hot oil

Stick a knife at random about 1 inch apart into roast. Mix bacon, pepper, allspice, onion, catsup, Worcestershire sauce and bay leaf. Stuff mixture into holes in roast.

Place roast in large mixing bowl and pour vinegar and water over it. Let marinate in refrigerator three days. Turn once. Drain and reserve liquid.

Dredge roast in flour and brown in hot oil. Make gravy from marinade and pour over roast. Cook 2½ to 3 hours covered at 325 degrees. Serves 4-6.

Mrs. Rudolph Geissler (Grey)

TURKEY BREAST CARDINAL

1 raw turkey breast
Flour
Salt and pepper
Butter and oil for frying
1 tablespoon Marsala,
   sauterne, or sherry

4-6 tablespoons chicken broth
6 thin slices prosciutto
½ pound mushrooms, sliced and
   sautéed
Parmesan cheese, grated

Skin turkey breast and carefully slice thinly into 6 fillets. Pound between wax paper and dredge in flour, salt and pepper. Cook slowly in butter and oil for about 5 minutes on each side. Have plenty to cook in but do not allow butter to burn. Add Marsala and chicken broth to pan, spooning liquid over turkey. Place a thin slice of prosciutto on each fillet, then a layer of sautéed mushroom slices. This much can be done ahead. Sprinkle with Parmesan cheese and heat until cheese melts and spreads. Serve immediately with pan juices spooned over top. Serves 6.

Mrs. Harry Gilham (Caroline)

CHICKEN CURRY

1 2 to 3 pound chicken,
   quartered
1 stalk celery, quartered
1 small onion, quartered
1 teaspoon salt
3½ cups water
1 green apple, diced

Chicken stock
½ medium onion, chopped
6 tablespoons butter, divided
4 tablespoons flour
3 tablespoons curry powder
Tabasco sauce

Place chicken in saucepan with celery, onion, salt and water and bring to a boil. Simmer until tender. Remove chicken, strain the stock and reserve. Remove skin and fat from the chicken and remove meat. Cut meat into strips about 1½ inches long.

Boil apple in ¼ cup chicken stock, mash, and set aside. Sauté onion in 2 tablespoons butter until transparent and set aside. Melt 4 tablespoons butter in saucepan and add flour and curry powder, mixing well. Add remaining chicken stock and stir until thickened like a cream sauce. Add cooked onion, and apple. Add Tabasco sauce by teaspoonfuls to taste depending on how hot you want the curry to be. Let boil slowly for 10 minutes. Add chicken and mix gently. Do not cover.

Serve over rice with condiments. Serves 6.

Mrs. C. A. Larsen, Jr. (Eleanor)

COLD CURRIED CHICKEN

3 onions, sliced
2 cloves garlic, crushed
2 tablespoons butter
1 heaping teaspoon curry
   powder
Salt and pepper
½ teaspoon turmeric
3 or 4 cardamon seeds,
   crushed

1 bay leaf
1½ chickens, boiled and boned
Just over ½ cup chicken stock
¾ cup heavy cream
½ cup mayonnaise
Cold cooked rice
Chutney

Sauté onions and garlic in butter but do not brown. Add curry powder and other spices and fry a minute or two longer. Add cooked chicken and chicken stock, simmer gently for 15 minutes; cover if it seems to be getting too dry. Cool. Combine cream and mayonnaise and stir into chicken mixture. Serve with cold cooked rice and chutney. Serves 6-8.

Mrs. Thomas H. Truslow (Frances)

CURRIED ORANGE CHICKEN

6 chicken breasts
2 tablespoons butter
Salt and pepper
1½ cups orange juice
½ cup raisins

¼ cup chutney, chopped
½ cup almonds, slivered
½ teaspoon curry
Dash of thyme
Bananas and parsley, garnish

Arrange chicken breasts in greased, shallow roasting pan, skin side up. Dot with butter. Sprinkle with salt and pepper. Bake at 425 degrees for 15 minutes. Meanwhile, combine orange juice, raisins, chutney, almonds, curry and thyme. Simmer slowly for 10 minutes. Pour over chicken and reduce heat to 350 degrees. Bake for 1 hour . Serve on bed of rice and garnish with bananas and parsley, if desired. Serves 6.

You may make sauce the day before. Do not over cook.

Mrs. William D. Huyler (Jo)

CHICKEN ORANGE

4 pound chicken fryer, cut into
    pieces
Salt and lemon pepper
½ cup onions, chopped
1 12-ounce can frozen orange
    juice, undiluted
½ cup butter

¾ cup orange marmalade
1 tablespoon Worcestershire sauce
Rind of 1 orange, grated
Orange slices
1 tablespoon parsley flakes
½ cup slivered almonds

Preheat oven to 350 degrees. Salt and lemon pepper each piece of chicken. Place in roasting pan. Cover with onions. Melt orange juice, butter and orange marmalade over low heat. Add Worcestershire sauce and orange rind. Pour over chicken. Top each chicken piece with a slice of orange, parsley flakes and almonds and cover with aluminum foil. Bake 1½ hours. Remove cover for last 15 minutes of baking. Serves 4-6.

Mrs. Mark Fordham (Virginia)

LEMON CHICKEN

1 fryer chicken, cut up
½ teaspoon salt
Pinch black pepper
3 lemons

2 tablespoons butter
1 cup water
1 pinch thyme leaves
½ pint heavy cream

Pour juice of 2 lemons over chicken. Sprinkle salt and pepper over and let sit for 2 hours in refrigerator. Dry the chicken pieces lightly with paper towels and sauté in butter until golden brown. Add water, lemon juice left in dish and thyme. Bring to a boil then cover and reduce heat and cook until tender, 20 to 30 minutes. Remove chicken to serving dish and keep warm. Add cream and the third lemon cut into thin slices to the pan. Reduce the sauce until it starts to thicken. Pour over the chicken. Serves 6.

Mrs. William S. Tilley (Mary Ann)

PEACH CHICKEN

2 fryers, cut up
¼ cup peach syrup
2 tablespoons lemon juice

1 teaspoon soy sauce
2 tablespoons butter
8 peach halves

Arrange chicken in shallow pan. Combine peach syrup, lemon juice and soy sauce and pour over chicken. Dot with butter. Bake at 375 degrees and baste often. After 1 hour, place peach halves around chicken and cook another ½ hour. Serves 8.

Mrs. H. E. Trask (Margaret)

HONEY CHICKEN

1 3-pound chicken, cut up	¼ cup prepared mustard
4 tablespoons butter	1 teaspoon salt
½ cup honey	1 teaspoon curry powder

Wash chicken pieces; pat dry. Melt butter in oblong baking dish. Combine other ingredients and add to baking dish. Roll chicken in mixture to coat on both sides. Then arrange in single layer. Bake at 375 degrees for 1 hour or until chicken is tender and glazed.

Mrs. John W. Gray, III (Molly)

COQ AU VIN

1 chicken, disjointed	¼ pound mushrooms, sliced
Flour	Thyme, to taste
Salt and pepper	Bay leaf
½ cup butter	Parsley, to taste
2 tablespoons sliced salt pork	2 tablespoons brandy
8-10 small white onions	1 cup red wine
1 clove garlic, crushed	

Roll chicken in flour, salt and pepper, or shake together in paper bag. In a large skillet brown chicken in butter with salt pork. Add onions, garlic, and mushrooms and brown a bit more. Add thyme, bay leaf and parsley. Transfer to heavy casserole; add brandy and wine; cover and bake at 325 degrees for 1½-2 hours. Good to make a day ahead and refrigerate overnight to skim off excess fat. Serves 4-6.

Mrs. Thomas H. Truslow (Frances)

POULET PROVENÇAL

1 uncooked chicken, boned and
    cut up
1 teaspoon salt
½ teaspoon pepper
8 tablespoons butter, divided
4 garlic cloves, crushed

½ cup wine vinegar
¼ cup water
2 tablespoons tomato paste
3 tablespoons fresh parsley,
    chopped

Rub chicken with salt and pepper. Melt 4 tablespoons butter in casserole dish on medium heat and brown chicken for approximately 10 minutes. Add garlic, vinegar, water, and tomato paste. Cover and cook until tender, about 20 minutes. Remove chicken to a platter and reduce sauce by boiling it for a minute. Whisk remaining 4 tablespoons butter in to thicken the sauce. Taste to correct seasonings. Pour sauce over chicken and sprinkle with parsley. Serves 8.

Mrs. John M. Trask, Jr. (Caroline)

CHICKEN MORNAY

3 tablespoons butter, melted
3 tablespoons flour
3 cups light cream
Cayenne pepper and salt to
    taste
2 pounds chicken, cooked and
    cut up
1½ cups rice, cooked in
    chicken broth and 1
    tablespoon chopped
    parsley

4 tablespoons butter, melted
¼ cup Parmesan cheese, grated
½ cup Gruyére cheese, grated
Parmesan cheese, grated
Paprika

Combine 3 tablespoons butter with flour, blend well. Add cream and season-ing, stirring constantly until thick to make a cream sauce. Mix chicken with 1 cup sauce. Put cooked rice in well buttered shallow casserole. Cover with chicken. Heat remaining sauce until bubbly. Beat with wire whisk and add alternately butter and two cheeses. Pour over chicken. Dust with Parmesan and paprika. Brown lightly in 350 degree oven. Serves 6-8.

Mrs. Kenneth Hutton (Phyllis)

HOT CHICKEN SALAD

3 cups cooked chicken, diced
1 cup mayonnaise
2 cups celery, finely chopped
2 tablespoons grated onion
2 tablespoons lemon juice
½ cup chopped almonds,
    toasted

½ teaspoon salt
1 teaspoon Accent
1 teaspoon tarragon
1 cup crushed potato chips
½ cup grated Cheddar cheese

Mix well and turn into 11 x 7 x 1-inch baking dish. Top with potato chips and cheese that have been combined. Bake at 450 degrees for 10 minutes and serve immediately. Serves 8-10.

Beaufort County Open Land Trust

HOT CHICKEN MOUSSE WITH MUSHROOM SAUCE

1½ pounds raw chicken
    breasts, boned and skinned
2 cups heavy cream
2 egg whites

1 3-4 ounce package dry chicken
    broth mix
¼ teaspoon cayenne pepper
Salt and pepper

Purée the chicken and put in the blender a little at a time with some of the cream. Mix well with the rest of the cream. Add the unbeaten egg whites and remaining ingredients, salting generously. Butter a 1½ quart mold and fill with mixture. Cover with waxed paper and refrigerate until ¾ hour before serving time. Place mold in a shallow pan of hot water in a 350 degree oven. Bake for 25-35 minutes. Unmold onto a hot platter. Pour over some of the sauce, garnish and serve remaining sauce separately. Serves 4.

MUSHROOM SAUCE:

½ pound mushrooms, chopped
½ cup onion, chopped
6 tablespoons butter
6 tablespoons flour

1 cup rich chicken stock
1 cup heavy cream
¼ cup sherry
Salt and pepper

Sauté the mushrooms and onion in the butter. Add the flour and stock gradually to the simmering mixture. Add the cream and bring to the boiling point. Add the sherry and season to taste with salt and pepper. Serve over hot chicken mousse.

Mrs. Edwin H. Marks, Jr. (Mildred)

CHICKEN BREASTS SUPREME

3 whole chicken breasts,
   boned, skinned to make 6
   pieces
7 tablespoons butter, divided
2 tablespoons flour
¼ teaspoon salt
White pepper

¾ cup chicken stock
¼ cup sherry
¼ cup heavy cream
½ pound fresh mushrooms,
   sliced
Butter

Sprinkle boned breasts lightly with salt. Using 5 tablespoons butter, sauté chicken breasts. Cook 4 minutes over medium heat, turn and cook another 4 minutes. Test to see if they are springy. Remove from skillet and keep warm. In a separate saucepan, melt 2 tablespoons butter. Blend in flour, salt and white pepper. Stir in chicken stock and cook over medium heat, stirring until thickened. Add sherry and simmer 2 minutes. Stir in heavy cream and remove from heat. Place chicken breasts on platter. Cover with mushrooms that have been sautéed in butter. Pour sauce over chicken and mushrooms. Can be frozen. (To serve: thaw completely and heat for 30 minutes in 350 degree oven.) Serve on brown and wild rice or toast points with tossed salad and white or rosé wine. Serves 6.

Mrs. C. A. Larsen, Jr. (Eleanor)

CHICKEN CASSEROLE

2 cups cold boiled chicken,
   diced
1 cup cooked rice
1 cup celery, chopped
½ cup onion, minced
¾ cup mayonnaise
¾ cup water chestnuts, drained
   and sliced

¾ cup almonds, slivered
1 10½-ounce can cream of chicken
   soup
½ teaspoon salt
½ cup Cheddar cheese, grated
1 cup Pepperidge Farm herb
   seasoned stuffing, crushed

Mix all ingredients except cheese and stuffing. Put in casserole. Add stuffing and cheese to top. Bake at 350 degrees until bubbly; 20-25 minutes. Serves 6.

Mrs. Harry Lightsey, Sr. (Ellen)

CHICKEN AND RICE AMANDINE

1 tablespoon onion, minced
4 tablespoons butter
⅓ cup flour
2 cups chicken stock
1 cup heavy cream
3 cups chicken, cooked and
   diced
3 cups cooked rice

½ cup almonds, blanched, slivered
   and toasted
2 tablespoons pimento, minced
1 tablespoon parsley, minced
¼ teaspoon nutmeg
¼ teaspoon thyme
⅓ teaspoon marjoram
1 teaspoon salt

Sauté onion in butter until golden but not brown. Add flour and blend. Add stock gradually, stirring until sauce thickens. Simmer 10 minutes. Add cream and heat, but do not boil. Add chicken, rice and remaining ingredients and mix well. Pour into a 2-quart casserole and bake at 375 degrees for 20 minutes, or until well heated through. This freezes well. Serves 8.

Mrs. Thomas H. Truslow (Frances)

CHICKEN DIVINE

2 10-ounce packages frozen
   broccoli spears, coarsely
   chopped
4 chicken breasts, cooked and
   chopped
2 10¾-ounce cans cream of
   chicken soup

1 cup mayonnaise
1 lemon (juice only)
1 teaspoon curry powder
1 cup grated sharp Cheddar
   cheese
1 cup bread crumbs, toasted
1 teaspoon paprika

Cook broccoli slightly in little salt water. Drain. Debone chicken and cut into bite size pieces. Put broccoli in layer in buttered casserole. Put layer of chicken over broccoli.

Mix a sauce of the soup, mayonnaise, lemon juice and curry powder. Cover the chicken and broccoli with sauce.

Top with grated cheese. Sprinkle with bread crumbs and then paprika. Bake 35 to 40 minutes at 350 degrees.

Rita Van Pelt

BARBECUE CHICKEN

1 chicken, cut up	2 tablespoons onion, grated
½ cup catsup	2 tablespoons sugar
1 tablespoon vinegar	½ cup water
2 tablespoons lemon juice	4 tablespoons butter, melted

Mix above sauce and pour over chicken in baking dish. Bake in covered dish at 350 degrees for 1¼ hours. Serves 6-8.

Lois Fuller

CHICKEN STEW

4 or 5 pound chicken	¼ teaspoon red pepper
3 cups water	1 teaspoon salt
4 slices bacon	3 cups chicken stock
6 large onions, sliced	½ cup butter
1 20-ounce bottle catsup	½ cup flour mixed with ½ cup
4 tablespoons Worcestershire	water
sauce	4 hard boiled eggs, sliced
1 tablespoon black pepper	Rice

Steam chicken in water until tender. Save stock. Remove skin, debone chicken and cut into bite size pieces. Cut bacon in small pieces and fry; add onions and cook until tender—not brown. Add catsup, Worcestershire sauce, peppers, salt, and chicken stock. Thicken with butter and flour and water mixture. When smooth, add chicken and eggs. Let stand on low heat until ready to serve. Serve over rice. Serves 10.

Mrs. Omar Beasley (Sadie)

CHICKEN GUMBO

1 4-pound chicken, cut up
6 cups cold water
1 carrot, sliced
2 stalks celery
1 onion, sliced
½ bay leaf
¼ teaspoon peppercorns

1 12-ounce can tomatoes
2 cups okra, sliced
½ medium green pepper, finely
  chopped
Salt and pepper to taste
Cooked rice

Clean and wipe chicken. Place in kettle, add water, cover and cook until tender. Skim and remove fat. Add vegetables and seasonings, simmer 40 minutes. Serve over steamed rice. Serves 8.

Mrs. W. W. Airar (Eugenie)

CUBAN CHICKEN

2 tablespoons olive oil
1 frying chicken, cut up
Flour
1 medium onion, chopped
1 green pepper, chopped
1 garlic clove, minced
1 15-ounce can tomato sauce

1 teaspoon capers
½ cup raisins
1 2¾-ounce bottle pimento
Stuffed olives
Rice
Saffron or Bijol

Heat olive oil in skillet. Flour chicken on all sides. Brown quickly in olive oil, turning until sides are golden brown. Remove chicken from pan. If necessary add more olive oil to skillet and fry onion, pepper and garlic until transparent. Add tomato sauce, capers and raisins. Blend thoroughly. Add chicken. Cover skillet and let simmer covered until chicken is tender. Just before serving add stuffed olives.

Serve with rice flavored with saffron or Bijol.

This dish freezes very well if olives are omitted. Add olives after defrosting while heating.

Mrs. Benjamin G. Weil (Bebe)

CHICKEN OF INDIA

1 whole chicken, cut up
1 quart buttermilk
2 tablespoons salt
1 teaspoon garlic powder
1 tablespoon lemon juice

1 teaspoon red pepper
1 tablespoon ground comino
    (cumin)
1 tablespoon ground coriander

Place the chicken in a large baking dish. Mix all the spices and lemon juice with the buttermilk and pour over the chicken. Leave in the refrigerator for 3 days or more before cooking. Cook outside over an open grill until done. Serves 4-6.

Mrs. P. J. Jones (Tanya)

CHICKEN ENCHILADAS

3 whole chicken breasts or one
    2½ pound chicken
Salt
Celery top
Onion studded with whole
    cloves
2 onions, chopped
3 tablespoons salad oil
1 clove garlic, finely chopped
Pepper

3 canned green chilis, chopped and
    seeded
1 tablespoon sugar
3 cups tomato puree
12 corn tortillas
¼ cup salad oil
2 cups half and half cream
6 chicken bouillon cubes
½ pound Monterey Jack cheese,
    grated

Simmer chicken until tender in water in which salt, celery top and onion studded with cloves have been added. Cool chicken in stock. Remove the skin and cut chicken into bite-size pieces. Sauté chopped onion in 3 tablespoons salad oil until soft. Add garlic, chili, sugar, tomato puree, pepper, and the chicken. Simmer 10 minutes. Fry tortillas in ¼ cup salad oil until soft. Do not let them get crisp. Drain on paper towels. Fill each tortilla with ½ cup of the chicken mixture. Roll and place in a shallow greased casserole, in a single layer with seam side down. Heat cream and bouillon cubes in a saucepan. Do not let them boil but be sure cubes are dissolved. Pour over the enchiladas and sprinkle with cheese. Bake at 350 degrees for 45 minutes or until hot and bubbly. Serves 6.

Mrs. J. E. McTeer, Jr. (Gail)

ARROZ CON POLLO (PUERTO RICAN STYLE)

1 chicken, cut into serving
    pieces
⅓ cup country ham, diced
3 tablespoons olive oil
½ cup water
1 8-ounce can tomato sauce
4 teaspoons capers
¼ cup olives, chopped

½ green pepper, chopped
2-3 cloves garlic, mashed
1 medium onion, diced
8 stuffed olives
Cooked rice
1 2-ounce jar pimentos
White asparagus

Brown chicken and ham in olive oil. Add water and simmer. Combine tomato sauce, capers, chopped olives, green pepper, garlic, and onion in blender. Add to chicken mixture and simmer until tender. Add whole olives to chicken. Add a few tablespoons sauce to rice as well as pimento juice. Garnish rice with pimento strips and white asparagus. Serve with chicken. Baked bananas is a good accompaniment with Arroz con Pollo. Serves 4-6.

Mrs. Reese W. Lindsay (Annie Sue)

ITALIAN CHICKEN BREASTS

4 large chicken breasts (8
    halves), boned
8 thin slices Mozzarella cheese
¼ teaspoon garlic powder
¼ teaspoon onion powder

¼ teaspoon paprika
¼ teaspoon seasoned salt
¼ teaspoon oregano
1 cup saltine crackers, crumbled

Pound each chicken breast flat. Place one slice of cheese on top of each half chicken breast and fold chicken over. Combine garlic powder, onion powder, paprika, seasoned salt and oregano and sprinkle on each chicken breast. Roll chicken in crumbs and place in a greased 8 x 14-inch pyrex dish. Bake 45 minutes in a 350 degree oven. Serves 6-8.

Mrs. Preston W. McElveen (Madlyn)

CHICKEN LIVERS IN SOUR CREAM SAUCE

4 slices bacon
1 onion, sliced
½ pound fresh mushrooms,
    sliced
½ pound chicken livers
¼ teaspoon rosemary leaves

1 cup chicken broth or bouillon
¼ teaspoon salt
⅛ teaspoon black pepper
1 cup sour cream
1 tablespoon flour

In a large skillet, fry bacon until crisp and brown. Remove from pan, crumble and set aside. In same skillet, add onions and mushrooms. Sauté until tender, about 5 minutes. Stir in chicken livers and rosemary. Sauté briefly until livers are brown. Add broth, salt and pepper. Cover and simmer 15 minutes, or until tender. Combine sour cream and flour. Stir into skillet, mixing until smooth. Simmer about 5 minutes or until hot and bubbly. Serve livers and sauce on noodles, rice or toast points. Top with bacon. This freezes well and may be doubled. Serves 4.

Mrs. John Achelis

Meats

ROAST BEEF

1 6-pound tenderloin   6 slices bacon
2 teaspoons black pepper

Allow roast to stand at room temperature for 30 minutes. Place roast in open pan. Sprinkle with pepper. Arrange bacon slices on top, skewering with toothpicks. Put into 450 degree oven. Allow 10 minutes per pound for rare roast, 12 minutes per pound for medium. Remove from oven and allow to stand 15 minutes before carving. Serves 10.

Mrs. J. E. McTeer (Lucille)

DIVINE BEEF ROAST

1 clove garlic, crushed   1 cup water
1 cup soy sauce   1 tablespoon meat tenderizer
1½ tablespoons vinegar   1 6-pound roast (any cut)
¼ cup bourbon

Combine crushed garlic, soy sauce, vinegar, bourbon, water and meat tenderizer. Pour over roast and marinate for 24 hours in refrigerator. Charcoal 45 minutes on an open grill, or 30 to 35 minutes on a covered grill.

Mrs. Raymond Stocks (Jerry)

DRUNKEN ROAST

1 roast (rump or sirloin tip)   1 12-ounce can beer
   approximately 4 pounds   1 large onion, sliced
1 20-ounce bottle tomato
   catsup

Brown roast. Mix catsup, beer and onion. Add to roast. Simmer covered for 2 hours. Uncover and simmer for 1 more hour. Serves 6 to 8.

Mrs. F. W. Boye (Page)

SPICY POT ROAST

4 pound pot roast (use chuck, rump, etc.)
2 tablespoons cooking oil
2 cups water
1 or 2 16-ounce cans tomatoes (use only 1 if you don't like things with too much of a tomato flavor)
3 teaspoons salt

1½ teaspoons pepper
2 teaspoons chili powder
⅛ teaspoon red pepper
1 large onion, sliced
2 bay leaves
1 teaspoon thyme
¼ cup red wine or sherry, if desired
Parsley

Brown roast in oil. Add other ingredients and simmer for 2½ hours, covered. Cover with sauce and parsley when serving. It is as good the next day and freezes well. Serves 6.

Mrs. J. L. Mavretic (Ruth)

BEEF STEW

5 large onions, peeled and sliced
½ cup butter, divided
1½ pounds of lean beef, cut into bite-size pieces
Flour
Pepper, to taste
Water

5 small carrots, peeled and sliced
5 stalks celery, sliced
1 16-ounce can tomatoes
Salt, to taste
3 bay leaves
3 medium potatoes, peeled and cut into bite-sized pieces
Flour, optional

Brown the onions slowly in butter until very brown. Remove from frying pan to stew kettle. Roll beef pieces in flour and pepper and brown quickly in butter in frying pan and add to onions. Then add enough water to frying pan to absorb the browned flour and fat and add that to the meat. Next add to kettle carrots, celery, tomatoes, salt and bay leaves. Simmer about 1 hour. Add potatoes and continue simmering until done. This may be thickened with flour if desired. Correct seasonings. Remove bay leaves. Serve over rice or in casserole with biscuits on top. Serves 4-6.

Mrs. George Tucker (Martha)

BEEF BURGUNDY

2 tablespoons salad oil
2½ pounds boneless chuck, cut
    into 1½-inch cubes
2 tablespoons cornstarch
1 beef bouillon cube, diluted in
    1 cup of water

½ pound small white onions
3 potatoes, chopped
3 carrots, chopped
1 cup Burgundy
Salt and pepper to taste
Parsley

Slowly heat in Dutch oven. Brown the beef well on all sides and remove from pan. Add cornstarch to pan drippings stirring until well blended. Gradually stir in beef bouillon. Bring to boil, stirring constantly. Add browned beef, onions and vegetables. Add Burgundy, salt and pepper. Reduce heat and simmer covered 3 hours. Serve garnished with parsley. Serves 3 to 4.

Mrs. W. N. Redling (Phylis)

BOEUF BOURGUIGNONNE

Butter
Flour
3 pounds beef, cubed
½ cup fresh mushrooms, sliced
5 medium carrots, cut into
    1-inch sections
¼ teaspoon rosemary

¼ teaspoon thyme
¼ teaspoon oregano
¼ teaspoon tarragon
1 10¾-ounce can consommé
1 cup Burgundy wine
1 10-ounce can boiled onions,
    drained

Flour cubes of stewing beef, and brown in butter. Place beef, mushrooms, carrots, rosemary, thyme, oregano and tarragon in large casserole. To drippings left from browning beef, add the can of consommé and the wine. Heat liquid only until it steams, then pour over meat. Cover and bake at 350 degrees for 1½ hours. Add drained onions. Cover and bake for additional 30 minutes. Serves 4 to 6.

Mrs. G. G. Cumming (Carol)

BEEF STROGANOFF

2 large onions, thinly sliced
6 tablespoons butter, divided
½ pound mushrooms, thinly
    sliced
2 pounds sirloin tip, cut into
    ¼-inch slices and then into
    bite-sized pieces
½ cup seasoned flour

⅔ cup tomato juice
⅓ cup sherry
¼ cup beef broth
Salt, pepper, and dash of nutmeg
¼ teaspoon prepared mustard
1 cup sour cream
Paprika

Cook onions in 2 tablespoons butter until soft and yellow. Transfer to large bowl. Cook mushrooms in 2 more tablespoons butter until just tender and place with onions. Dredge meat in flour. Brown meat pieces over high heat a few at a time in the remaining butter, adding more if needed. Transfer browned meat to bowl with onions and mushrooms. When all pieces are browned, add tomato juice, sherry, and broth, scraping pan. Add salt, pepper, mustard and nutmeg. Return meat, onions and mushrooms to pan. Reduce heat to low. Cover and cook 25 minutes or until meat is tender. Stir in sour cream; dust with paprika. Serves 5 or 6.

Mrs. Richard G. Price, Jr. (Mary Jo)

BRAISED BEEF SHORT RIBS WITH VEGETABLES
Succulent, juicy ribs braised to perfection in the oven
with no watching necessary!

5 pounds beef short ribs, cut in
    serving size pieces
1½ cups onion, chopped
½ cup celery, finely chopped
1 10¾-ounce can condensed
    beef broth
1 cup water

1 teaspoon salt
¼ teaspoon pepper
½ teaspoon leaf marjoram,
    crumbled
1 tablespoon flour
2 tablespoons water

Heat dutch oven. Rub fat edges of meat over hot surface to grease. Brown ribs well on all sides. Drain off most of fat. Remove ribs. Add onion, celery and carrot to dutch oven. Sauté until lightly browned. Add beef broth, water, salt, pepper and marjoram. Return ribs to kettle and cover. Bake in slow oven at 325 degrees for 2½ hours, or until meat is very tender. Remove ribs to serving platter and keep warm. Pour liquid from kettle into quart measure. Skim off fat. Return liquid to kettle. Bring to a simmer. Combine flour with water and stir into simmering liquid. Cook, stirring constantly until sauce thickens and bubbles for 3 minutes. Serves 6.

Mrs. Jack D. Pollitzer (Toni)

MARINADED BEEF KEBABS

½ cup salad oil
2 tablespoons cider vinegar
1 teaspoon celery salt
1 teaspoon onion salt
¾ teaspoon garlic salt
¾ teaspoon oregano leaves
½ teaspoon salt

½ teaspoon black pepper
2 pounds boneless shoulder or top round of beef, cut into 1½-inch cubes
8 medium mushroom caps
2 zucchini, cut into ½-inch pieces

Combine oil, vinegar, celery salt, onion salt, garlic salt, oregano, salt and pepper in saucepan. Heat to boiling and cool. Add meat to marinade along with mushrooms and zucchini. Toss lightly. Cover and marinate at room temperature 4 to 6 hours, turning occasionally to season. Alternate meat and vegetables on skewers. Place on grill over bed of medium slow burning coals. Cook 20 to 25 minutes, turning and basting with marinade frequently. Kebabs may be broiled in oven 4 to 6 inches from heat source for 8 to 10 minutes. Serves 6 to 8.

Mrs. Frank W. Tuckwiller (Barbara)

MARINADED STEAK

4 to 5-inch thick top round steak
4 teaspoons meat tenderizer
2 tablespoons sugar
4 tablespoons sherry

4 tablespoons soy sauce
2 tablespoons honey
2 teaspoons salt
2 teaspoons Accent

Marinate a round steak for 6 hours or longer. Charcoal to desired doneness. This is better served cold and sliced very thin. Perfect for a summer meal or a large cocktail party.

Mrs. Russel C. Harris, Jr. (Rena)

STUFFED FLANK STEAK

1 2½ pound flank steak
1 teaspoon seasoned instant
    meat tenderizer
2 tablespoons flour
2 teaspoons seasoned salt
¼ teaspoon Tabasco
½ cup herb-seasoned stuffing
1 egg, slightly beaten
½ cup canned sliced apples
1 teaspoon poultry seasoning

2 tablespoons butter, melted
½ teaspoon sage
¼ cup onion, chopped
¼ cup green pepper, seeded and
    chopped
¼ cup celery, chopped
2 tablespoons vegetable shortening
½ cup water
⅓ cup Worcestershire sauce

Trim steak and score on one side. Sprinkle tenderizer on both sides. Sprinkle flour that has been mixed with salt and Tabasco on both sides of meat. In a bowl, combine stuffing, egg, apple, poultry seasoning, butter, sage, onion, green pepper, and celery. Spoon lengthwise onto center of unscored side of steak. Roll up steak lengthwise, enclosing stuffing. Tie or skewer steak very securely. Heat shortening in dutch oven and brown steak on all sides. Add water and Worcestershire sauce. Cover and bake 1 hour or until tender at 325 degrees. Baste occasionally. Transfer to heated platter, remove string and slice diagonally. Serves 4-6.

Mrs. Frank J. Kobes (Lydia)

WELSH PASTY

Pastry for 9-inch 2 crust pie
1 to 1¼ pounds beef round
    steak, trimmed of fat and
    cut into ½-inch cubes
3 cups raw all-purpose potatoes,
    peeled and cubed

½ cup onion, diced
½ cup carrots, diced
2 teaspoons salt
½ teaspoon ground pepper
1 tablespoon butter

Line deep 9-inch pie plate with half the pastry. In a large bowl, mix thoroughly the round steak, potatoes, carrots, onions, salt and pepper. Using a slotted spoon, transfer mixture to pastry-lined pie plate. Dot with butter, then cover with top crust and seal edges of crusts tightly. Make several small slits in top crust to allow steam to escape. Bake in preheated 300 degree oven for 1 hour. Then increase oven temperature to 375 degrees and bake 30 to 45 minutes longer. Crust should be golden brown. Cut in wedges to serve. Serves 4 to 6.

Mrs. Neil S. Williams (Sally)

BEEF CHUNKS POLYNESIAN

2½ pounds sirloin tips cut in
    bite size pieces
1½ teaspoons garlic salt
1 teaspoon paprika
1 teaspoon ground ginger
1 large clove garlic, minced
3 tablespoons oil
1 13½-ounce can pineapple
    chunks, drain and reserve
    juice
1 10½-ounce can condensed
    beef broth

¼ cup wine vinegar, divided
½ cup celery, sliced
2 medium onions, quartered
2 large tomatoes, cut in wedges
3 tablespoons brown sugar
2 tablespoons cornstarch
¼ cup water
2 tablespoons soy sauce
½ cup green pepper, sliced

Mix garlic salt, paprika and ground ginger. Toss with beef cubes to coat. Brown meat and garlic in hot skillet in oil. Stir in reserved pineapple juice, beef broth and ½ of the vinegar. Cover and simmer until meat is tender, or about 2 hours. Stir in celery, onions, tomatoes and pineapple chunks. Cook covered about 10 minutes. Stir in a mixture of brown sugar, cornstarch, water, soy sauce and remaining vinegar and cook 3 minutes. Serves 8.

Mrs. H. E. Walker (Murray)

ORIENTAL SKILLET SUPPER

1 medium onion, sliced
1 cup green pepper strips
⅔ cup celery pieces, bias cut
2 tablespoons shortening
2-3 cups beef, pork or shrimp,
    cooked and sliced
1⅓ cups cold water
2 tablespoons soy sauce

4 tablespoons cornstarch
1 teaspoon sugar
½ teaspoon salt
2 medium tomatoes, sliced in
    wedges
4-6 cups hot cooked rice
1-1½ teaspoons powdered ginger

In heavy skillet, cook onion, pepper and celery in shortening until crisp-tender. Remove vegetables from skillet and set aside. Add meat to hot skillet and brown quickly. Combine water, soy sauce, cornstarch, sugar, and salt and add to skillet. Cook and stir until thick and bubbling. Add tomatoes and onion mixture and heat. Serve with hot rice that has been tossed with ginger.

Mrs. Stanley Bond (Bernice)

CHINESE BEEF

1 pound sirloin tips
4 teaspoons sugar
2 teaspoons cornstarch
4 teaspoons soy sauce
2 teaspoons Burgundy wine
¼ cup cooking oil

3 green peppers, cut in bite size
   pieces
2 stalks celery, chopped
1 onion, thinly sliced
6 cups hot cooked rice

SAUCE:
1 teaspoon cornstarch
1 tablespoon catsup
½ teaspoon Worcestershire
   sauce

2 teaspoons sugar
1 teaspoon soy sauce

Cut sirloin tips in thin strips. Mix together sugar, cornstarch, soy sauce and wine. Pour over meat. Marinate at least 30 minutes. Drain beef. Cook in oil for 2 minutes over high heat and remove beef. Add vegetables to pan. Cook until tender crisp or about 5 minutes. Add beef. Mix together all sauce ingredients. Stir in sauce. Cook 1 minute. Serve over hot cooked rice. Serves 4.

Mrs. Albert Ahrenholz (Roma)

CHILI

4 slices bacon, browned
3 onions, sliced
1 tablespoon green pepper,
   diced
1½ pounds ground beef
3 16-ounce cans kidney beans

1½ cups celery, diced
1 16-ounce can tomatoes, drained
   and chopped
2 teaspoons chili powder
1 teaspoon nutmeg
Salt and pepper to taste

Brown bacon in frying pan. Remove to crisp and break into small pieces. Sauté onion and green pepper in bacon fat. Remove. Sauté ground beef in same pan until well done. Combine cooked ingredients in large casserole and add celery, kidney beans, tomatoes and seasonings. Bake in 325 degree oven for 1½ hours. It is delicious served with applesauce. Serves 6 to 10.

Mrs. Donald J. Guthridge (Nancy)

CHALUPA CHILI

12 pounds ground meat
Flour
1 ounce chili powder
2 ounces comino seeds or
   cumin
4 28-ounce cans tomatoes

Salt and pepper to taste
4 8-ounce cans tomato sauce
1 14-ounce bottle catsup
1 large onion, chopped
3 pods garlic, crushed

Brown ground meat. Thicken with flour to absorb all grease. Add other ingredients. Cook, covered, all day on low heat. Serves 24.

Mrs. Edwin H. Marks, Jr. (Mildred)

CHALUPA BEANS

6 cups pinto beans, cooked
   with ham bone or salt pork
3 pods garlic, crushed
3 8-ounce cans tomato sauce

1 ounce comino powder (cumin)
1 large onion, chopped
24 tortillas, deep fried
Longhorn cheese, grated

Cook beans, ham bone or salt pork, garlic, tomato sauce, cumin and onion all day. To serve, spoon bean mixture onto tortillas. Top with cheese. Spoon on chili. Top with more cheese, chopped onion and shredded lettuce. Serves 24.

Mrs. Edwin H. Marks, Jr. (Mildred)

ENCHILADA CASSEROLE

1 pound ground beef or
   sausage
1 teaspoon oregano
½ teaspoon salt
1 clove garlic, minced
1 16-ounce can tomato sauce

1 10-ounce can enchilada sauce
12 tortillas
1 onion, finely chopped
1 pound sharp cheese, grated
1 4-ounce can ripe olives, chopped

Brown meat and oregano, salt and garlic. Combine tomato sauce and enchilada sauce in pan and heat. Dip tortillas in heated sauce. Spread 3 coated tortillas in greased casserole. Combine onions, cheese, and olives. Proceed to make layers on the tortillas of meat mixture, onion mixture, then the sauce. Between each layer make a layer of the dipped tortillas. Pour remaining sauce over entire casserole. Bake at 325 degrees for 40 minutes.

Mrs. J. E. McTeer, Jr. (Gail)

TACO SAUCE
AND
MEAT FILLING FOR TACOS

TACO SAUCE:

1 16-ounce can tomatoes, mashed
1 medium onion, finely chopped
Pinch of salt and pepper

½ cup water
3 jalapeño peppers, finely chopped
½ teaspoon garlic salt
Dash of Accent

FILLING:

2 medium potatoes, grated
3 pounds lean beef, ground
1 tablespoon oregano
½ cup chili powder

Salt and pepper to taste
3 cloves garlic, finely cut
1 teaspoon Accent
1 medium onion, chopped

Sauce:
Combine all ingredients. Simmer until thick (about 30 minutes).

Meat Filling:
Combine all ingredients and simmer 2 hours. Enough to fill 24 taco shells.

Mrs. W. N. Redling (Phylis)

TAMALE PIE

1 pound ground beef
½ pound pork sausage
2 cups celery, chopped
1 cup onion, chopped
2 1-pound can tomatoes
1 12-ounce can whole kernel corn and juice
1 clove garlic, minced

¾ cup yellow corn meal
1 cup ripe olives, pitted
½ cup olive juice
1½ cups Cheddar cheese, grated
1 tablespoon salt
2 tablespoons chili powder
Grated Cheddar cheese, garnish

In large skillet brown beef and sausage with celery and onions. Place meat and vegetables with juices in large baking dish. Add all other ingredients and mix well. Bake at 350 degrees for 1 hour. Cheese may also be added on top of dish. Serves 6.

Mrs. Owen Chambers (Dorothy)

"BETSY'S" ITALIAN CASSEROLE

3 green peppers, chopped
1 stalk celery, chopped
2 large onions, chopped
2 garlic cloves, chopped
3 pounds lean ground beef
1 pound sharp Cheddar
   cheese, grated and divided
1 28-ounce can tomato purée
2 10¾-ounce cans tomato soup
1 12-ounce bottle chili sauce

1 24-ounce bottle catsup
2 4-ounce cans mushrooms,
   drained
1 4½-ounce bottle stuffed
   green olives
1 8-ounce box wide noodles,
   cooked and divided
Salt and pepper
Parsley
Paprika

Cook ground beef in large skillet. Remove, drain and place in large mixing bowl. Sauté peppers, celery, onions and garlic in frying pan. More oil may be added if necessary. Add vegetables and cheese to meat and mix thoroughly. Salt and pepper to taste. Stir in purée, soup, chili sauce, catsup, mushrooms and green olives. Line baking dish with noodles. Pour mixture on top of noodles. Place thin layer of noodles on top. Sprinkle cheese on top of noodles and garnish with parsley and paprika. Bake in 350 degree oven until bubbly hot. Serves 12.

Mrs. Frank Linnell (Harriet)

LASAGNA

2 pounds lean ground beef
1 clove garlic, mashed
2 6-ounce cans tomato paste
2 cups tomatoes
1 tablespoon parsley
1 tablespoon basil
1½ teaspoons salt
Pepper to taste

1 pound Mozzarella cheese, grated
2 12-ounce cartons cottage cheese
½ cup Parmesan cheese
2 tablespoons parsley
2 eggs, beaten
2 teaspoons salt
1 16 ounce package lasagna
   noodles, cooked

In an uncovered saucepan, brown ground beef. Drain off excess grease. Add garlic, tomato paste, tomatoes, parsley, basil, salt and pepper. Simmer 45 minutes, stirring occasionally. Combine Mozzarella, cottage cheese, Parmesan cheese, parsley, eggs and mix well. Cover bottom of baking dish with ⅓ sauce. Place ½ lasagna lengthwise over sauce. Cover noodles with ½ cheese mixture. Repeat. Cover with remaining sauce and cook at 375 degrees for 30 minutes. Let stand 10 minutes before serving. Serves 8.

Mrs. John Hart (Lakie)

SPAGHETTI GOULASH

1½ pounds ground round steak
Salt, pepper, Accent
1 medium onion, chopped
Flour
Hot oil
2 16-ounce cans tomatoes
1 8½ ounce jar English peas
1 large green pepper, chopped
1 large onion, chopped
1 4½ ounce bottle stuffed olives, chopped
Tabasco sauce to taste
1 8-ounce package thin spaghetti, cooked
10 ounces sharp cheese, grated

Season ground steak with salt, pepper, Accent and onion. Shape into balls approximately 1 inch in diameter. Dredge balls in flour and brown in hot oil. Remove balls and make thick, brown gravy adding additional flour as needed. In saucepan bring tomatoes, peas, green pepper, onion, olives and Tabasco sauce to a boil. In 3-quart casserole place meat balls and gravy, pour vegetable mixture over this and top with spaghetti. Top with grated cheese. Cover and cook in 350 degree oven until bubbly. Serves 8.

Mrs. John C. Sease (Margaret)

HEAVENLY HAMBURGER

1½ pounds ground beef
1 15-ounce can spaghetti sauce
1 teaspoon sugar
1 tablespoon salt
1 tablespoon chili powder
1 6-ounce can button mushrooms, drained
8 ounces sour cream
6 green onions, chopped
1 3-ounce package cream cheese
4-ounces small egg noodles, cooked
Grated Cheddar cheese

Brown meat and add spaghetti sauce, sugar, salt, chili powder, and mushrooms. Cook noodles and drain. Mix sour cream, onions, and cream cheese (softened to room temperature). In casserole layer noodles, meat mixture and sour cream mixture, ending with noodles. Sprinkle cheese generously on top. Bake thirty minutes at 350 degrees. Freezes well. Serves 8.

Mrs. Day Surles (Ellen)

HAMBURGER, NOODLE, CREAM CHEESE CASSEROLE

2 pounds ground beef
1 tablespoon butter
1 8-ounce can tomato sauce
1 cup cottage cheese
8 ounces cream cheese

¼ cup sour cream
⅓ cup green onions, chopped
8 ounces noodles, cooked
2 tablespoons butter, melted

Brown and crumble meat in butter. Stir in tomato sauce and remove from heat. Combine cheeses, sour cream and green onions until softened. In a greased casserole dish, layer noodles, cheese mixture and meat. You may layer one or more times according to size and depth of your dish. Pour 2 tablespoons melted butter over top. Bake at 350 degrees for 30 minutes. Serves 8.

Mrs. L. Brent Kuhnle (Terry)

LAYERED HAMBURGER BAKE

4 ounces medium noodles
1 pound ground beef
1 15-ounce can tomato sauce
1 teaspoon sugar
½ teaspoon salt
¼ teaspoon garlic salt
⅛ teaspoon pepper
1 8-ounce package cream
cheese, softened

½ cup sour cream
3 tablespoons milk
2 tablespoons onion, finely
chopped
1 10-ounce package frozen
chopped spinach, cooked and
drained well
½ cup Cheddar cheese, shredded

Cook noodles in boiling salted water about 10 minutes. Drain. Brown meat in skillet; drain off fat. Add meat, tomato sauce, sugar, salt, garlic salt and pepper to the cooked noodles. Set aside. Stir together cream cheese, sour cream, milk and onion. In 2-quart casserole, layer half of the ground beef-noodle mixture; half of the cream cheese mixture, all of the spinach and the rest of the ground beef mixture. Cover and bake in 350 degree oven for 40 minutes or until bubbly. Uncover and spread rest of cream cheese mixture on top. Sprinkle with Cheddar cheese. Bake 10 minutes more or until cheese is melted. Serves 6.

Mrs. Ronald Dodge (Lee)

MOUSSAKA

2 medium size eggplants,
  peeled and cut in ½ inch
  slices
½ cup butter, divided
3 large onions, finely chopped
2 pounds ground beef
3 tablespoons tomato paste
½ cup red wine
½ cup chopped parsley
¼ teaspoon cinnamon

Salt to taste
Freshly ground black pepper to
  taste
6 tablespoons flour
1 quart milk
4 eggs, beaten until frothy
Nutmeg
2 cups cottage cheese or Ricotta
1 cup fine bread crumbs
1 cup Parmesan cheese

Brown the eggplant slices quickly in 2 tablespoons of butter. Set aside. Heat 2 tablespoons of butter in the same skillet and cook the onions until they are brown. Add the ground meat and cook 10 minutes. Combine the tomato paste with the wine, parsley, cinnamon, salt and pepper. Stir this mixture into the meat and simmer over low heat, stirring frequently, until all the liquid has been absorbed. Remove the mixture from the fire. Make a white sauce by melting 4 tablespoons of butter and blending in the flour, stirring with wire whisk. Meanwhile, bring the milk to a boil and add it gradually to the butter and flour mixture, stirring constantly. When the mixture is thickened and smooth, re-move from the heat. Cool slightly and stir in beaten eggs, nutmeg and cottage cheese. Grease a casserole (13½ x 8¾ x 1¾-inch) and sprinkle the bottom lightly with bread crumbs. Arrange alternate layers of eggplant and meat sauce in the pan, sprinkling each layer with Parmesan cheese and bread crumbs. Pour the cottage cheese sauce over the top and bake 1 hour at 375 degrees, or until top is golden. Remove from the oven and cool 20 to 30 minutes before serving. Cut into squares and serve. The flavor of this dish improves on standing 1 day. Reheat before serving. Freezes well. Serves 8 to 10.

Mrs. Herbert Keyserling (Harriet)

JUICY MEAT LOAF

1½ pounds ground beef
¾ cup rolled oats
½ teaspoon salt
¼ teaspoon pepper
¼ cup onion, chopped

1 egg, beaten
¾ cup milk
⅓ cup catsup
1 tablespoon brown sugar
1 tablespoon prepared mustard

Combine beef, oats, salt, pepper, onion, egg and milk. Shape into loaf and put in deep casserole. Combine catsup, brown sugar and mustard. Mix well. Spread over beef loaf. Bake uncovered in oven 350 degrees for 1 hour. Serves 6.

Mrs. Laurance Davis (Sarah)

BEEF BARBEQUE

3 pounds lean stew beef
2 cups water
1 large onion, chopped
2 tablespoons butter
1 cup catsup
2 tablespoons vinegar
2 tablespoons brown sugar

4 tablespoons lemon juice
3 tablespoons Worcestershire
    sauce
1 teaspoon mustard
2 teaspoons salt
Dash red pepper

Cook beef in water for 4 hours. Mash meat. Brown onion in butter. Add catsup, vinegar, brown sugar, lemon juice, Worcestershire sauce, mustard, salt and red pepper to onion mixture and cook 20 minutes. Mix this with meat and let stand overnight. Reheat slowly. May be frozen.

Mrs. Graeme Keith (Gloria)

BARBEQUED BEEF

1 tablespoon oil
1½ pounds ground beef
1 large Bermuda onion,
    chopped
1 green pepper, chopped
2 teaspoons sugar

1 tablespoon prepared mustard
¼ teaspoon ground cloves
1 teaspoon salt
1 cup catsup
1 tablespoon vinegar

Brown the meat in oil until it is crumbly but not hard. Add the remaining ingredients, cover and simmer gently for 30 minutes. Serve on toasted buns. Serves 6.

Mrs. H. C. Rose (Marjorie)

BARBEQUED MEAT

2 pounds each pork and beef,
    cubed and cut ½ inch thick
Olive oil
2 28-ounce cans tomatoes,
    mashed
1 cup onion, diced

⅓ cup Worcestershire sauce
⅓ cup white vinegar
1 teaspoon salt
½ teaspoon crushed red pepper
¼ teaspoon black pepper
¼ teaspoon liquid smoke

Brown the meat in a little olive oil. In a heavy pot, place all the ingredients, boil, reduce heat and simmer at least 4 hours or until mixture is thick. Serve on heated hamburger buns with sliced dill pickles. Serves 10 to 12.

Mrs. W. W. Elliott (Martha)

GRILLED MINTED LEG OF LAMB

1 cup dry white wine
¼ cup fresh mint, finely
    chopped or 2 teaspoons
    dried mint
2 cloves garlic, crushed

1 teaspoon salt
½ teaspoon freshly ground black
    pepper
7 to 8 pound butterflied leg of lamb

Combine wine, mint, garlic, salt and pepper in a large shallow glass or ceramic dish. Put in lamb and turn to coat. Cover the dish with plastic wrap and refrigerate 3 or 4 hours. Turn the lamb once during this time. Grill the lamb about 4 inches from medium hot coals for about 15 minutes per side. Brush often with remaining marinade during grilling. Remove from grill and slice the lamb crosswise in ¼ thick slices. Serves 8.

Mrs. Robert Poitras (Louise)

GIGOT FARCI (STUFFED LEG OF LAMB EN CROUTÉ)
A lot of work but excellent!

4-5½ pound leg of lamb (have butcher remove inner bone, leaving end bone intact)
6 tablespoons butter, divided
½ pound mushrooms, finely chopped
6 cloves garlic, crushed
6 shallots, finely chopped
2 heaping tablespoons parsley, finely chopped
½ teaspoon salt
¼ teaspoon pepper
½ pound puff pastry
1 egg, beaten
Wine, vermouth or chicken broth
Watercress

Sauté mushrooms in 2 tablespoons butter. Reserve mushrooms, pouring off the juices. Melt 2 tablespoons butter and sauté the garlic, shallots, and parsley. Add ¼ teaspoon salt and pepper and mix with mushrooms. Stuff lamb with above mixture, sprinkle with remaining ¼ teaspoon salt and 2 tablespoons butter, and tie with string. Unwaxed dental floss is good to use. This can be done a day ahead. Preheat oven to 425 degrees and cook lamb 35-40 minutes. Remove from oven and allow to cool 20 minutes before putting pastry on lamb. Roll out dough into two pieces (⅓" to ½" thick) placing the smaller piece on a cookie sheet and the lamb, bone up, on this piece. Lamb should not be hot or dough will melt. Take the larger piece and place it over the lamb like a blanket and close the 2 edges together, sealing with a fork but leaving the bone exposed. Top may be decorated with remaining pastry. Glaze with egg using pastry brush. Bake at 425 degrees for 15 minutes and 375 degrees for 10 minutes. Allow to cool for 20 minutes or more before cutting. Make gravy from pan juices using necessary amounts of wine, vermouth or chicken broth. Serve lamb on bed of watercress. Serves 4-6.

Mrs. John M. Trask, Jr. (Caroline)

LEG OF LAMB NANETTE

½ cup wild rice
6 tablespoons butter, divided
1¼ cups bouillon
2 onions, chopped
¼ cup currants
¼ cup pine nuts

¼ cup parsley
Salt and pepper to taste
4-6 pounds leg of lamb, boned
6 cloves garlic, halved
Lemon juice

Sauté rice in 4 tablespoons butter. Add bouillon and cook until tender. Sauté onions in remaining butter and mix with rice, currants and pine nuts. Season with parsley and salt and pepper. Place atop lamb, roll and tie with natural twine as nylon will melt. Pierce roast making 12 slits. Insert 1 garlic piece deeply in each slit. Rub lamb with lemon juice and place on rack. Roast in 350 degree oven for 1¼ hours or until blush pink in center. Serves 8.

Mrs. Sam Stafford III (Nancy)

DIRECTIONS FOR COOKING COUNTRY HAM

Country ham
1 cup vinegar
1 cup molasses
1 cup brown sugar
2 tablespoons whole cloves

3 tablespoons prepared mustard
Cold water
Glaze: brown sugar, orange
    juice and cloves

Scrub ham. In turkey roaster or ham boiler combine the above ingredients. Place ham in liquid, skin side up. Liquid should reach level about 1 inch below rim of boiler. Cover. Place in 450 degree oven and bring to a boil. You can hear it in about 1 hour. Let boil for approximately 1 hour and 15 minutes to 1 hour and 30 minutes. Don't open door after timing period begins. Cut oven off. Let stay overnight. Next morning take off skin and glaze with brown sugar, orange juice and cloves.

Mrs. William C. Pitt, Jr. (Alta)

COUNTRY HAM

Country ham
Water

Brown sugar
Cloves

Scrub country ham with brush and warm water. Line a roaster with extra strength heavy duty foil. Place ham on foil, fat side up. Place 1½ cups water over ham and secure with foil tightly to retain juices. Bake at 350 degrees for 20 to 25 minutes per pound. Let ham cool in foil and remove skin and fat carefully. When ham is cool, cover with brown sugar and cloves and run under broiler.

The Editors

BARBEQUED HAM
Good for cocktail buffet

1 10-pound ham, cooked	1 cup butter
2 cups vinegar	2 lemons, thinly sliced
2 cups water	1 teaspoon cayenne
8 tablespoons sugar	6 teaspoons salt
4 tablespoons mustard	2 cups catsup
4 large onions, thinly sliced	8 tablespoons Worcestershire
2 teaspoons pepper	sauce

Put first 10 ingredients, except ham in a pan and simmer over low heat uncovered for 20 minutes. Add catsup and Worcestershire sauce. Slice ham and alternate ham with sauce in a baking dish. Prepare a day before using. Ham can also be frozen. Reheat before using.

Mrs. Marshall B. Garth (Martha)

HAM WITH PECAN STUFFING

6 to 8 pound shank end pre-cooked ham, boned	½ teaspoon salt
	½ teaspoon white pepper
1 cup celery, diced	1 cup sherry
2 tablespoons butter	½ cup brandy
1½ slices stale bread, crumbled	½ cup raisins
	¼ cup honey
1 cup pecans	½ cup orange marmalade

To make dressing, sauté celery and butter in a pan until soft. Add bread crumbs, nuts, salt and pepper. Stuff bone cavity, packing firmly. Reroll meat and tie with string every 2 inches. Place in roaster and cover with sherry, brandy and raisins. Bake covered in 275 degree oven for 30 minutes basting frequently. Remove lid, coat with honey, and continue baking 30 minutes. Remove to serving platter. Skim fat from liquid in roaster, add marmalade and serve separately as sauce. Serves 8-10.

Mrs. Henry Merriman (Marge)

HAM DELIGHTS

1 cup butter
3 tablespoons poppy seed
1 teaspoon Worcestershire
    sauce
3 tablespoons mustard

1 medium onion, minced
3 packs Pepperidge Farm party
    rolls, split
1 pound boiled ham, sliced
¾ pound Swiss cheese, sliced

Cream butter, poppy seed, Worcestershire sauce, mustard and onions. Spread tops and bottoms with creamed mixture. Then add 1 pound boiled ham and ¾ pound Swiss cheese divided evenly over the rolls. Wrap in foil. Bake at 400 degrees for 10 minutes. To serve, cut into individual rolls. Yields 60. Freezes well.

Mrs. John Wiley (Ann)

PORK TENDERLOINS WITH ORANGE SAUCE

2 pork tenderloins, 2 pounds
    each
2 tablespoons butter
¾ cup onion, chopped
2 teaspoons salt
¼ teaspoon pepper
½ cup white wine

3 oranges
3 tablespoons sugar
1 bay leaf
1 tablespoon parsley, chopped
1½ teaspoons arrowroot or
    cornstarch
4 cups hot cooked rice

Sauté tenderloins in butter until golden. Remove from pan and cook onion, salt and pepper in the butter until tender. Return meat to pan. Pour wine and juice from 2 oranges over meat. Add sugar, bay leaf and parsley. Cover and simmer until meat is tender, about 45 minutes. Peel remaining orange and section. Cut peel in very thin strips and boil in a small amount of water until tender. Remove meat from pan. Mix arrowroot or cornstarch with a tablespoon of water and add this to the broth, stirring until thick and smooth. Cut tenderloin in thick slices and place on platter of cooked rice. Pour sauce over meat and garnish with orange slices and cooked peel. Serves 6.

Mrs. O. Stanley Smith (Connie)

ROAST LEG OF PORK

7 to 9 pound leg of fresh pork   2 cups red wine
Salt   ¼ teaspoon nutmeg
½ cup onions, chopped

Preheat oven to 325 degrees. Line roaster pan with aluminum foil. Put rack in roaster. Skin ham. Rub meat well with salt. Stuff crevices with onion, put any leftover on top of meat. Put meat on rack in roaster with fat side up. Mix together the wine and nutmeg. Pour mixture into bottom of roaster. Ladle a few spoonfuls over the top of meat. Cover. Place in oven. Cook 20 or 25 minutes per pound. Baste every 15 or 20 minutes. Serves 10 to 12.

Miss Katharine W. Kroeg

OVEN-COOKED SPARERIBS

3 pounds lean spareribs   1 teaspoon nutmeg
1 small onion, chopped   1 teaspoon allspice
1 tablespoon butter   1½ teaspoons cinnamon
1 cup catsup   1 teaspoon salt
1 tablespoon dry mustard   1 teaspoon white pepper
4 tablespoons brown sugar

Trim and cut ribs into serving size pieces. Wash, pat dry, and lightly salt and pepper. Put in covered roasting pan. Cook for 1 hour at 300 degrees. Drain off excess fat. Sauté onion in butter. Mix all other ingredients. Pour ½ of sauce over ribs and bake 30 minutes. Turn, and pour on remainder of sauce. Cook for an additional 30 minutes. Serves 4.

Mrs. J. C. Gibbs (Marjorie)

BARBEQUED SPARERIBS

SAUCE:
¼ cup butter   ⅓ cup catsup
1 onion, chopped   2 tablespoons Worcestershire
¼ cup lemon juice   sauce
¼ cup vinegar   Salt and pepper to taste

3 pounds spareribs   Oil
Flour

Sauté onion in butter until lightly browned. Add remaining sauce ingredients and bring to a boil. Flour and brown ribs in frying pan. Pour sauce over meat. Bake uncovered in a 350 degree oven for 1 to 2 hours or until meat is tender. Baste with sauce while cooking. Serves 4.

Mrs. George L. Tucker, Jr. (Vickie)

SAVORY SAUSAGE CASSEROLE

1 pound pork sausage
1 16-ounce can red kidney
   beans
1 cup tart apples, sliced
¼ cup packed brown sugar

1 onion, sliced
½ cup tomato juice
⅛ teaspoon pepper
½ teaspoon chili powder (or more)

Cook sausage lightly in skillet. Pour off the fat. Mix sausage and remaining ingredients and pour into a 1½-quart casserole. Cover and bake in 350 degree oven for 1 hour and 15 minutes. May be served with or without rice. Serves 4.

Mrs. Peter Neidig (Daune)

VEAL SUPREME

1 pound veal, cut into 1-inch
   cubes
Flour
3 tablespoons cooking oil
½ cup onion, diced
½ cup celery, diced
2 tablespoons green pepper,
   diced
½ cup mushrooms, sliced

1 cup consommé or 1 bouillon
   cube dissolved in 1 cup water
1 8-ounce can tomato sauce
1 bay leaf
2 pinches cumin
¼ teaspoon thyme
1 teaspoon salt
¼ teaspoon pepper
Small clove garlic, crushed

Dredge veal in flour. Heat oil in heavy skillet and brown veal. Add onion, celery, green pepper, mushrooms and brown. Mix liquids and spices together. Pour over veal cubes and cook over low heat. Remove bay leaf after 2 hours and continue cooking until veal is tender. Serves 4.

Mrs. James Payette (Marie)

VEAL WITH CREAM

3 pounds veal shoulder or leg
2 tablespoons butter
2 tablespoons sherry
1 small onion, chopped
1 clove garlic, chopped
4 tomatoes, skinned and sliced
1 tablespoon tomato paste

3 tablespoons flour
1 cup chicken stock
¾ cup sour cream
Dash salt and pepper
2 tablespoons chopped chives
1 bay leaf

Cut veal into large squares. Brown in butter. Pour sherry over veal and remove from heat. Place in a pan the onion and garlic and cook for 2 minutes. Add tomatoes; cook for 3 minutes. Remove from heat and stir in tomato paste and flour very slowly with whisk. Add stock; stir over heat until mixture comes to a boil. Mix in sour cream, salt, pepper, chives, bay leaf and veal. Cook slowly ¾ hour or until veal is tender. Serves 6-8.

Mrs. Nöel Seeburg (Alice)

VEAL MARENGO

3 pounds lean veal, cubed
3 tablespoons flour
1 teaspoon salt
¼ teaspoon pepper
6 tablespoons butter, divided
2 onions, chopped
2 garlic cloves, crushed
1½ cups dry Chablis

1 cup chicken broth
¼ teaspoon thyme
2 bay leaves
6 tomatoes, unpeeled and
    quartered
1 cup whipping cream
1 pound small mushrooms
Fresh parsley

Dredge veal in flour, salt and pepper. Melt 4 tablespoons butter and brown meat. Add onions and garlic and toss. Add wine, chicken broth, thyme, bay leaves and tomatoes. Cover and cook about 1 hour. Remove meat and strain sauce. Replace sauce in pan and boil fast to reduce juice to about 1½ cups. Add cream and meat to sauce. Melt 2 tablespoons butter and sauté mushrooms. Add mushrooms to meat and sauce. Before serving, sprinkle liberally with fresh parsley. Good with steamed Red Bliss potatoes. Serves 4 to 6.

Mrs. John M. Trask, Jr. (Caroline)

ROAST VEAL WITH BING CHERRIES

4 pound leg of veal, boned
2-3 teaspoons cinnamon
3 teaspoons ground cardamon
2¼ pounds Bing cherries,
    pitted and divided

¼ pound butter
2 tablespoons vegetable oil
¼ cup sweet vermouth

Rub outside of roast with ½ of the cinnamon and cardamon. Stuff leg with 2 pounds of cherries and rest of spices. Brown in a casserole in butter and oil. Add vermouth and ¼ pound of cherries to casserole and place in preheated 350 degree oven. Baste every half hour with pan juices. Roast about 2 hours and 20 minutes. Skim fat from pan juices and serve as a sauce with the meat. Serves 6-8.

Mrs. Sam Stafford, III (Nancy)

VEAL CACCIATORE

2 cloves garlic
¼ to ⅓ cup oil
1½ pounds veal, cut into small
    pieces and sprinkled with
    ½ teaspoon salt

3-5 green peppers, cut into strips
3-5 onions, sliced
1 16-ounce can tomatoes
1 teaspoon savory herbs (thyme,
    oregano and bay leaves)

Fry garlic in oil. Remove garlic and fry veal or beef in oil. When slightly browned, remove meat to large pan. Fry peppers and onions in the oil until wilted and add all of this to the meat. Add tomatoes, garlic, herbs, pepper and salt to taste. Cover and cook slowly for 2 hours or more. Serve over hot rice or spaghetti. Serves 6.

Mrs. F. Bethea Rogers (Flora)

VIOLET

Sauces

SAUCE FOR ASPARAGUS

2 teaspoons catsup
4 teaspoons white wine
1 teaspoon parsley, chopped
2 eggs, hard boiled and
    chopped

1 teaspoon olive oil
½ cup cracker crumbs
½ cup butter, melted

Mix and cook in a saucepan until sauce thickens. Serve over cooked asparagus.

Mrs. Russel C. Harris, Jr. (Rena)

BARBEQUE SAUCE

½ cup butter
1 cup onion, chopped
3 cloves garlic, crushed
½ cup catsup
¼ cup brown sugar
1 teaspoon salt

1½ teaspoons pepper, freshly
    ground
¼ teaspoon Tabasco
1 tablespoon lemon juice
1 teaspoon basil
1 tablespoon chili powder

Saute onions in butter until tender but not brown. Add all other ingredients and cook 5 to 10 minutes. Great on charcoaled country style pork spareribs and chicken. Serve with yellow rice.

Dale Hryharrow Friedman

BEST-EVER BARBEQUE SAUCE

2 tablespoons butter
1 medium onion, finely
    chopped
1 clove garlic, minced
½ cup celery, finely chopped
¾ cup water
1 cup catsup
2 tablespoons vinegar

2 tablespoons lemon juice
2 tablespoons Worcestershire
    sauce
2 tablespoons brown sugar
1 teaspoon dry mustard
1 teaspoon salt
½ teaspoon pepper

Melt butter. Add onion, garlic and celery and simmer until onion is light brown. Add water, catsup, vinegar, lemon juice, Worcestershire sauce, brown sugar, dry mustard, salt and pepper. Simmer 20 minutes. Keeps well when refrigerated. Yields approximately 2¼ cups or enough for 3 to 4 pounds of meat.

Mrs. R. E. Beaty (Kathy)

BARBEQUE SAUCE FOR CHICKEN OR SPARERIBS

1 teaspoon ginger
1 clove garlic
¾ cup sugar
¼ cup sherry

½ cup soy sauce
½ cup catsup
1 teaspoon salt
Dash of Tabasco

Pour over ribs or chicken and marinate 3 hours. Cover with foil. Cook at 350 degrees for 1½ hours.

Mrs. H. E. Trask (Margaret)

CHUCKWAGON BARBEQUE SAUCE

1 cup strong coffee
1 cup Worcestershire sauce
1 cup catsup
½ cup butter

¼ cup lemon juice
2½ tablespoons sugar
1 teaspoon salt
1 teaspoon pepper

Combine ingredients and bring to a boil. Lower heat and simmer for 30 minutes. Good with any kind of beef. Baste with the sauce while barbequing. Can be stored in the refrigerator.

Mrs. Ray Williams (Hedy)

BEEF FONDUE SAUCE

¼ cup parsley, chopped
¼ cup dill pickles, chopped
¼ cup onion, chopped
2 teaspoons capers
3 tablespoons paprika
1 cup mayonnaise

2 tablespoons catsup
2½ tablespoons dry sherry
1 teaspoon Worcestershire
Few drops lemon juice
2 eggs, hard boiled and chopped

Mix the first 9 ingredients together and chill for several hours. Before serving, add lemon juice and chopped eggs. Serves 4 to 6.

Mrs. Frank Mears (Jeanne)

BENIHANA GINGER SAUCE

½ cup soy sauce
¼ cup cider vinegar
1 medium sized onion, chopped

3 thin slices fresh ginger root
½ teaspoon monosodium
    glutamate

In container of electric blender, place soy sauce, cider vinegar, onion, ginger and monosodium glutamate. Process at high speed for 2 minutes or until mixture is smooth. Good with steak, chicken or shrimp.

Mrs. Emil Klatt (Alice)

BÉARNAISE SAUCE

½ cup white wine
2 tablespoons wine vinegar
2 tablespoons shallots,
    chopped
1 teaspoon chervil
1 teaspoon tarragon
½ teaspoon salt

Fresh white pepper
3 egg yolks
2 tablespoons white wine
3 tablespoons parsley, chopped
½ teaspoon chervil
½ teaspoon tarragon
½ cup butter, melted and clarified

Cook wine, wine vinegar, shallots, chervil, tarragon, salt and white pepper for 15 minutes or until volume is reduced by one half. Cool. Blend egg yolks, white wine, parsley, chervil and tarragon. Strain first mixture into second mixture. Slowly add the butter in very small amounts while mixture is warm, blending constantly. Transfer mixture to double boiler and cook over warm—not boiling—water until sauce begins to thicken rapidly.

Mrs. C. A. Larsen, Jr. (Eleanor)

HOLLANDAISE SAUCE

3 egg yolks
2 tablespoons lemon juice
½ teaspoon salt

½ cup butter, melted
½ cup water, boiling

Combine egg yolks, lemon juice, salt and butter in blender. Blend until smooth or about 5 seconds. Remove cover and gradually add boiling water. Pour all in top of double boiler and cook until sauce is like soft custard. Remove double boiler from heat and serve warm. This hollandaise sauce will keep for days in refrigerator and can be reheated. Yields 1 cup.

Mrs. William W. Elliott (Martha)

FOOLPROOF MOCK HOLLANDAISE SAUCE

4 tablespoons butter
2 tablespoons flour
1 egg yolk, beaten
½ teaspoon salt

½ cup water
5 tablespoons mayonnaise
1½ teaspoons vinegar or lemon
  juice

Melt butter and blend in flour. Add egg yolk, salt and water. Stir until mixture thickens. Remove from stove and add mayonnaise and vinegar or lemon juice. Reheat over hot water. Yields 1 cup.

Mrs. Harold O. Danielson (Mary)

LONDON BROIL MARINADE

1 cup soy sauce
1 onion, finely chopped
1 teaspoon Accent
1 teaspoon lemon pepper

Juice of ½ lemon, including a few
  slivers of rind
½ teaspoon garlic salt
2 teaspoons ground ginger

Combine the above and boil for three minutes. Pour this mixture over 1-inch thick London Broil. Marinate from morning until dinner turning often. Broil on charcoal grill 10 minutes on each side. Cut on slant. The favorite meal of my entire family and closest friends; so easy too.

Mrs. Graham Keith (Gloria)

TOMATO MEAT SAUCE
A favorite of children

1 pound ground meat
½ teaspoon bacon drippings
½ cup bell pepper, chopped
1 large onion, chopped
½ cup celery, chopped

3 sprigs parsley, chopped
1 16-ounce can tomatoes
1 10½-ounce can tomato sauce
Salt and pepper

Brown ground beef in bacon drippings in large skillet. Pour off excess grease. Add bell pepper, onion, celery, parsley and mix with browned ground meat, then add tomatoes and tomato sauce. Salt and pepper to taste before serving. Cook over medium heat for 30 minutes. Spoon over cooked rice or noodles. Serves 8.

Mrs. James B. Easterling (Mary)

CURRANT SAUCE FOR GAME

8 ounces currant jelly
2 tablespoons brandy

½ cup fresh mint leaves
or ¼ cup dried mint leaves

Melt jelly with brandy. When warm and smooth, add mint leaves. Serve over hot game. Yield 1 cup.

Mrs. Sam Stafford, III (Nancy)

LAMB SAUCE

4 tablespoons butter
2 tablespoons lemon juice
2 tablespoons wine vinegar

½ teaspoon black pepper
½ teaspoon red pepper

Combine all ingredients, heat until blended. Serve in sauce boat over lamb.

Mrs. DeAlton Ridings (Jane)

JEZEBEL SAUCE

1 10-ounce jar pineapple
    preserves
1 8-ounce jar hot mustard

1 10-ounce jar apple jelly
1 5-ounce bottle horseradish

Heat all ingredients until mixed, stirring constantly. Store in refrigerator in glass jar. Will keep a month or longer. Serve over hot or cold ham.

Mrs. George G. Trask (Connie)

RAISIN SAUCE FOR HAM

¾ cup seedless raisins
1 cup water
4 whole cloves
¾ cup brown sugar

1 tablespoon cornstarch
¼ teaspoon salt
1 tablespoon butter
1 tablespoon lemon juice

Cook raisins, water and cloves for 10 minutes. Add brown sugar, cornstarch and salt. Cook until it thickens. Add butter and lemon juice. Serve over ham slices.

Mrs. Eugene Spears (Lillian)

MUSTARD SAUCE FOR HAM OR TONGUE

½ cup sugar
2 tablespoons ground mustard
¼ teaspoon turmeric
1 teaspoon flour

½ cup vinegar
1 egg, thoroughly beaten
1 tablespoon butter

Place all ingredients except butter in small saucepan and boil for 1 minute, stirring constantly. Strain and add butter. Stir in thoroughly. Place in refrigerator to get cold. Will keep for a month.

Mrs. William W. Elliott (Martha)

MUSTARD SAUCE

3 egg yolks
½ cup vinegar
½ teaspoon salt

½ cup sugar
2 tablespoons dry mustard
½ pint cream

Beat egg yolks. Add rest of ingredients adding cream last. Cook in double boiler until thickened. Serve with ham.

Mrs. Badger Perrin (Chris)

SPICY RAISIN SAUCE

1 cup light or dark raisins
¼ cup butter
2 cups water
4 tablespoons vinegar
2 teaspoons prepared mustard

2 tablespoons flour
½ cup brown sugar
¼ teaspoon salt
1 teaspoon cinnamon
¼ teaspoon cloves, ground

Rinse and drain raisins. Combine butter, water, vinegar and mustard. Heat to boiling. Blend together flour, sugar, salt and spices and stir into hot mixture. Add raisins and simmer 10 minutes. Serve hot. Yields 3 cups.

Mrs. Stanley E. Waskiewicz (Betty)

SWEET SAUCE FOR EGG ROLLS

2 12-ounce jars apple jelly
1 5-ounce jar Mr. Mustard

1 9-ounce jar pineapple sauce
1 5-ounce jar horseradish, drained

Mix all ingredients in blender and refrigerate. Serve with egg rolls.

Mrs. Edward Holt (Kitty)

SOUR CREAM DILL SAUCE

1 egg
1 teaspoon salt
Fresh ground pepper
Pinch of sugar

4 teaspoons lemon juice
1 teaspoon grated onion
2 tablespoons fresh dill
1½ cups sour cream

Blend first seven ingredients. Lastly blend in sour cream. Good on fish.

Mrs. John Pratt (Janey)

TARTAR SAUCE

2 teaspoons capers
3 tablespoons mayonnaise

¼ teaspoon onion juice
5 drops lemon juice

Crush capers and mix all ingredients. May be kept in small tightly covered jar in refrigerator for a few days. Excellent on scallops, shrimp, crabmeat, etc.

Mrs. Rudolph Geissler (Grey)

CRAB OR LOBSTER VELOUTÉ FOR FISH

2 tablespoons butter
3 tablespoons flour
¼ teaspoon salt
Pepper to taste
1 cup rich chicken broth

½ cup cream
2 egg yolks
1 cup crab or lobster, flaked
Baked or broiled fish

Melt butter. Blend in flour, salt and pepper. Whisk in chicken broth. Bring to a boil and add cream. Let mixture partially cool and beat in egg yolks. Add lobster or crab and serve warm on fish. Yields 1½ cups.

Mrs. Sam Stafford, III (Nancy)

PROCESSOR SAUCE VELOUTÉ

2 tablespoons butter
2 tablespoons flour

1 cup hot stock (meat or fish)
Salt and pepper to taste

Place flour and butter in food processor bowl, using the steel blade and process until well blended. Add hot stock through the tube and process until smooth. Cook and stir until thick and season. Yields 1 cup.

Mrs. Sam Stafford III (Nancy)

HARD SAUCE

1 cup confectioners' sugar or
    ¾ cup granulated sugar
⅓ cup butter

½ teaspoon vanilla or other
    flavoring
¼ cup heavy cream, optional

Sift sugar. Cream sugar and butter until mixture is smooth and fluffy. Add flavoring. Chill and serve on bread pudding, fruit cobblers, etc. For a richer sauce, beat in ¼ cup heavy cream.

Mrs. Malcolm Goodwin (Barbara)

ROMANOFF SAUCE

1 pint vanilla ice cream
3 tablespoons lemon juice
6 tablespoons rum

2 tablespoons Cointreau
½ pint cream, whipped

Soften ice cream in a bowl and mix in other ingredients. The mixture should be the consistency of marshmallow sauce. Serve over fresh fruit.

Mrs. William W. Elliott (Martha)

ORANGE SAUCE FOR ANGEL FOOD CAKE

4 egg yolks, beaten
⅔ cup sugar
Juice and rind of 2 small or 1
    large orange

½ pint heavy cream, whipped

Cook egg yolks, sugar, juice and rind of orange in top of double boiler until it begins to thicken. Place in refrigerator. One hour before using sauce, add whipped cream.

Mrs. H. E. Trask (Margaret)

LEMON SAUCE FOR GINGERBREAD

1 cup sugar
½ cup butter
1 egg

1 lemon, juice and grated rind
1 teaspoon nutmeg
3 tablespoons boiling water

Mix all ingredients in top of double boiler and cook until thick. Serve hot on gingerbread. Will keep in refrigerator and can be reheated. Yields 1 cup.

Mrs. S. N. Clark, Jr. (Carolyn)

RICH CHOCOLATE SAUCE

3 ounces unsweetened
    chocolate
¾ cup white sugar
¼ cup brown sugar
½ teaspoon salt

1 tablespoon cornstarch
½ cup light corn syrup
½ cup light cream
3 tablespoons butter
3 tablespoons brandy

Mix chocolate, sugar, salt and cornstarch in a bain marie or double boiler. Add syrup and cream. Cook until thickened, about 15-20 minutes. Add butter and brandy. Serve warm. Makes 2½ cups.

Mrs. Sam Stafford, III (Nancy)

Rice and Hominy

Nancy Rhodes Rhett

FRIED GRITS

1 cup cooked grits
1 egg, beaten
¼ cup cracker crumbs, finely
   crushed

Salt to taste
Shortening or bacon grease

Pour hot cooked grits into chilled tall glass. Refrigerate until cold. Slide knife around inside of glass to remove. Slice in ½ inch slices. Dip into egg and then into crumb and salt mixture. Heat shortening in skillet and cook grits' slices over medium heat until golden brown on both sides. Serve with bacon or syrup for breakfast.

The Editors

GRITS SOUFFLÉ

2 tablespoons butter
¼ cup onion, finely chopped
2 cups water
½ teaspoon salt
½ cup quick grits

1 teaspoon Tabasco
Black pepper, freshly ground
1¾ cups Cheddar cheese, grated
3 tablespoons butter
2 egg whites

Melt 2 tablespoons butter and add onion. Cook about 4 minutes. Do not brown. Boil 2 cups water. Add salt and pour grits in slowly. Boil about 1 minute, stirring constantly. Then reduce heat and cook another 2 minutes. Add onions, Tabasco, a few grinds black pepper and 1½ cups grated cheese. Combine with 3 tablespoons soft butter. Lightly butter casserole dish. Beat egg whites until they form stiff peaks. With rubber spatula, thoroughly fold egg whites into grits mixture. Pour into casserole dish and sprinkle top with remaining cheese. Bake in 400 degree oven for about 30 minutes or until puffed and lightly browned. Serve at once. Serves 3 to 4.

Mrs. William Hyland (Mary)

GRITS CASSEROLE

1 cup grits
1 quart water, salted
¾ pound Cheddar cheese,
  diced

½ cup butter
1 cup light cream
6 egg yolks
½ teaspoon garlic powder

Cook grits in salted water according to the directions on the package. When the grits are done, add cheese and butter. Combine cream with egg yolks and garlic powder. Beat well and stir into grits. Bake covered about 25 minutes at 350 degrees. Serves 8.

Mrs. George O'Kelley (Yancey)

ROCKBRIDGE COUNTY GRITS

1 cup quick grits
4 cups water, boiling
1 teaspoon salt
1 6-ounce roll garlic cheese
4 tablespoons butter

2 eggs, beaten
½ cup milk
½ teaspoon Tabasco
½ cup corn flakes, coarsely
  crushed

In 3-quart saucepan slowly stir grits into boiling, salted water. Reduce heat and cook 5 minutes, stirring frequently. Remove from heat. Add cheese and butter, stirring until melted and smooth. Cool 5 minutes. Combine eggs, milk and Tabasco and add to grits mixture, beating well. Pour into 9 x 13-inch baking dish, which has been greased and sprinkled with corn flakes. Bake in 350 degree oven about 45 minutes, or until set. Serves 8 to 10.

Mrs. Paul Emmons (Ellen)

COLD CURRIED RICE RING

1 cup rice, raw
1 tablespoon salad oil
¼ teaspoon saffron or turmeric
2 teaspoons onion, diced

½ cup mayonnaise
1 teaspoon curry powder
Raw vegetables, diced

Cook rice, adding oil, saffron or turmeric and onion while cooking. Cool. Combine mayonnaise and curry powder. Mix into cooled rice. Pack into 1-quart ring mold and refrigerate at least 2 hours. Unmold and fill center with diced tomatoes, green pepper, green onions, cucumber, avocado or any combination you want. Serve with cold meat or chicken. Serves 6 to 8.

Mrs. Thomas H. Truslow (Frances)

CHINESE RICE

3 cups raw rice
1 10½ ounce can beef bouillon, diluted
2 or more tablespoons peanut oil
3 bunches scallions, chopped (include parts of tops)

8 ounches mushrooms, chopped
1 8½-ounce can water chestnuts, drained and sliced
Soy sauce
8 ounces whole mushrooms

Cook rice in bouillon. Sauté onions and chopped mushrooms in peanut oil. Do not brown. Add to rice along with water chestnuts. Stir in soy sauce to taste. Place in casserole. Sauté whole mushrooms and use as garnish. Heat thoroughly in 350 degree oven. Serves 14.

Mrs. Sam Greenly (Lucille)

CONFETTI RICE

1 cup fresh mushrooms, sliced
½ cup onion, chopped
⅓ cup butter
3 cups hot cooked rice
1 10-ounce package frozen peas, cooked and drained

1 teaspoon salt
¼ teaspoon pepper
¼ teaspoon rosemary, crushed
¼ cup slivered almonds, toasted

Cook mushrooms and onions in butter until tender. Add rice, peas and seasonings. Cook about 5 minutes stirring occasionally. Sprinkle with almonds and serve. Serves 6 to 8.

Mrs. Ernest S. Collins (Sue)

CRAB RICE

1 pound bacon, cooked and drained
1 pound crabmeat, lump or claw

1 cup onion, diced
3 cups cooked rice
Salt and pepper to taste

Crumble bacon and mix with crabmeat, onion and rice. Add salt and pepper to taste. Pour into casserole. Bake 25 to 30 minutes in 350 degree oven. Serve with tossed salad and garlic bread. Serves 6 to 8.

Mrs. A. R. McAfee (Lydia)

GREEN RICE

1 10-ounce package frozen
   chopped spinach
2½ cups cooked rice
¾ cup milk
½ cup Cheddar cheese, grated
¼ cup parsley, chopped

¾ teaspoon Worcestershire sauce
2 eggs, well beaten
3 tablespoons butter
1 small onion, chopped
1½ teaspoons salt

Cook and drain spinach. Blend together spinach, rice, milk, cheese, parsley, Worcestershire sauce, eggs, butter, onion and salt. Place in greased casserole. Bake at 325 degrees for 45 minutes. Serves 6.

Mrs. Frank Tuckwiller (Barbara)

JALAPEÑO RICE

2⅓ cups rice, raw
½ cup butter
¾ cup green onions, chop tops
   and bottoms

½ teaspoon oregano
¼ cup Parmesan cheese
1 8-ounce Jalapeño pepper cheese
Salt to taste

Cook rice. Melt butter and wilt onions. Add oregano and Parmesan cheese. Pour over rice and toss with fork. Cut up half the Jalapeño pepper cheese into cubes and mix into rice. Put in greased 2-quart casserole. Arrange slices of rest of Jalapeño cheese on top. Bake at 400 degrees until cheese melts. This may be made the day before. Serves 10.

Mrs. J. Bernard Credle (Shirley)

HOPPING JOHN

1 cup dried field peas
4 cups water
2 teaspoons salt
1 cup rice, uncooked and
   washed

⅓ pound bacon
Bacon grease
1 large onion, chopped

Boil peas in water and salt until tender. Fry bacon until crisp. Remove from pan and crumble. Pour off half the grease and cook onion until tender. Combine peas, 1½ cups pea liquid, rice, bacon and onion. Put in rice steamer and cook until done or about 1 hour. Remove top from steamer the last 10 to 15 minutes of cooking time and fluff. Serves 6.

Mrs. Hugh O. Pearson, Jr. (Nancy)

ORANGE RICE

¼ cup butter	½ teaspoon salt
1 cup celery, diced with leaves	2 tablespoons orange juice
3 tablespoons onion, chopped	concentrate
2 tablespoons orange peel,	1¾ cups Minit rice
slivered	

Melt butter. Add celery, onion and orange peel. Cook until tender but not brown. Add salt. Put concentrate in measuring cup and add water to make 1½ cups. Add to celery mixture and bring to a boil. Add rice, mixing just to moisten. Cover and remove from heat. Let stand at least 5 minutes before serving. Serves 6 to 8.

Mrs. Bruce Whitney (Mary Olive)

ORIENTAL RICE

1 cup onion, chopped	2 tablespoons soy sauce
1 cup celery, chopped	1 3-ounce can mushrooms, drained
1 6-ounce package long grain	⅓ cup slivered almonds, toasted
and wild rice, cooked	Salt
3 tablespoons butter	

Sauté onion and celery in butter until tender. Mix all ingredients. Bake in 1½-quart casserole at 350 degrees for 20 minutes or until hot. Better when not doubled. Serves 6 to 8.

Mrs. Eugene Spears, Jr. (Lillian)

RED RICE I

2 onions, chopped	10 ounces water
1 cup bacon drippings	Salt and pepper to taste
1 15-ounce can tomato sauce	2½ cups rice, raw

Cook onions in bacon drippings until tender. Add tomato sauce and water. Add salt and pepper to taste; cook 15 minutes. Rinse rice and drain off as much water as possible. Add rice and tomato sauce mixture together. Put in rice steamer. Steam hard for 1 hour before opening. Open and mix rice in sauce that settled on top. Serves 6.

Mrs. Charles Aimar (Jeanne)

RED RICE II

¼ pound bacon
1 medium onion, chopped
1 cup rice, uncooked
2 cups red tomatoes

½ teaspoon salt
¼ teaspoon pepper
⅛ teaspoon Tabasco
1 cup cooked ham, diced

Fry bacon until crisp and remove from pan. Sauté onions in bacon grease until tender. Add rice, tomatoes, seasonings and crumbled bacon and ham. Cook over low heat about 10 minutes, then pour into 1-quart casserole and cover tightly. Bake at 350 degrees for 1 hour and stir with fork several times during the baking process. Serves 6 to 8.

Mrs. Bruce Whitney (Mary Olive)

VENETIAN RICE AND PEAS

1 tablespoon olive oil
¼ cup butter
1 small onion, chopped
½ slice bacon, diced
¾ cup rice, raw

1¾ cups chicken broth
2 cups frozen peas
Salt and pepper to taste
1 tablespoon Parmesan cheese

Heat oil and butter together. Brown onion and bacon. Add rice and cook 3 minutes, until coated. Add broth, peas, salt and pepper. Cook over low heat, covered, for about 15 to 20 minutes, or until all liquid is absorbed. Toss with cheese. Serves 4.

Mrs. Frank Mears (Jeanne)

SHRIMP AND RICE

1 cup rice, raw
2 cups water
2 tablespoons butter
1 cup celery, chopped
½ cup green pepper, chopped

½ cup carrots, chopped
1 8-ounce can mushrooms, drained
1 pound shrimp, boiled and peeled
½ cup soy sauce

Cook rice with 2 cups water. Sauté celery, green peppers, onions, carrots and mushrooms in butter slowly for 30 minutes. Mix rice, vegetables, shrimp and soy sauce. Serves 4.

Mrs. Michael M. Hynes (Tanya)

SHRIMP RICE

2 cups rice, raw
1 egg, beaten
4 tablespoons butter
1 bell pepper, chopped

1 teaspoon prepared mustard
Salt and pepper to taste
1 pound shrimp, boiled and peeled

Cook rice. Mix hot rice with egg, butter, bell pepper, mustard, salt and pepper. Stir in shrimp. Place in large baking dish, cover and bake until hot in 350 degree oven. Serves 6 to 8.

Mrs. Joe Perkins (Priscilla)

WILD RICE

1 cup wild rice
12 cups water, boiling and
    divided

1 teaspoon salt
Pepper
Butter

Wash the wild rice thoroughly in cold water. Place rice in saucepan. Cover rice with 4 cups of rapidly boiling water. Put the lid on pan and let the rice stand for 30 minutes. Drain. Repeat this twice, adding salt to the last 4 cups of water. Be certain to use fresh boiling water each time. Season with salt, pepper and generous amounts of butter when serving. This rice may be done early in the day and kept warm in a covered double boiler. This is a foolproof way to cook wild rice. Serves 6.

Mrs. John M. Trask (Flora)

WILD RICE PECAN CASSEROLE

½ cup butter
½ pound mushrooms, sliced
2 tablespoons onion, chopped
2 tablespoons green pepper,
     chopped
1 clove garlic, minced
     (optional)

1 cup pecans, coarsely chopped
1 cup wild rice
3 cups chicken broth
Salt and pepper
1 or 2 cups chicken, turkey or
     roast pork (optional)

Heat butter. Add mushrooms, onion, green pepper and garlic. Cook about 5 minutes stirring often. Add pecans and cook about 1 minute. Wash rice well and drain. Add to mushroom mixture. Add broth and season to taste with salt and pepper. Turn into a greased casserole, cover and bake in a slow oven about 325 degrees for about 1 hour. Chicken, turkey or roast pork which has been cut into cubes or julienne strips, may be added before turning into the casserole. Serves 4.

Mrs. John S. Osborne (Betty)

BUCKWHEAT GROATS (KASHE)

2 cups medium groats (Kashe)
1 egg, beaten
1 onion, diced
2 tablespoons vegetable oil or
     chicken fat

2 cups boiling water
1 teaspoon salt

Pour Kashe into heavy pan. Pour egg over grains and mix thoroughly with fork until all grains are coated with egg. Place heavy pan in moderate oven 300-325 degrees, stir occasionally until all grains are dried. Meanwhile, dice and brown onion in oil or fat. Set aside. Bring to a boil 2 cups water and 1 teaspoon salt. When water is rolling, pour in, stirring constantly, 2 cups Kashe. Reduce heat, stir constantly until mixture begins to thicken. Then cover, stir occasionally with fork until all the water has been absorbed. Should be slightly dry with grains easily separated. Stir in browned onions and fat. Keep warm until served. Remaining dried, uncooked groats may be stored in jar with tight cover.

Mrs. Sol Neidich (Evelyn)

BLACKBERRY

Vegetables

FRENCH FRIED ARTICHOKE

4 artichokes, washed and
    drained
3 egg yolks, beaten
½ cup milk
¾ teaspoon salt
½ teaspoon nutmeg

Pepper to taste
Dash of Tabasco
Flour
Fine bread crumbs
Vegetable shortening for frying

Cut off top half of artichokes and trim stem. Snip off outer leaves until all pale green leaves are exposed. Slice artichokes in half and remove choke. Cut ¼-inch slices lengthwise. Blend yolks, milk and seasonings. Coat artichoke slices with flour, dip into egg mixture and coat with bread crumbs. Drop into skillet or deep fat fryer set at 375 degrees. Fry until golden brown or about 1 minute. Drain and serve hot.

Mrs. Sam Stafford III (Nancy)

ASPARAGUS PLUS

5 tablespoons butter
5 tablespoons flour
2½ cups milk or cream
Salt and white pepper to taste
2 14½-ounce cans green
    asparagus, drained
1 8-ounce can water chestnuts,
    sliced

1 4-ounce jar chopped pimento
½ pound mushrooms, sliced and
    sautéed in butter
1 pound shrimp, peeled and
    slightly cooked
4 hard boiled eggs, sliced
Bread crumbs
3 tablespoons butter

Make a white sauce of butter, flour, milk or cream, salt and pepper. Alternate vegetables, eggs and shrimp in 2-inch deep 8 x 12-inch casserole with the white sauce. Make sure there is enough white sauce to cover top. Sprinkle with the bread crumbs and dot with butter. Bake at 325 degrees for 35-40 minutes. Serves 6-8.

Mrs. Hugh Pearson (Nancy)

CURRIED ASPARAGUS STICKS

2 pounds fresh asparagus
Salt and pepper
1 cup butter, melted
2 tablespoons lemon juice
1 teaspoon curry powder

½ cup ground almonds
1½ cups unseasoned whole wheat
　breadcrumbs
Melted butter

Steam asparagus until done, but still quite crisp. Salt and pepper asparagus. Combine butter and lemon juice. Dip asparagus in butter mixture. Mix curry, almonds, and breadcrumbs. Roll asparagus in crumb mixture. Serve with additional butter dribbled on top. Serves 6-8.

Mrs. Sam Stafford, III (Nancy)

PINTO BEAN POT

2 cups (1 pound) pinto beans,
　washed and picked over
6 cups water
1 tablespoon oil
1 meaty ham bone
1 tablespoon bacon grease
1 cup onion, chopped
2 cloves garlic
1 teaspoon salt

½ teaspoon black pepper
½ teaspoon oregano
½ teaspoon cumin (ground or
　crushed seeds)
3 teaspoons chili powder
1 8-ounce can tomato sauce
Onion and green pepper rings
½ cup provolone cheese, grated

Cover beans with water. Soak overnight. Place in a deep kettle with oil and ham bone. Simmer, covered until tender, about 2 hours. Remove bone, cut off meat and reserve. Sauté onion in bacon fat until tender. Mash garlic with salt and add to onions. Cook for 2 or 3 minutes. Add seasonings and tomato sauce to onion. Add one cup liquid from cooked beans. Cook 5 minutes. Drain cooked beans. Combine sauce and reserved ham with beans and turn into a casserole or bean pot; cover and bake at 325 degrees for two hours. Check seasoning. Garnish with onion and pepper rings and grated cheese. A spicy main dish that serves 6-8.

Dale Hryharrow Friedman

BROCCOLI WITH MUSTARD SAUCE

3 pounds broccoli
2 tablespoons onion, finely
   chopped
½ cup butter
½ cup flour
1½ cups milk

1½ cups chicken stock
3 tablespoons lemon juice
2 tablespoons prepared mustard
2 tablespoons sugar
1 teaspoon salt

Cut buds and stems from broccoli. Cook buds and stems in boiling salted water until just tender. Sauté onion in butter until tender. Stir in flour. Gradually add milk and chicken stock, stirring constantly until thickened. Season with lemon juice, mustard, sugar and salt. Pour sauce over broccoli. Serves 8.

Mrs. O. Stanley Smith (Connie)

BROCCOLI CASSEROLE

2 10-ounce packages frozen
   broccoli
2 tablespoons butter, melted
2 tablespoons flour
2 cups milk
¾ cup Cheddar cheese, grated

1 teaspoon salt
¼ teaspoon pepper
¼ cup slivered almonds
4 slices crisp cooked bacon
½ cup buttered bread crumbs

Cook broccoli until just tender. Drain and place in casserole dish. Combine butter and flour in saucepan. Add milk stirring constantly until almost thickened. Add cheese, salt and pepper. Continue to stir until thickened. Sprinkle broccoli with almonds and crumbled bacon. Pour sauce over all. Top with buttered bread crumbs. Bake at 350 degrees for 20 minutes. Serves 6-8.

Mrs. L. Brent Kuhnle (Terry)

SAUCY CABBAGE WEDGES

1 head cabbage, cut into 8
   wedges
⅓ cup mayonnaise
¼ cup milk

4 teaspoons cider vinegar
1 teaspoon sugar
½ teaspoon prepared mustard
Paprika

Boil cabbage in salted water 8 to 10 minutes. Drain. Combine mayonnaise and milk in saucepan until smooth. Add vinegar, sugar and mustard to sauce and mix well. Heat well over low heat. When hot, pour over cabbage. Sprinkle paprika over top. Serves 8.

Mrs. Gene Grace (Beth)

CANTONESE CARROTS

2 tablespoons oil
12 to 14 young carrots, peeled
   and cut on bias ¼-inch
   slices
3 stalks celery, cut ⅛-inch
   slices

½ medium sweet green pepper,
   thinly sliced
1 scallion, finely chopped including
   top
Pinch monosodium glutamate
¾ teaspoon salt

Heat oil in heavy skillet over medium-low heat for 1 minute. Add carrots and celery and stir fry for 4 minutes. Add green pepper and scallion. Stir fry for 5 minutes until carrots are crisp and tender. Sprinkle vegetables with monosodium glutamate and salt. Toss and serve. Serves 4.

Mrs. Charles P. Graham (Jean)

MARINADED CARROTS

5 cups carrots, cooked and
   sliced
1 medium onion, thinly sliced
1 small green pepper, finely
   chopped
1 10¾-ounce can tomato soup
½ cup salad oil

¾ cup cider vinegar
1 cup sugar
1 teaspoon dry mustard
1 teaspoon Worcestershire sauce
1 teaspoon salt
1 teaspoon pepper

Combine all ingredients, tossing vegetables. Marinate overnight in tightly covered bowl. Serves 8 to 10.

Mrs. Walter E. Jenkins (Louise)

COLD CAULIFLOWER NIVERNAIS

2 heads cauliflower
1¼ cups mayonnaise
¼ cup sour cream

4 ounces Dijon mustard
Salt and freshly ground pepper
Fresh parsley, chopped

Break cauliflower into small flowerettes. Cook in boiling water for 3 minutes ONLY. Blanch in cold water. Drain. Combine all other ingredients except parsley. Whisk until light and creamy. Pour dressing over cauliflower until all pieces are well coated. Chill. Garnish with parsley. Serves 5 to 6.

Dale Hryharrow Friedman

CHINESE CELERY CASSEROLE

4 cups celery, diagonally cut
Water
½ pound fresh mushrooms,
   sliced
1 8-ounce can water chestnuts,
   sliced
1 4-ounce can pimento,
   chopped

1 10¾-ounce can undiluted cream
   of chicken soup
Salt, pepper and MSG
1 cup Pepperidge Farm herb
   dressing
3-4 ounces slivered almonds
Butter

Cook celery in water 8 minutes and drain. Combine with mushrooms, water chestnuts, pimento, chicken soup, salt, pepper, and MSG. Place in 1-quart greased casserole. Top with herb dressing. Dot with butter and almonds. Cook uncovered 20-25 minutes in 400 degree oven. Serves 6.

Mrs. H. C. Stelling (Martha)

CELERY AU GRATIN

2 tablespoons butter
2 tablespoons flour
1 cup chicken stock
¼ cup light cream
Salt and pepper to taste

2 cups celery, sliced and parboiled
¼ cup blanched almonds, chopped
Cheddar cheese, grated
Bread crumbs, buttered

Make a cream sauce of the butter, flour, chicken stock, cream, salt and pepper. Add celery and almonds. Place in a buttered casserole. Top with cheese and crumbs. Bake 20 to 30 minutes in 350 degree oven. Serves 6.

Mrs. C. Blackburn Brewer (Frances)

CORN CASSEROLE

1 cup evaporated milk
4 tablespoons butter or
   margarine
½ cup flour
1 12-ounce can whole kernel
   golden corn, drained

½ teaspoon dry mustard
1 teaspoon paprika
1 tablespoon Worcestershire sauce
1 egg, beaten
1 cup buttered crumbs

Dilute evaporated milk to about 1½ cups. Melt butter, add flour and make cream sauce with the milk. Add corn. Add all flavorings and beaten egg. Top with layer of buttered crumbs. Heat in 300 degree oven for 20 minutes. Just before serving, brown crumbs quickly under broiler. Serves 4.

Mrs. William Montgomery (Marjorie)

CORN FRITTERS

1½ cups corn kernels
2 eggs
¾ cup flour
1 teaspoon baking powder

½ teaspoon salt
2 tablespoons butter
2 tablespoons oil

Use Cuisinart fitted with plastic blade. Place corn and eggs into work bowl and turn on and off twice. Mix flour, baking powder and salt together. Add to work bowl. Process only long enough to mix. Melt oil and butter in large skillet. When hot, drop spoonful of batter to form fritters. Fry until golden turning once. Serves 4 to 6.

The Editors

CORN PUDDING

1 dozen ears of corn
1 cup heavy cream
3 tablespoons sugar

3 eggs, separated
Salt and pepper
2 tablespoons butter, melted

Score and scrape kernels of raw corn. Add cream, sugar, beaten egg yolks, salt and pepper. Fold in stiffly beaten egg whites. Pour into a buttered baking dish. Pour melted butter over top. Bake in 350 degree oven for 45 minutes. Serves 6.

Mrs. John W. Stoddard (Katrina)

EGGPLANT ALCASIENNE

1 medium green pepper, diced
1 clove garlic, crushed
½ cup onion, finely chopped
2 tablespoons olive oil
1 pound eggplant, peeled and
    diced
2 cups tomatoes, coarsely
    diced

1 teaspoon salt
½ teaspoon pepper
½ teaspoon oregano
1 tablespoon capers
Pimento, anchovies, sliced stuffed
    olives

Sauté green pepper, garlic and onion in oil until tender. Add eggplant, tomatoes, and salt to sautéed vegetables. Cover and cook slowly 15 minutes. Add pepper, oregano, and capers. Increase heat and cook until almost all the liquid is gone. Cool. Garnish with pimento, anchovies, and olives. Serves 6-8.

Mrs. Frederic W. Boye, Jr. (Page)

EGGPLANT CASSEROLE

1 large eggplant, peeled
1 small green pepper, chopped
2 ribs celery, chopped
1 large onion, chopped
4 tablespoons butter
1 teaspoon Worcestershire
    sauce
1 dash Tabasco

½ cup sharp cheese, grated
¼ cup ripe olives, chopped
½ teaspoon salt
Dash of pepper
2 tablespoons milk
2 tomatoes, chopped and peeled
18 saltine crackers, crumbled

Cut eggplant and cook in boiling salted water for 10 minutes. Sauté green pepper, celery and onion in butter. Add cooked eggplant, Worcestershire sauce, hot sauce, cheese, olives, salt, pepper, milk and tomatoes. Mix lightly and turn into a 2-quart baking dish. Cover with cracker crumbs. Bake 35-40 minutes in 350 degree oven. Serves 6.

Mrs. W. K. Pillow, Jr. (Anne)

EGGPLANT PARMIGIANA

1½ cups olive oil
1 clove garlic, minced
1 cup onion, chopped
1 35-ounce can peeled Italian
    tomatoes, drained
½ teaspoon dried basil
½ teaspoon freshly ground
    pepper
¼ teaspoon salt

4 tablespoons flour
2 eggs, beaten
2 eggplant, peeled and cut into
    ⅓-inch slices
1 cup Parmesan cheese, freshly
    grated
1 cup Mozzarella cheese, diced
Butter

Heat ¼ cup of the olive oil in a heavy skillet, add the garlic and onions and sauté until the onion is transparent. Add the tomatoes, basil, pepper and salt, and cook, stirring occasionally, 30 minutes. Combine the flour and eggs. Dip the eggplant slices in the batter and fry in the remaining oil until lightly browned on both sides. Drain slices on paper towels. Place alternate layers of eggplant, sauce, and cheeses in a large casserole. Dot top with butter. Freeze. To serve, defrost completely and bake in a preheated oven at 350 degrees for 30 minutes. Serves 6.

Mrs. C. A. Larsen, Jr. (Eleanor)

EGGPLANT SUPREME

4 small eggplant, peeled and
    cut up
2 large onions, chopped
8 tablespoons butter, divided
1 pound sharp cheese, grated

2 eggs, beaten
Salt and pepper
1 teaspoon sugar
Cracker crumbs

Boil eggplant in salted water until soft, drain off water and mash. Sauté onions in 4 tablespoons butter. Combine eggplant, onions, cheese, eggs, salt, pepper and sugar. Place in greased 2-quart casserole. Cover with cracker crumbs and dot with remaining butter. Bake at 350 degrees for 45 minutes. Serves 8.

Mrs. Jack Duncan (Norma)

MUSHROOM CHEESE BAKE

½ cup celery, chopped
¼ cup onion, chopped
3 tablespoons butter
½ pound mushrooms, sliced
4 cups day old wheat bread,
    cubed

2 cups cheese, grated
2 eggs
2 cups milk
2 teaspoons dry mustard
1 teaspoon salt
½ teaspoon pepper

Sauté celery and onion in butter. Stir in mushrooms and cook until tender. In buttered 2-quart casserole, layer ½ of bread, mushroom mixture and cheese; repeat layers. Beat together egg, milk and seasonings. Pour evenly over layers. Bake in 325 degree oven about 45 minutes. Let casserole stand about 5 minutes before serving. Serves 4-6.

Mrs. H. K. Stoneman (Lucia)

MUSHROOM CASSEROLE

1 pound fresh mushrooms, sliced	½ cup butter, melted
2 cups French bread, cubed	Salt and pepper
	⅓ cup dry white wine

Butter 2-quart round casserole. Layer ⅓ mushrooms, ⅓ bread and spoon on ⅓ melted butter. Sprinkle with salt and pepper. Repeat process. Pour wine evenly over casserole. Cover and bake at 325 degrees for 25 minutes. Uncover and continue baking until brown. Serves 6.

Mrs. Robert N. Hughs (Ria)

MUSHROOM PIE FILLING

Pastry dough sufficient for 2 pie crusts	2 tablespoons flour
2 medium onions, sliced	¾ cup half and half
1½ pounds mushrooms, sliced	3 tablespoons sherry
½ cup butter	1 teaspoon salt
	¼ teaspoon pepper

Sauté onions and mushrooms in butter until soft. Add flour, half and half, sherry, salt and pepper. Cool.

Using slightly more than half of pastry dough, roll out a thin crust and line 9 inch pie pan. Pour in mushroom filling. Roll out remaining pastry dough and slice in ½ inch wide strips. Place on top of filling in lattice pattern moistening at edges. Bake in 400 degree oven for 30 minutes or until brown. Serves 6-8.

Mrs. L. Brent Kuhnle (Terry)

MUSHROOM AND CELERY MEDLEY

3 cups celery, sliced	Salt and pepper to taste
1 cup chicken broth	1 tablespoon soy sauce
1 pound fresh mushrooms, sliced	½ cup almonds, slivered and toasted
4 tablespoons butter	

Simmer celery in chicken broth until tender but crisp. Drain. Sauté mushrooms in butter. Season with salt and pepper. Add soy sauce. Add to cooked celery. Toss with almonds. Serves 6.

Mrs. Gene Grace (Beth)

OKRA PILAU

2 cups raw rice
2 teaspoons salt
2 cups water
8 slices bacon, cut into 4 or 5
    pieces each

1 onion, chopped
2 pounds okra, sliced crosswise

Put rice, salt and water to steam in rice steamer. Cook bacon and onion in skillet for 5-8 minutes. Add okra to bacon and onion and cook until okra browns on edges. When all of water has been absorbed by rice, add okra mixture and mix thoroughly. Add more salt if needed. Let mixture cook 20-30 minutes. Serves 8-10.

Mrs. T. Ladson Webb (Ann)

MARINADED BLACK-EYED PEAS

2 16-ounce cans cooked
    black-eyed peas
1 cup salad oil
1 clove garlic

¼ cup wine vinegar
½ cup onion, thinly sliced
½ teaspoon salt
Freshly ground pepper

Drain peas. Add ingredients and mix. Store in a jar in refrigerator. Remove garlic the second day. Keeps for 2 weeks in refrigerator.

Mrs. C. W. Mayo, III (Miriam)

DEVONSHIRE POTATO MUSHROOM PIE

3 cups mashed potatoes,
   seasoned
1½ cups mushrooms, sliced
¼ cup onion, chopped
2 tablespoons butter

1 teaspoon lemon juice
¼ teaspoon salt
Dash white pepper
½ cup sour cream

Preheat oven to 350 degrees. Put ½ of the mashed potatoes in a buttered 9-inch pie pan. Sauté mushrooms and onions in butter. Add lemon juice, salt, and pepper. Spoon over potatoes. Spread with sour cream. Top with remaining potatoes. Bake for 45 minutes. Cut into wedges to serve. Serves 6.

Mrs. McDonald Dixon (Phyllis)

GOLDEN POTATO CASSEROLE

2 cups Cheddar cheese,
   shredded
¼ cup butter
2 cups sour cream
⅓ cup chives, chopped

1 teaspoon salt
¼ teaspoon white pepper
6 medium potatoes, baked,
   skinned, cooled and shredded
2 tablespoons butter

In a large saucepan, over low heat, combine cheese and butter until almost melted. Remove from heat and blend in next 4 ingredients. Add potatoes, stir lightly and dot with butter. Put into greased casserole; bake 25 minutes at 350 degrees uncovered. Serves 6-8.

Mrs. William Knepp (Helen)

HOT POTATO SALAD CASSEROLE

3 large baking potatoes (baked
   in skin)
Salt to taste
1 cup sour cream
1 cup creamed cottage cheese

1 garlic clove, minced
½ cup green onion, diced
1 tablespoon parsley, chopped
1 cup sharp cheese, grated
Paprika

Add salt to potatoes that have been baked then peeled and diced. Mix well. Add sour cream, cottage cheese, garlic, onion and parsley. Mix together. Put in a buttered 2-quart casserole dish. Add cheese and top with paprika. Bake at 350 degrees for 40 to 45 minutes. Serves 6.

Mrs. Gary Fordham (Joan)

POTATOES ANNA

1 cup butter, melted
3 pounds Red Bliss or new
    potatoes, peeled and sliced

Salt
White pepper

Use an 8-inch by 3-inch mold that can go in oven or a cast iron skillet with a fitted lid. Place ¼ of the butter in skillet or mold and set over medium heat. Arrange potatoes starting in middle. Sprinkle with salt and pepper. Arrange a second circle in other direction and baste with melted butter. Continue until all are used. Butter inside of lid and press down on potatoes. Place in 375 degree oven for 25 minutes. Take off lid and bake at 350 degrees for 20 minutes longer. Unmold and reserve dripping butter for other use. Slice like a pie. Serves 6 to 8.

The Editors

PUFFED POTATOES

Small new potatoes
Vegetable oil

Salt

Wash and dry the potatoes. Rub the skins with vegetable oil. Cut each potato in half lengthwise; salt the cut surfaces. Bake in a 450 degree oven until browned and puffed, about 10 minutes.

Mrs. Richard H. Bateson (Lois)

LITHUANIAN-STYLE POTATO KUGEL

1 cup (6 ounces) slab bacon,
    diced
1 onion, minced
4 potatoes, peeled and grated

4 eggs, lightly beaten
1 cup milk
1 tablespoon parsley, minced
Salt and pepper to taste

In a skillet, sauté bacon for 3 minutes. Add onion and sauté mixture until onion is soft and bacon crisp. Put potatoes in a bowl. Stir in bacon mixture, eggs, milk, parsley, salt, and pepper. Transfer mixture to shallow 1½-quart buttered baking dish. Bake in preheated 375 degree oven for 1 hour or until top is brown. Serves 6.

Mrs. Gene Grace (Beth)

SWEET POTATO PONE

½ cup butter
1½ cups white sugar
½ cup brown sugar
¼ cup milk
¼ cup flour
2 eggs, beaten

1 teaspoon vanilla
1 teaspoon nutmeg
½ teaspoon cinnamon
¼ teaspoon cloves
2 cups raw sweet potatoes, grated

Melt butter in 2-quart casserole dish. Add sugar, milk and flour to eggs and blend. Add spices and grated potatoes. Mix well. Put in casserole with butter. Bake at 325 degrees for 1 hour or until not soupy in center of casserole. Serves 4 to 6.

Mrs. Doadie Johnson

BOURBON SWEET POTATOES

4 pounds yams or sweet
    potatoes
½ cup margarine or butter
½ cup bourbon
⅓ cup orange juice

¼ cup light brown sugar
1 teaspoon salt
½ teaspoon apple pie spice
⅓ cup pecans, chopped

Cook and mash yams or sweet potatoes. Add butter, bourbon, orange juice, sugar, salt and spice and beat well. Put in buttered 2-quart casserole and sprinkle with pecans. Bake at 350 degrees for 45 minutes until brown. Serves 8.

Mrs. Badger Perrin (Chris)

PUMPKIN MOUSSE

3 cups cooked pumpkin
2-3 tablespoons rum
1 tablespoon honey
1 teaspoon salt
¼ cup light cream

2 tablespoons flour
¼ teaspoon nutmeg
¼ teaspoon white pepper
3 egg yolks
3 egg whites, stiffly beaten

Combine all above ingredients, except egg yolks and egg whites. Mix well and beat in egg yolks vigorously. Fold in beaten egg whites. Pour the mixture into a 1-quart oiled baking dish and set dish in a pan of hot water. Bake the mousse in a 375 degree oven for 20-25 minutes. Serve mousse hot, with roast chicken, turkey or duck. Serves 6.

Mrs. L. E. Lovette (Louise)

RAVIOLI NUDI

4 10-ounce packages frozen
spinach, chopped
1 pound Ricotta cheese
4 egg yolks
Salt and freshly ground pepper

½ teaspoon nutmeg, freshly grated
1½ cups Parmesan cheese, freshly
grated
Flour
4 tablespoons butter

Cook spinach according to directions. Cool in running water and squeeze very dry. Mix spinach with Ricotta, egg yolks, salt, pepper, nutmeg and 1 cup Parmesan. Mix thoroughly. Make little balls about 1-inch diameter. Coat lightly with flour and put into very slowly boiling water. In less than a minute each will rise to the top of the water at which point it should be removed with a slotted spoon. Place in a serving dish, with the melted butter, over hot water to keep Ravioli warm and moist until they are all in the dish. Sprinkle with ½ cup Parmesan and serve hot. Can make ahead and keep in serving dish in refrigerator and warm up in 350 degree oven. Serves 8.

Mrs. Harry Gilham (Caroline)

SPINACH CASSEROLE

2 10-ounce packages frozen
spinach, cooked and
drained
½ pound bacon, fried and
crumbled
2 eggs, beaten

2 cups milk
1 teaspoon salt
⅔ cup seasoned Italian bread
crumbs
1½ cups Provalone cheese, grated
½ teaspoon paprika

To the spinach add the bacon, eggs, milk, salt, bread crumbs and ¾ cup of the cheese. Mix thoroughly. Pour into greased 1½-quart baking dish. Sprinkle remaining cheese and paprika on top. Bake in 375 degree oven for 30-35 minutes. Serves 8.

Mrs. H. W. Coupland (Sue)

SAVORY CHOPPED SPINACH

1 10-ounce package frozen
  chopped spinach, cooked
  and drained
1 3-ounce package cream
  cheese, softened

3 slices bacon, cooked, drained
  and crumbled
1 tablespoon green onion, minced
1 tablespoon horseradish
Salt to taste

Add spinach to cream cheese and stir until blended. Add bacon, onion, horseradish and salt. Place in a greased 1½-pint casserole. Bake in 350 degree oven for 20-30 minutes. Serves 3.

Mrs. Edward Herendeen (Marguerite)

SPINACH PIE

1 3-ounce package cream
  cheese
1 cup half and half
½ cup bread cubes, lightly
  packed
⅓ cup Parmesan cheese
2 eggs, beaten
1 10-ounce package frozen chopped
  spinach, cooked and drained

4 tablespoons butter
1 large onion, finely chopped
¼ pound mushrooms, finely
  chopped
1 teaspoon tarragon
Salt
Unbaked 9-inch pie shell

Mash cream cheese and gradually blend in half and half. Add bread, Parmesan cheese, and eggs. Beat to break up bread cubes. Stir in spinach. Melt butter and cook onions and mushrooms until lightly browned. Add tarragon and salt. Blend mushroom-onion mixture into spinach mixture. Pour into pie shell. Bake at 400 degrees for 25 minutes or until done. Let stand 10 minutes and then cut. Good hot or cold. Serves 6-8.

Mrs. Hunter Wyatt-Brown (Nancy)

SPINACH WITH SOUR CREAM AND PARMESAN

2 10-ounce packages frozen
   chopped spinach
4 tablespoons onion, grated
4 eggs
1 cup sour cream

2 cups Parmesan cheese, grated
4 tablespoons butter
2 tablespoons flour
¼ teaspoon salt

Bring spinach and onion to a boil and drain. Beat eggs and add to spinach. Mix and add remaining ingredients. Bake in a greased, small casserole for 25 minutes in 350 degree oven. Do not over cook. Serves 8.

Mrs. Joel Patrick (Mary)

STUFFED YELLOW SQUASH

8 medium yellow squash
1 10-ounce package frozen
   peas or spinach
4 tablespoons butter, melted
¼ cup light cream

¼ teaspoon pepper
1 teaspoon salt
¾ cup buttered bread crumbs
¾ cup Parmesan cheese, grated

Cook squash whole in boiling water for 10 minutes. Drain. Cut lengthwise and remove pulp. Cook peas and drain. Combine pulp, peas, butter and seasonings in blender and blend. Spoon into shells and sprinkle with bread crumbs and cheese. Bake at 350 degrees for 15 minutes or until brown. Serves 8.

Mrs. William Elliott (Martha)

SOUFFLÉD SQUASH

2 eggs, separated
2 tablespoons water, divided
2 cups cooked, mashed, and
   drained yellow squash
¼ cup celery, finely chopped
¼ cup onion, finely chopped
1 teaspoon sugar

1 teaspoon baking powder
1 tablespoon flour
⅓ cup milk
Salt and pepper, to taste
3 tablespoons butter, melted
⅛ cup dried bread crumbs or
   grated sharp cheese

Beat egg yolks with 1 tablespoon of water and beat egg whites with 1 tablespoon water. To squash add celery, onion, sugar, baking powder, flour, milk, salt and pepper and butter. Add egg yolks and whites separately. Pour into buttered greased casserole. Bake at 350 degrees for 20 minutes or until crumbs brown or cheese melts. Serves 6.

Mrs. W. T. Miars, Jr. (Emma)

SQUASH CASSEROLE I

½ cup butter, melted
1 8-ounce package Pepperidge
   Farm herb dressing
2½ cups cooked and drained
   squash

1 10¾-ounce can mushroom soup
1 cup sour cream
1 small white onion, grated
1 2-ounce jar pimento
Salt and pepper

Grease 3-quart glass casserole dish. Pour melted butter over stuffing and mix well. Line bottom of casserole with ½ of the stuffing mixture. Mix all other ingredients and add on top of stuffing. Put remainder of stuffing on top of squash mixture. Bake at 350 degrees for 40 minutes. Fifteen minutes after baking begins, cover lightly with foil to avoid overcrusting.

Mrs. Robert McDowell (Becky)

SQUASH CASSEROLE II

2 pounds yellow squash or
   zucchini, steamed, drained
   and mashed
1 10½-ounce can cream of
   chicken soup, undiluted
1 cup sour cream

¼ cup butter or margarine
2 carrots, peeled and grated
1 medium onion, grated
Pepperidge Farm herb stuffing
   (reserve some to use as a
   topping for the casserole)

To squash add other ingredients and mix well. Put into shallow baking dish and top with reserved stuffing mix. Bake at 350 degrees for 30-45 minutes or until top is brown.

Mrs. J. S. Douglass (Margaret)

LEMON ZUCCHINI

3 pounds zucchini, sliced
Butter
2 tablespoons lemon pepper
   seasoning
¾ teaspoon salt

1½ cups bread crumbs
3 tablespoons butter
1½ teaspoons grated lemon rind
Parsley

Sauté zucchini in butter until barely done. Add lemon pepper and salt. Brown bread crumbs in butter. Add to zucchini. Add lemon rind and toss. Place in 1-quart casserole and top with parsley. Bake at 350 degrees for 20 minutes. Serves 6.

Mrs. R. L. Huffines, III (Douglas)

PARMESAN ZUCCHINI

4 or 5 small zucchini,
   quartered and sliced in
   2-inch lengths
Salt

Pepper
¼ cup Parmesan cheese
2 tablespoons butter

Drop zucchini into boiling water. Reduce heat to simmer and cook 5 to 10 minutes. Do not overcook. Drain and run under cold water. Butter a shallow baking dish and arrange zucchini in 1 layer. Sprinkle with salt, pepper and Parmesan cheese. Dribble butter over top. Cook under broiler until zucchini is hot and golden. Serves 6.

Mrs. Robert Poitras (Louise)

ZUCCHINI CASSEROLE

4 pounds zucchini, unpeeled
   and diced
½ teaspoon garlic salt
1 large onion, chopped
1 bell pepper, chopped
1 cup water
4 eggs, beaten
1 cup bread crumbs

¼ cup Parmesan cheese, grated
¼ cup Monterey Jack cheese,
   grated
2 tablespoons parsley, chopped
½ cup salad oil
Salt and pepper to taste
Italian seasoning to taste

Combine zucchini, garlic salt, onion, bell pepper and cook in water until tender. Drain well; mash. Combine remaining ingredients. Mix with zucchini mixture. Place in a casserole and bake at 400 degrees for 30 minutes.

Mrs. Jack W. Gray (Cile)

BAKED TOMATOES

6 firm tomatoes
6 tablespoons onions, minced
4 tablespoons butter
1½ cups bread crumbs

1 teaspoon salt
¼ teaspoon pepper
4 tablespoons brown sugar
Butter

Cut tomatoes in half. Place cut side up in greased baking dish. Sauté onions in butter until tender. Stir in bread crumbs with ½ of the salt and pepper and all of the sugar. Sprinkle tomatoes with remaining salt and pepper and cover with onion mixture. Dot with butter. Bake for 15 to 20 minutes in 450 degree oven. Serves 6.

Mrs. Ed Holt (Kitty)

SCALLOPED TOMATOES

1½ cups soft brown bread
   crumbs
5⅓ tablespoons butter, melted
1 14½-ounce can whole
   tomatoes

¼ cup brown sugar
½ teaspoon salt
¼ teaspoon basil

Put bread crumbs into a 1-quart baking dish. Pour butter over the crumbs and toss to coat. Mix the juice from tomatoes with brown sugar, salt and basil. Nest the tomatoes down in the bread crumbs and pour the juice mixture over the top. Bake at 425 degrees for 25 to 30 minutes. Serves 4.

Mrs. Beecher Hoogenboom (Irene)

Similar recipe submitted by *Mrs. James Ranger (Jane)*

MUSHROOM STUFFED TOMATOES

6 medium tomatoes
1 pound fresh mushrooms,
   chopped
2 tablespoons butter
½ cup sour cream
2 egg yolks, beaten

¼ cup fine dry bread crumbs
1 teaspoon salt
Dash of pepper and thyme
1 tablespoon butter
3 tablespoons bread crumbs

Cut stems from tomatoes. Scoop out pulp. Turn shells upside down to drain. Chop pulp fine. Measure 1 cup and set aside. Cook mushrooms in butter until tender. Combine sour cream and egg yolks. Add to mushrooms with tomato pulp and mix well. Stir in the crumbs, salt, pepper and thyme. Cook and stir until mixture thickens and boils. Place tomato shells in 10-inch by 6-inch by ½-inch baking dish. Spoon mushroom mixture into tomatoes. Combine melted butter and fine dry bread crumbs. Sprinkle on top of tomatoes. Bake in 325 degree oven for 25 minutes. Serves 6.

Ms. Paula Battey

SPINACH IN TOMATOES

1 10-ounce package frozen
   chopped spinach, cooked
   and drained well
1 cup sharp cheese, grated
1 egg, well beaten

1 teaspoon sugar
1 teaspoon salt
8 tomatoes
Pepperidge Farm dressing

Mix spinach with cheese, egg, sugar and salt. Scoop out tomatoes and drain well. Stuff tomatoes with spinach mixture. Top tomatoes with dressing. Bake at 350 degrees for 15 to 20 minutes. Serves 8.

The Editors

STUFFED TOMATOES

8 medium tomatoes, unpeeled
1 medium onion, diced
1 tablespoon butter
2 eggs
1 teaspoon dried tarragon
1 tablespoon parsley, minced

2 cloves garlic, crushed
1 cup Swiss cheese, grated
Salt
Pepper
Chives or parsley, chopped

Slice off the top of tomatoes and scoop out inside pulp. Reserve pulp. Sauté onions in butter with tomato pulp until soft. Beat the eggs and mix with herbs, garlic and cheese. Add the tomato and onion mixture. Salt and pepper to taste and fill the hollowed tomato shells. Arrange in greased baking dish and cook at 350 degrees for approximately 15 minutes. Sprinkle chives or parsley before serving. Serves 8.

Mrs. Paul Trask (Marjorie)

TOMATO PIE

1 9-inch pie shell, baked and
   cooled
2 or 3 large tomatoes, thickly
   sliced
Salt
Pepper

Sweet basil
Chives
2 or 3 green onions, chopped
1 cup mayonnaise
1 cup sharp cheese, grated

Fill pie shell with tomatoes. Sprinkle with salt, pepper, basil, chives and green onions. Mix mayonnaise and cheese. Spread over tomatoes. Bake for 30 minutes at 350 degrees. Serves 6.

Mrs. Michael Ragsdale (Laura)

BAKED CHERRY TOMATOES

24 cherry tomatoes
4 tablespoons butter
1 teaspoon sugar

Dash salt
Fresh parsley, chopped

Slice tomatoes almost through and place in baking dish. Add butter, salt and sugar. Bake in 350 degree oven for 8 to 10 minutes. Shake the pan occasionally so the tomatoes turn in the butter. Sprinkle parsley on top when done. Serves 4 as an accompaniment.

Mrs. F. W. Boye (Page)

BAKED FRUIT CASSEROLE

1 #2½ can peaches, drained
1 #2½ can pears, drained
1 #2½ can sliced or chunk
   pineapple, drained

¾ cup brown sugar
⅓ cup margarine or butter
1 teaspoon ground ginger

Cut fruit into bite sized pieces. Place in buttered 3 quart casserole. Combine brown sugar, margarine and ginger; stir over low heat until margarine has melted. Pour over fruit and bake at 350 degrees about 30 minutes or until mixture is hot and syrup bubbles. Serves 8.

Mrs. E. E. Woods (Theo)

COOKED APPLES

3 pounds cooking apples, cored
   and quartered
6 tablespoons butter

2 teaspoons cinnamon
1 cup sugar
½ cup water

Layer apples in a 2-quart casserole. Cover each layer with butter, cinnamon and sugar. Pour water over top. Bake at 350 degrees for 1 hour or until done. Serves 6 to 8.

Mrs. Frank Chaplin (Louise)

Salads
and Salad Dressings

BOMBAY GARDEN SALAD

SALAD:

4 cups salad greens
1 cup bean sprouts, drained
½ cup water chestnuts, drained
    and thinly sliced

¼ cup slivered almonds, toasted

DRESSING:

½ cup green onions, chopped
½ teaspoon coriander
¼ cup parsley, chopped
2 teaspoons water
1 teaspoon ground ginger

1 tablespoon soy sauce
½ teaspoon curry powder
2 tablespoons mayonnaise
1 cup sour cream or plain yogurt

Place greens, sprouts, water chestnuts and almonds in a large bowl. Toss. In a blender, put all of the ingredients for the dressing. Blend on a low speed for a few seconds. Just before serving, pour dressing over greens and toss lightly to give a thin coating throughout the salad. Serve immediately. Serves 6 to 8.

Mrs. Fred Trask (Mary Louise)

CAESAR SALAD

1 egg
Salt, to taste
2 cloves garlic
1 1-ounce can anchovies
½ teaspoon Worcestershire
    sauce
1 cup oil

2 tablespoons lemon juice
6 teaspoons Parmesan cheese,
    divided
3 grinds whole peppercorns
1 head lettuce or Romaine, torn
    apart
1 cup croutons

Coddle egg by leaving it in hot water 1 minute. Sprinkle salt in bottom of salad bowl. Rub garlic into salad bowl and crush. Cut and mash anchovies into paste and add to salad bowl. Add to anchovies, Worcestershire sauce, oil, lemon juice, 3 teaspoons cheese, pepper and lettuce. Add egg, remaining cheese and croutons. Toss ingredients.

Mrs. DeAlton Ridings (Jane)

GARDEN SALAD

½ pound fresh spinach, in bite
   size pieces
½ head cauliflower, broken in
   flowerets
1 small green pepper, thinly
   sliced
1 small carrot, shaved

6 to 8 radishes, thinly sliced
1 medium tomato, chopped
½ head Bibb lettuce
1 medium cucumber, sliced
½ cup French dressing
1 egg, hard boiled and chopped

Combine vegetables. Combine French dressing and egg. Pour this over salad. Serves 8.

Mrs. Robert Poitras (Louise)

SPINACH SALAD

SALAD:
10 ounces fresh spinach,
   washed, dried and
   de-stemmed
¾ pound fresh mushrooms,
   sautéed in butter

1 bunch scallions, chopped
8 strips bacon, cooked crisp and
   crumbled

DRESSING:
6 tablespoons olive oil
2 tablespoons lemon juice
1 egg yolk
1 clove garlic, minced

½ teaspoon salt
⅛ teaspoon pepper
⅛ teaspoon dry mustard

Mix salad ingredients well. Mix dressing ingredients well. Combine just before serving. Serves 6.

Mrs. William J. Catlett, Jr. (Toni)

COTTAGE FARM CANAPÉ SALAD

4 toast rounds, buttered
½ cup mayonnaise
½ cup sour cream
2 tablespoons prepared
   horseradish
Salt and pepper to taste

Bibb lettuce
Anchovy paste
4 slices fresh tomato
2 eggs, hard boiled
Paprika

Prepare toast rounds by cutting rounds from 4 slices of bread. Butter them, and toast in 300 degree oven until crisp. Prepare dressing by mixing together mayonnaise, sour cream and horseradish. Salt and pepper to taste. For each serving, assemble as follows: arrange bed of Bibb lettuce on salad plate. Spread each toast round with anchovy paste liberally and place on lettuce bed. Next, place 1 slice tomato on each round and top with ½ hard boiled egg, sliced horizontally. Cover each serving with the dressing and decorate with paprika. This is ideal as a first course prior to the main entreés, or as a luncheon salad. Serves 4.

Mrs. Donald McChesney (Marian)

SEVEN LAYER SALAD

1 head lettuce, shredded
½ cup celery, chopped
½ green pepper, chopped
½ cup onion, chopped
1 10-ounce package frozen
   peas, cooked and drained

2 cups mayonnaise
2 tablespoons sugar
1 cup Cheddar cheese, shredded
¼ cup bacon, crumbled

Place first 5 ingredients in bowl in the order listed. Combine mayonnaise and sugar and spread over top. Sprinkle shredded cheese and bacon crumbs over mayonnaise mixture. Cover with plastic wrap and refrigerate 24 hours.

Mrs. John Staggs (Shirley)

BISHOP'S SALAD

6 slices bread, buttered, garlic
  salted, and toasted
½ head Iceberg lettuce,
  shredded
½ head Romaine, shredded

12 slices bacon, cooked and
  crumbled
4 eggs, hard boiled and chopped
4 ounces bleu cheese, crumbled

DRESSING:
⅓ cup sour cream
½ cup mayonnaise

1 teaspoon sugar
⅓ cup vinegar

Break up toast into small pieces. Combine all salad ingredients and toss with dressing mixture. Serve immediately. Serves 10 to 12.

Mrs. Royal G. Luther (Helen)

CAESAR DRESSED VEGETABLES

VEGETABLES:
1 pound green beans, ends
  trimmed
1 basket cherry tomatoes,
  halved

1 pound pitted black olives
Black pepper, freshly ground
¼ cup Parmesan cheese, grated

PROCESSOR CAESAR DRESSING:
2 egg yolks
½ cup olive oil
¼ cup wine vinegar
2 garlic cloves, minced

1 teaspoon Dijon mustard
½ teaspoon onion powder
¼ teaspoon garlic powder

Steam beans until barely crisp and then plunge beans in cold water to stop cooking. Chill. Arrange beans, tomatoes, and olives. Pour dressing over all. Grind pepper on top and sprinkle with grated cheese. Serves 4-6.

Place all dressing ingredients in food processor and blend until smooth. Makes 1 cup.

Mrs. Sam Stafford, III (Nancy)

MARINADED SLICED TOMATOES

4 large tomatoes
¼ cup salad oil
1 tablespoon lemon juice

½ teaspoon garlic, chopped
½ teaspoon salt
½ teaspoon dried oregano leaves

Peel and slice tomatoes. Arrange in a shallow dish. Combine oil, lemon juice, garlic, salt and oregano; mix well. Pour over tomatoes. Refrigerate, covered, several hours, or until very well chilled. Serves 6.

Mrs. Richard H. Bateson (Lois)

MARINADED TOMATOES

3 tomatoes, peeled and cut in
wedges
2 tablespoons tarragon vinegar
3 tablespoons olive oil
½ teaspoon salt

¼ teaspoon dried tarragon
1 tablespoon parsley, chopped
1 tablespoon chives, chopped
Ground pepper to taste

Place tomatoes in a bowl. Combine all other ingredients. Pour over tomatoes. Marinate at room temperature 1 hour. Refrigerate until shortly before serving time.

Mrs. L. Brent Kuhnle (Terry)

MARINADED VEGETABLES

1 head cauliflower, broken into
flowerettes
1 bunch broccoli, broken into
flowerettes
2 bell peppers, sliced into strips
1 5.8-ounce jar of whole pitted
black olives
Bunch of green onions,
trimmed

1 8-ounce box mushrooms,
trimmed
1 cup olive oil
1½ cups white wine vinegar
1½ tablespoons salt
¾ teaspoon pepper
3 tablespoons sugar
2 cloves garlic

Wash and dry all vegetables. Drain olives. Boil together for 2 minutes the olive oil, wine vinegar, salt, pepper, sugar and garlic cloves. Pour this mixture over the vegetables which have been placed in a large ceramic or glass bowl. Refrigerate at least 6 hours. Turn or mix the vegetables occasionally to insure all are marinated. To serve, remove from the marinade with a slotted spoon and arrange attractively. Serves 8-10.

Ms. Cathy Mallard

CUCUMBER SALAD

2 large cucumbers, peeled and
    thinly sliced
2 teaspoons salt
1 cup sour cream

2 tablespoons vinegar
¼ teaspoon paprika
1 large onion, thinly sliced

Sprinkle cucumbers with salt and let stand in refrigerator for several hours. Rinse in cold water to remove salt. Blend sour cream, vinegar and paprika. Add cucumbers and onions to mixture. Return to refrigerator. Serves 6.

Mrs. Jimmie Brantly (Phyllis)

BEAN SALAD

½ cup salad oil
½ cup lemon juice
½ cup wine vinegar
¼ cup soy sauce
Dash Tabasco
1 tablespoon salt
2 teaspoons pepper
1 garlic clove, mashed
2 16-ounce cans green beans,
    drained

2 16-ounce cans kidney beans,
    drained
1 16-ounce can wax beans, drained
2 large purple onions, sliced in
    rings
2 4-ounce jars button mushrooms,
    drained

Mix marinade of salad oil, lemon juice, vinegar, soy sauce, Tabasco, salt, pepper and garlic together. Pour over vegetables and chill for several hours before serving. Shrimp may be added but also add 1 teaspoon thyme and 1 teaspoon rosemary. Serves 6 to 8.

Mrs. Walter E. Jenkins (Louise)

SCHNITZELD BEAN SALAD

SALAD:

1 pound green beans
4 slices bacon
½ cup onions, chopped

½ cup red wine vinegar
Salt and pepper to taste
1 red onion, sliced

DRESSING:

1 cup sour cream
2 tablespoons red wine vinegar

2 tablespoons chopped chives
Sugar, salt and pepper to taste

Cook green beans until barely tender. Fry bacon until crisp. Crumble while still warm, reserve. Cook chopped onions in bacon drippings until tender. Add vinegar, bring to boil. Add drained beans, bacon, salt and pepper and toss gently. To make dressing: mix sour cream, vinegar and chopped chives. Add sugar, salt and pepper to your taste. Combine with bean mixture. Garnish with red onion rings. Serves 6.

Mrs. W. N. Redling (Phyllis)

LUCY NEVILLE'S RING MOLD SALAD

TOMATO ASPIC PART:

1 envelope plus 2 teaspoons
　　unflavored gelatin
2¼ cups tomato juice
⅔ cup tomato sauce
½ teaspoon salt

¼ teaspoon sugar
1 tablespoon Worcestershire sauce
¼ teaspoon Tabasco
¼ cup lemon juice

SOUR CREAM PART:

1 envelope unflavored gelatin
¼ cup milk
¾ cup chicken broth
½ teaspoon salt

¼ teaspoon Worcestershire sauce
⅛ teaspoon celery salt
⅛ teaspoon garlic
1 cup sour cream

Add gelatin to 1 cup of tomato juice. Stir over low heat until dissolved. Add tomato sauce, remaining juice and other ingredients. Pour half of tomato mixture into a 5-cup ring mold and put in refrigerator. Reserve other half of tomato mixture. Add gelatin to milk. Stir over low heat to dissolve. Add chicken broth. Stir well. Add all other ingredients except sour cream. Cool this mixture to egg white consistency. Fold in sour cream. Spoon into ring mold on top of tomato aspic that has already set. When first 2 layers are set, pour remaining tomato mixture on top and return to refrigerator. Serves 8.

Mrs. Nöel Seeburg (Alice)

TOMATO ASPIC I

2½ envelopes unflavored
    gelatin
2 cups V-8 juice
1 bay leaf
Celery tops
1½ cups tomato juice
½ cup tarragon vinegar

Salt, red pepper, Tabasco to taste
1 teaspoon lemon juice
1 3-ounce bottle capers
Juice of 1 onion
1 cup celery, diced
½ cup stuffed olives, chopped

Soak gelatin in ½ cup V-8 juice. Heat 1½ cups V-8 juice with bay leaf and celery tops. Strain and add gelatin. When gelatin has dissolved, add cold tomato juice and vinegar, salt, red pepper, Tabasco and lemon juice. When cool add capers, onion juice, celery and olives. Pour in ring mold and chill thoroughly. Serves 8.

Mrs. Neil Trask, Jr. (Rebecca)

TOMATO ASPIC II

1¼ tablespoons gelatin
2 cups tomato juice
2 tablespoons lemon juice
1 teaspoon sugar

½ teaspoon salt
1 teaspoon Worcestershire sauce
½ cup celery, chopped

Soak gelatin in ¼ cup of tomato juice. Heat remaining juice to boiling and pour over the above and stir until dissolved. Then add the lemon juice, salt, sugar, and Worcestershire sauce. When slightly thickened add the celery and mold. Serves 4.

Mrs. John K. Hollins (Sallie Mae)

CONGEALED VEGETABLE ASPIC

2 tablespoons gelatin
½ cup cold water
2 cups water, boiling
2 tablespoons lemon juice
2 teaspoons Worcestershire
  sauce
¼ cup sugar

1 teaspoon salt
1 medium onion, grated
1½ cups cabbage, shredded
1 cup celery, diced
¼ cup pimento, chopped
1 cup green peas
1 cup tiny whole green beans

Soften gelatin in cold water. Add to boiling water and stir until dissolved. Add all other liquids and cool. Mix vegetables with sugar and salt. Pour liquid over vegetable mixture, stir well and put into mold. Refrigerate until congealed. Serves 10-12.

Mrs. Lion G. Mason (Jean)

ASPARAGUS SALAD

1½ envelopes unflavored
  gelatin
½ cup cold water
1 cup water, boiling
¾ cup sugar
⅓ cup vinegar
1 teaspoon salt
1 2-ounce jar chopped
  pimento, drained

1 14-ounce can asparagus tips, cut
  and drained
Juice of 1 lemon
1 cup celery, chopped
½ cup English walnuts, broken up
1 small onion, finely chopped

Soften gelatin in cold water. Bring to boil 1 cup water, sugar, vinegar and salt. Add softened gelatin to hot mixture. When it begins to thicken, fold in the pimento, asparagus, lemon juice, celery, walnuts and onion. Pour into a wet mold or individual molds and chill. Serves 8.

Mrs. George M. Scott (Helen)

BROCCOLI SALAD MOLD

1 envelope gelatin
5 ounces consommé
1 10-ounce package frozen
   chopped broccoli, cooked
   and drained

½ cup mayonnaise
½ lemon, juice only
3 eggs, hard boiled and grated
1 teaspoon salt
1 teaspoon wine vinegar

Soak gelatin in ¼ cup consommé. Heat remaining consommé and add to gelatin mixture. Add other ingredients. Pour into salad mold. Chill until firm. Serves 6.

Mrs. James Ingram (Berta)

BROCCOLI MOLD

1 10-ounce package frozen
   chopped broccoli
1½ envelopes unflavored
   gelatin
½ cup water
1 10¾-ounce can condensed
   chicken broth

⅔ cup mayonnaise
⅓ cup sour cream
1 tablespoon lemon juice
1 tablespoon onion, minced
3 eggs, hard boiled and chopped
Taste for salt

Cook broccoli; drain well. In medium saucepan, soften gelatin in water and add chicken broth. Heat and stir gelatin until dissolved. Add mayonnaise, sour cream, lemon juice and onion. Beat smooth with beater or whisk. Chill until partially set resembling a consistency of unbeaten egg white. Fold eggs into gelatin along with broccoli. Turn into 4-cup mold. Chill 4 hours or overnight. Unmold onto lettuce. Serves 6.

Mrs. Frank Tuckwiller (Barbara)

EMERALD SALAD RING

1 3-ounce lime flavored gelatin
¾ cup water, hot
1 cup cucumber, unpeeled and
   shredded

2 tablespoons onion, grated
1 cup cream-style cottage cheese
1 cup mayonnaise
⅓ cup blanched almonds, slivered

Dissolve gelatin in hot water; cool to slightly set syrup. Combine cucumber and onion; drain well and add to gelatin. Add cottage cheese, mayonnaise and almonds. Turn into 5-cup ring mold. Chill until set. Unmold and fill center with parsley. Serves 6 to 8.

Mrs. Hooks K. Johnston (Kathleen)

CUCUMBER MOUSSE

1 envelope gelatin
¼ cup cold water
1 beef bouillon cube
¼ cup water, boiling
½ cup mayonnaise
1 tablespoon onion, grated

1 tablespoon vinegar
1 teaspoon Worcestershire sauce
1 teaspoon salt
White pepper
3½ cups cucumber, diced
1 cup heavy cream, whipped

Lightly oil 6-cup mold. Soften gelatin in cold water. Dissolve bouillon in hot water and add gelatin, stirring until it dissolves. Cool slightly. Add mayonnaise, onion, vinegar, Worcestershire, salt and white pepper to taste. Blend carefully and chill until thick, about 5 to 10 minutes. Remove from refrigerator and beat well. Fold in cucumbers and whipped cream. Turn into mold and chill. Serves 10 to 12.

Mrs. Mary L. McDowell

BLEU CHEESE SLAW

1 cup bleu cheese, crumbled
½ cup dairy sour cream
2 tablespoons light cream
1 tablespoon lemon juice
½ teaspoon sugar

Dash of salt
6 cups red and white cabbage,
    shredded and chilled
3 tablespoons green onion,
    chopped and chilled

Beat the first 6 ingredients together. Just before serving, toss lightly with cabbage and green onion. Serves 7 to 8.

Mrs. Paul Trask (Marjorie)

COLE SLAW SALAD

1 medium head white cabbage,
    chopped
½ bell pepper, chopped
1 medium ripe tomato,
    chopped
2 medium sweet pickles,
    chopped

1 small onion, chopped
1 clove garlic, chopped
1 egg, hard boiled and chopped
1 teaspoon sugar
Mayonnaise to taste
Salt to taste
Red pepper to taste

Combine first 7 ingredients. Add sugar; mix together. Add mayonnaise and salt to taste. Sprinkle with red pepper, refrigerate until chilled. Serves 6 to 8.

Mrs. R. L. Furr (Mora)

GERMAN COLE SLAW

SLAW:

1 large head cabbage, finely
    chopped
1 large onion, finely chopped

1 or 2 mango peppers, finely
    chopped

DRESSING:

1 tablespoon salt
2 tablespoons honey
½ cup sugar

1 cup vinegar
⅔ cup salad oil

Combine slaw ingredients. Combine salt, honey, sugar, vinegar, and oil and bring to a boil. Pour over cabbage mixture. Do not stir until very cold. Will keep in covered container in refrigerator for several days. Serves 6 to 8.

Mrs. Neil Trask, Jr. (Rebecca)

GERMAN SLAW

1 large cabbage, finely cut
1 green pepper, finely cut
2 medium onions, finely cut
1 2-ounce jar pimento,
    finely cut
2 cups sugar

2 cups apple cider vinegar
1 tablespoon salt
1 teaspoon mustard seed
1½ teaspoons celery seed
1¼ teaspoons turmeric

In a large bowl place all vegetables. In separate container mix sugar, vinegar, salt, mustard seed, celery seed, and turmeric; bring to a boil and pour over vegetables. Put into container and let stand in refrigerator for 12 hours before using. This slaw will keep indefinitely in refrigerator. Do not freeze.

Miss Eileen Hunter

CONGEALED CRANBERRY SALAD

2 3-ounce packages lemon
   gelatin
1 16-ounce can whole berry
   cranberry sauce
2 cups boiling water
1 8¼-ounce can crushed
   pineapple, drained and
   liquid reserved

½-1 cup celery, finely chopped
Mayonnaise
Nutmeg

Dissolve gelatin and cranberry sauce in boiling water. Add pineapple. When gelatin begins to jell, add celery. Serve topped with mayonnaise which has been softened with reserved pineapple juice. Sprinkle with ground nutmeg. Serves 8.

Beaufort County Open Land Trust

CRANBERRY SALAD

2 oranges
2½ cups fresh cranberries
3 3-ounce packages orange
   gelatin
3 cups water, boiling
2 tablespoons lemon juice

1 cup sugar
Pinch salt
1½ cups celery, chopped
1 cup crushed pineapple, undrained
½ cup pecans, chopped (more if
   desired)

Peel oranges, put peeling and cranberries through food grinder. Remove white membrane from oranges and section them, breaking each section into 3 or 4 pieces. Dissolve gelatin in boiling water, add lemon juice, sugar and salt. Stir until dissolved. Add orange pieces, the ground mixture, celery, pineapple and nuts. Pour into mold and chill until set. This salad should be made at least 2 days before serving. Serves 12 to 15.

Mrs. Henry V. Boyce, Jr. (Frances)

GRAPEFRUIT-PINEAPPLE SALAD

2 grapefruit
1 8-ounce can crushed
  pineapple
1 3-ounce package orange
  flavored gelatin

1 3-ounce package cream cheese
3 tablespoons milk
¼ cup nuts, chopped

Cut grapefruit in half and scoop out pulp; drain pulp well and reserve all juice. Drain pineapple; reserve juice. Combine grapefruit juice and pineapple juice. If necessary, add enough water to make 2 cups liquid. Heat 1 cup liquid and dissolve gelatin. Add remaining juice. Cool until partially set. Stir in pineapple and grapefruit pulp. Pour into grapefruit halves and chill until firm. Soften cream cheese with milk until of spreading consistency. Spread on congealed gelatin mixture. Top with finely chopped nuts. Keep in refrigerator until ready to serve. Cut each half in half again. Serves 6 to 8.

Mrs. Ed Howle (Katherine)

FRESH STRAWBERRY-GRAPEFRUIT CONGEALED SALAD

1 3-ounce package of either
  lemon, lime or orange
  gelatin
1 cup water, boiling
½ teaspoon salt
½ cup orange juice
½ cup grapefruit juice
2 cups grapefruit sections,
  diced

Sprigs of watercress
1 cup strawberries, sliced
Grapefruit sections, whole for
  garnish
Strawberries, whole for garnish
Watercress for garnish

Dissolve gelatin in boiling water and add fruit juices to gelatin. Let cool. Add salt and divide into thirds. Pour a thin layer into a slightly oiled mold. Chill until firm. Place diced grapefruit and a few sprigs of watercress on gelatin and cover with additional gelatin. Arrange sliced strawberries on this after it has set and pour remaining gelatin over it. Chill until firm. Unmold and garnish with grapefruit sections, whole strawberries and watercress. Serves 6-8.

Mrs. C. Blackburn Brewer (Frances)

PINEAPPLE CHERRY SALAD

1 8-ounce can crushed
   pineapple
½ cup sugar
1 envelope gelatin
½ cup water, cold

1 3-ounce package cream cheese,
   softened
½ pint cream, whipped
½ cup nuts, chopped
1 6-ounce bottle red cherries

Drain juice from pineapple. Add juice to sugar and let boil until syrupy (3 or 4 minutes). Dissolve gelatin in ½ cup cold water and add to warm syrup, stirring until completely dissolved. Mash cheese and add to pineapple. When syrup is cool, add cheese, pineapple, whipped cream, nuts and cherries. Place in molds and chill.

Mrs. John Gale (Cynthia)

ORANGE DAIRY DELIGHT SALAD

1 6-ounce package orange gelatin
1 cup hot water
2 cups small marshmallows
½ cup sugar
1 6-ounce can frozen orange
   juice, thawed
1 3-ounce package cream
   cheese

1 15-ounce can crushed pineapple
1 cup cottage cheese
2 bananas, mashed
1 11-ounce can mandarin oranges
1 cup heavy cream, whipped
Lettuce, for garnish
Cottage cheese, for garnish

Dissolve gleatin in hot water. Add the marshmallows and mix. Stir sugar in orange juice. Add this to gelatin mixture. Blend cream cheese and pineapple; add to gelatin mixture. Add cottage cheese, bananas and orange sections. Fold in whipped cream and pour into large or small gelatin molds. Let set overnight. Turn out on platter of lettuce and fill center with cottage cheese if desired. Serves 12-15.

Mrs. Walter Taylor (Evelyn)

SUNSET SALAD

2 envelopes gelatin
¼ cup sugar
½ teaspoon salt
1 20-ounce can crushed
   pineapple, drain and
   reserve juice

½ cup water
1 cup orange juice
¼ cup vinegar
1½ cups shredded carrots

FRUIT DRESSING:
1 cup sour cream
1 teaspoon orange rind, grated

2 tablespoons honey

Mix gelatin, sugar, and salt in saucepan; stir in juice from pineapple and water. Heat slowly, stirring constantly until gelatin dissolves. Stir in orange juice and vinegar. Pour into large bowl. Refrigerate about 1 hour. Stir in pineapple and carrots; pour into 6-cup mold or 8-inch square dish. Refrigerate. Serve with fruit dressing. Serves 6.

Mrs. James M. Gray (Doris)

SPICED PEACH SALAD

2 3-ounce boxes lemon gelatin
1 tablespoon plain gelatin
2½ cups boiling water
½ cup lemon juice
1½ cups peach juice

1 13-ounce can spiced peaches,
   drained
1 cup nuts, chopped
1 cup celery, chopped

Add lemon gelatin and gelatin to boiling water and dissolve. Add lemon and peach juice. Stir well and let set until cool. Add peaches, nuts and celery. Mold until firm. Serve with sour cream dressing. Serves 10-12.

SOUR CREAM DRESSING:
½ cup sour cream
1 tablespoon parsley or chives,
   chopped
3 tablespoons vinegar or lemon
   juice

¼ teaspoon salt
⅛ teaspoon paprika

Beat sour cream with fork. Add remaining ingredients. Serve over salad.

Mrs. J. A. Physioc (Florence)

CONGEALED FRUIT SALAD

2 3-ounce packages lemon
    gelatin
1¾ cups water, boiling
1 16-ounce can crushed
    pineapple, in syrup
1 6-ounce bottle cherries, cut
    in halves

½ cup cottage cheese
¼ cup mayonnaise
½ cup nuts, chopped
1 teaspoon lemon juice
1 cup whipping cream, whipped

Dissolve gelatin in boiling water. Let stand in refrigerator until thick but not firm. Stir well. Add pineapple, cherries, cottage cheese, mayonnaise, nuts and lemon juice. Mix well. Fold in whipped cream. Pour into 8-inch by 12-inch baking dish. Refrigerate overnight. Makes 24 generous servings.

Mrs. J. W. Logan, Jr. (Lois)

FROZEN BANANA SALAD

2 3-ounce packages cream
    cheese
1 teaspoon salt
1 cup crushed pineapple
3 medium bananas, sliced

½ cup nuts, chopped
½ cup maraschino cherries, sliced
1½ cups heavy cream, whipped
½ cup mayonnaise
Juice of 1 lemon

Mash cream cheese in bowl and stir in salt. When smooth, add pineapple, bananas, nuts and cherries. Fold whipped cream, mayonnaise and lemon juice into fruit and cheese mixture. Pour into refrigerator tray. Freeze until firm. Serve in slices on lettuce with garnish of whole cherries or strawberries. Serves 8 to 10.

Mrs. David P. Farrior, Sr. (Millie)

FROZEN FRUIT SALAD

1 3-ounce cream cheese
½ cup mayonnaise
1 cup crushed pineapple

½ cup nuts, chopped
½ cup cherries, halved
1 cup heavy cream, whipped

Soften cream cheese and mix well with mayonnaise. Add fruits and nuts. Fold in whipped cream. Put in container or mold and freeze. Let sit out 15 to 30 minutes before slicing and serving. Serves 4 to 6.

Mrs. James M. Gray (Doris)

SOUR CREAM POTATO SALAD I

5 pounds boiled potatoes
2 bunches spring onions,
   chopped, including tops
2 tablespoons dried parsley

2 teaspoons dried dill weed
4 cups sour cream
Salt and pepper to taste

Peel and slice potatoes, keeping size fairly uniform. Combine spring onions, parsley, dill weed, sour cream, salt and pepper. Mix with potatoes. Chill before serving. The flavor is better if allowed to chill for several hours. May be prepared the day before serving. Serves 16 to 20.

Mrs. Benjamin Durham (Rita)

SOUR-CREAM POTATO SALAD II

7 medium potatoes, cooked in
   jackets, peeled and sliced
   (6 cups)
⅓ cup clear French or Italian
   dressing
¾ cup celery, sliced
⅓ cup green onions and tops,
   sliced

4 eggs, hard boiled
1 cup mayonnaise
½ cup dairy sour cream
1½ teaspoons prepared
   horseradish mustard
Salt and celery seed to taste
⅓ cup cucumbers, pared and diced

While potatoes are warm, pour dressing over them. Chill 2 hours. Add celery and onions. Chop egg whites, add. Sieve yolks; reserve some for garnish. Combine remaining sieved yolk with mayonnaise, sour cream and horseradish mustard, fold into salad. Add salt and celery seed to taste. Chill 2 hours. Add cucumbers. Sprinkle reserved yolk over top. Makes 8 servings.

Mrs. Carl W. Elliott (Ginny)

GERMAN POTATO SALAD

1 tablespoon bacon drippings
1 medium onion, chopped
1¾ tablespoons flour
½ cup sugar
½ cup vinegar
½ cup water
5 medium potatoes, cooked,
    peeled and chopped

2 eggs, hard boiled (1 chopped and
    1 sliced)
6 slices bacon, cooked crisp and
    crumbled
Salt and pepper to taste

Heat bacon drippings in a skillet. Add onion and cook until tender, stirring occasionally. Stir in flour until smooth. Add sugar, vinegar and water; bring to a boil, stirring constantly. In a 2-quart casserole, pour onion mixture over potatoes, chopped egg and bacon. Season to taste with salt and pepper. Garnish with sliced egg. Serve immediately or cover and reheat in a slow oven. Never serve cold. Serves 4 to 6.

Mrs. Ted Ledford (Suzi)

COLD RICE SALAD

1 cup long grain rice
1 pound fresh string beans
Salt, cracked pepper and
    Monosodium glutamate
1 6-ounce package frozen
    Chinese pea pods

1 medium red onion, chopped
2 5-ounce cans water chestnuts,
    sliced

DRESSING:
½ cup mayonnaise
1 teaspoon curry powder, or to
    taste

1 tablespoon lemon juice

Cook rice just *al dente*. Place in large mixing bowl to cool. Cut string beans into 1-inch pieces (ends cut diagonally) and cook until crisp. Season with salt, pepper and monosodium glutamate, and add to rice. Cook Chinese pea pods until crisp and season separately and add to rice. Add onion and water chestnuts. Prepare dressing an hour or two in advance to develop flavor. Mix dressing into cold ingredients thoroughly. Serves 12-16.

Mrs. Donald A. Roberts (Ruth)

LADIES' LUNCHEON CHICKEN SALAD

1¼ cups mayonnaise
½ teaspoon curry powder
2 tablespoons soy sauce
1 tablespoon lemon juice
1 16-ounce can light seedless
  grapes

1 20-ounce can pineapple chunks
4 cups chicken, cooked and cubed
1 cup celery, sliced
½ cup almonds, slivered and
  toasted

Mix mayonnaise, curry powder, soy sauce, and lemon juice in a small bowl. Drain the grapes and pineapple. Combine the chicken, celery, grapes, pineapple and almonds in a large bowl. Add the mayonnaise mixture and stir well. Chill several hours before serving. Serves 8-10.

Mrs. Paul L. Siegmund (June)

CHICKEN SALAD

1 baking hen
2 large fryers
1 bunch green onions
4 stalks celery
Salt and pepper
1½ cups celery, finely chopped

¾ cup sweet mixed pickle
5 eggs, finely chopped
1 lemon, juice only
Salad dressing
Optional—a little mustard and/or a
  little Tabasco

In a big pot with a little water place 1 hen and 2 large fryers to which has been added 5 or 6 green onions and 3 or 4 stalks celery, salt and pepper to taste. Place the hen on the bottom. Boil moderately. When the fryers are tender, take them out of the pot. Continue to boil the hen until the meat is tender. Take the hen out of the pot. Remove and discard the onions and celery. Cool the stock. Put in the freezer or refrigerator until the grease rises to the top. Cut chicken in ¾-inch cubes. You do not want the pieces too small because you want to know you are eating chicken salad. To the coarsely cut up chicken, add enough of the jellied stock from the bottom of the stock to make the chicken moist. Stir carefully. Cover and put in the refrigerator for several hours, preferably overnight. Add celery, pickle and eggs to chicken. Add salad dressing to suit your taste. A little mustard or a shot or two of Tabasco may be added. Serves 12.

Mrs. Jack Gray (Ceil)

CHICKEN LUNCHEON SALAD

3 cups mayonnaise
2 tablespoons soy sauce
1 tablespoon curry powder
2 tablespoons lemon juice
2 quarts chicken, cut in bite
    size pieces
1 20-ounce can water
    chestnuts, diced

2 pounds seedless grapes
2 cups celery, chopped
1½ cups almonds, toasted and
    slivered
Boston or Bibb lettuce
½ cup almonds, slivered
1 16-ounce can pineapple chunks,
    drained

Mix mayonnaise, soy sauce, curry powder, lemon juice. Combine chicken, water chestnuts, grapes, celery, and 1½ cups almonds. Add mayonnaise mixture. Stir well. Chill several hours. Spoon on nests of lettuce. Sprinkle with remaining almonds and garnish with pineapple chunks. Serves 10 to 12.

Mrs. Walter E. Jenkins (Louise)

CHICKEN VEGETABLE SALAD

1 clove garlic
1 teaspoon salt
¼ teaspoon dry mustard
Dash of pepper and paprika
1 tablespoon catsup
1 tablespoon lemon juice
2 tablespoons vinegar

½ cup salad oil
1 head lettuce, broken into
    bite-sized pieces
6 tomatoes, quartered
1 10-ounce can artichoke hearts
2 cups chicken, cooked and cubed
6 black olives, chopped

Rub salad bowl with garlic. Add salt, mustard, pepper, paprika, catsup, lemon juice, vinegar and oil. Mix thoroughly with a fork. Add lettuce and chill. Arrange tomatoes, artichokes, chicken and olives over top and toss lightly. Makes a lovely summer meal. Serves 6.

Mrs. Edwin O. Merwin

HONEYDEW SHRIMP

1 large honeydew melon
1½ pounds shrimp, cooked and
    peeled
2 cups celery, chopped
1½ cups mayonnaise

2 tablespoons lemon juice
1½ teaspoons salt
2½ teaspoons curry powder
½ cup sour cream

Cut melon into 6 boatlike wedges. Scoop out as many melon balls as possible and set aside. Drain melon boats 2 hours. Marinate shrimp and celery in sauce made from remaining ingredients which have been blended together. Chill well. Before serving, put shrimp into boats and decorate with melon balls. Can also be served with chutney. Serves 6.

Mrs. Harold E. Trask (Margaret)

ORIENTAL SALAD

SALAD:
1 pound shrimp, cooked,
    peeled, deveined
½ cup onions, chopped
½ cup celery, chopped

½ cup green peppers, chopped
1 cup raw mushrooms, sliced
1 can bean sprouts, drained
Chow Mein noodles

DRESSING:
½ cup sour cream
½ cup mayonnaise
2 tablespoons ground ginger

2 tablespoons lemon juice
2 tablespoons lemon rind

Mix salad ingredients and refrigerate for 3 hours. Pour dressing mixture over salad and let stand for 30 minutes, then toss. Sprinkle top with chow mein noodles.

Mrs. Mac Donald Dixon (Phyllis)

SALMON MOLD

1 15½-ounce can red salmon	1½ tablespoons melted butter
1 teaspoon salt	¾ cup milk
1½ tablespoons sugar	¼ cup vinegar
1 tablespoon flour	2 tablespoons cold water
2 egg yolks	¾ tablespoon unflavored gelatin

Rinse salmon thoroughly with hot water and separate flakes. Mix salt, sugar, and flour. Add egg yolks, butter, milk, and vinegar to flour mixture. Cook flour-butter mixture over boiling water, stirring constantly until thickened. Add gelatin which has been soaked in cold water. Stir and strain mixture. Add salmon. Put in greased mold and chill. Serve with sauce. Serves 4-6.

SAUCE FOR SALMON MOLD:

½ cup heavy cream	2 tablespoons vinegar
½ teaspoon salt	1 cucumber, finely chopped
½ teaspoon pepper	

Beat cream until stiff. Add salt and pepper. Gradually add vinegar while continuing beating. Fold in cucumber. Pour over molded salmon.

Mrs. Marvin C. McCarthy (Allison)

MOLDED TUNA SALAD

2 tablespoons gelatin	1 7-ounce can tuna, drained
4 tablespoons cold water	3 small sweet pickles, diced
1 cup hot water	2 teaspoons pimento
3 tablespoons vinegar	3 eggs, hard boiled and diced
1 tablespoon sugar	3 stalks celery, diced
½ teaspoon salt	½ cup heavy cream, whipped
¼ teaspoon paprika	½ cup salad dressing
1 teaspoon onion juice	

Soften gelatin in cold water. Dissolve in hot water. Cool and add vinegar, sugar, salt, paprika and onion juice. When mixture begins to thicken, add tuna, pickles, pimento, eggs and celery. Fold in whipped cream and salad dressing. Pour into molds or 9-inch by 5-inch pan. Serves 6.

Mrs. John M. Patek (Doris)

HORSERADISH RELISH MOLDS
An accompaniment to a meat course

1 3-ounce package lemon
    flavored gelatin
¾ teaspoon salt
1 cup water, boiling
1 tablespoon vinegar

Dash of pepper
1 cup sour cream
¼ cup prepared horseradish
1 teaspoon onion, grated

Dissolve gelatin and salt in boiling water. Add vinegar and pepper. Chill until slightly thickened. Combine sour cream, horseradish and onion. Add gelatin. Chill until firm. Unmold. Serves 6 to 8.

Mrs. Ira B. Webber (Rosalie)

FRENCH DRESSING

⅔ cup olive oil
⅓ cup vinegar
2½ tablespoons catsup
1½ teaspoons sugar
1 bud garlic, peeled

1 teaspoon orange juice
½ teaspoon salt
10 shakes black pepper
2 cubes ice

Mix all ingredients except orange juice and ice cubes. Beat with a fork. Then add orange juice and beat again. Taste for seasoning of salt and pepper. Add 2 ice cubes. Beat for 2 minutes, and throw ice cubes away.

Mrs. C. A. Larsen, Jr. (Eleanor)

MEXICAN VILLAGE SALAD DRESSING

1 quart safflower or
    polyunsaturated oil
4 cloves garlic
5 tablespoons lemon juice
¼ pound Roquefort cheese

Pinch of Accent
1 tablespoon whole peppercorns
1 tablespoon salt
½ teaspoon dry mustard

Mix in blender. Age in refrigerator 3 weeks.

Mrs. Albert Schaufelberger (Virginia)

ROQUEFORT DRESSING

1 cup mayonnaise
⅞ cup buttermilk
4 ounces Roquefort cheese,
    crumbled

½ teaspoon garlic salt

Mix all ingredients in a jar, shake well, and refrigerate 6 hours prior to using. Will keep several weeks.

Mrs. C. I. Meeks III (Lila)

SOUTHERN SALAD DRESSING

⅓ cup tomato catsup
⅓ cup sugar
¼ cup vinegar

½ cup Wesson oil
1 teaspoon onion, grated
1 teaspoon paprika

Combine all ingredients in a pint jar. Shake well. Refrigerate. Delicious on grapefruit and avocado, on a green salad or canned artichokes. Will keep indefinitely in refrigerator. Before serving, let stand at room temperature and shake well.

Mrs. Reid Toms (Edith)

AVOCADO AND YOGURT SALAD DRESSING

1 very ripe avocado, peeled,
   pitted and cubed
1 cup plain yogurt
⅓ cup onion, diced
⅓ cup green pepper, diced
¼ cup mayonnaise

1 teaspoon dill, snipped
½ teaspoon lemon juice
¼ teaspoon sugar
¼ teaspoon garlic, minced
Salt and white pepper to taste

Blend in blender for 20 seconds the avocado, yogurt, onion and green pepper. Add mayonnaise, dill, lemon juice, sugar, garlic, salt and white pepper. Blend mixture until smooth. Makes 2½ cups.

Mrs. Gene Grace (Beth)

COLE SLAW DRESSING

2 tablespoons onion, minced
2 tablespoons vinegar
2 tablespoons oil
1 teaspoon salt

1 teaspoon pepper
⅓ cup sugar
1 tablespoon celery seed
½ pint sour cream

Mix together and pour over shredded cabbage. May be kept in refrigerator until needed.

Mrs. Harold E. Trask (Margaret)

COOKED SALAD DRESSING

½ cup sugar
½ teaspoon dry mustard
¼ teaspoon salt
Dash pepper

1 egg, beaten
⅓ cup milk
⅓ cup vinegar
1 tablespoon butter

In a heavy saucepan, combine dry ingredients. Add egg and milk and mix well. Add vinegar very slowly, stirring constantly. Over medium heat, cook and continue to stir until mixture boils. Add butter and stir until melted. Chill. Especially good over slaw.

Mrs. Joe Phinny (Hetty)

MAYONNAISE

1 whole egg	1 teaspoon dry mustard
1 egg yolk	Juice of 1 lemon
1 pint Wesson oil, divided	Red pepper, Tabasco and
1 teaspoon salt	Worcestershire sauce

Beat eggs well and add ½ pint Wesson oil. Mix salt and dry mustard in lemon juice. Add lemon juice mixture. Continuing to beat, add remaining oil slowly. Season to taste with red pepper, Tabasco and Worcestershire sauce.

The Editors

BLENDER MAYONNAISE

1 egg	½ teaspoon salt
1 cup oil, divided	Dash Tabasco
2 tablespoons lemon juice	

Drop egg into blender. Add ¼ cup oil and rest of ingredients in the order given (except ¾ cup oil). Turn on blender to a middle speed and pour remaining oil in finest possible steady stream. If oil pools on top of mayonnaise, cut off blender and run spatula down inside of blender to release air pocket. Then resume the mayonnaise making. Several batches of mayonnaise may be made at the same time without cleaning the blender between each one.

The Editors

SAUCE FOR FRUIT SALAD

¼ cup sugar	¾ cup pineapple juice
½ teaspoon salt	1 tablespoon butter
1½ tablespoons flour	1 egg yolk, beaten
2 tablespoons lemon juice	

Combine ingredients. Cook slowly, stirring constantly until thickened. Serve over fruit. Serves 8.

Mrs. B. L. Credle (Shirley)

CELERY SEED DRESSING FOR FRUIT SALAD

½ cup sugar
1 teaspoon dry mustard
1 teaspoon salt
½ tablespoon onion juice

⅓ cup vinegar
1 cup salad oil
1 tablespoon celery seed

Mix first 4 ingredients with half the vinegar. Gradually add salad oil and remaining vinegar alternately. Add celery seed.

Mrs. F. W. Scheper, Jr. (Margaret)

HONEY DRESSING

⅔ cup sugar
1 teaspoon dry mustard
1 teaspoon paprika
1 teaspoon salt
1 teaspoon celery seed

⅓ cup honey
1 teaspoon lemon juice
5 tablespoons white vinegar
1 teaspoon onion, grated
1 cup salad oil

Mix sugar, dry mustard, paprika, salt and celery seeds. Add honey, lemon juice, vinegar, onion and salad oil. Mix well with electric mixer, not a blender. Store in refrigerator. This dressing is especially good on fruit salads.

Mrs. W. R. Sawyer

MORNING GLORY

Bread

GOLD EAGLE CINNAMON ROLLS

2 packages yeast	1 teaspoon salt
½ cup warm water	2 eggs
½ cup milk, scalded and cooled	½ cup shortening
½ cup sugar	4½-5 cups flour

TOPPING:

1 cup light brown sugar	½ cup butter, melted
2 tablespoons cinnamon	

Dissolve yeast in warm water. Stir in milk, sugar, salt, eggs, shortening, and 2½ cups flour. Mix well. Add remaining flour or enough to make dough easy to handle. Turn dough onto floured board. Knead until smooth and elastic, 10 minutes or more. Place in greased bowl and turn greased side up. Let rise in warm place until double in size, 1½ hours or longer. Punch dough down. Shape dough into the size of a walnut. Cover. Let rise in warm place until double in size. Brush rolls with melted butter. Sprinkle 1 teaspoon of brown sugar-cinnamon mixture on top of each roll. Drizzle melted butter over each roll. Bake in preheated 375 degree oven for 20-30 minutes. Makes 5 dozen rolls.

Mrs. S. S. Stokes (Dreka)

WHOLE WHEAT ROLLS OR BREAD

¼ cup warm water	½ cup sugar
2 teaspoons sugar	2 eggs, beaten
2 packages yeast	5 cups whole wheat flour
2 cups milk, scalded	3 teaspoons salt
2 tablespoons shortening	

Combine water and sugar. Add yeast to water to soften. Pour milk over shortening and sugar. Allow to cool. Add eggs and yeast to milk mixture. Mix well with flour and salt. Allow to rise until double in bulk. Dough will be very soft. Place into 2 greased loaf pans or make into rolls. Bake at 400 degrees for approximately 15-18 minutes for rolls, a little longer for bread.

Mrs. Jack Bond (Elizabeth)

LAURIE'S YEAST ROLLS

2 cups milk, scalded
2 yeast cakes
3 tablespoons Wesson oil
3 tablespoons sugar

1 teaspoon salt
7-7½ cups flour, sifted
Softened butter

Dissolve yeast cakes in ½ cup scalded milk which has been cooled to luke-warm. In a large bowl mix remaining milk, Wesson oil, sugar, salt and yeast cakes mixture. Add flour and stir until well mixed. Cover and let rise in warm place until doubled in size. Turn on lightly floured board and knead. Roll and cut with biscuit cutter. Spread with softened butter and place on greased biscuit pan close together. Cover and let rise again. Bake in 375 degree oven for 15-20 minutes or until lightly brown.

Laurie Adger

ONE HOUR YEAST ROLLS

1½ cups warm milk
2 tablespoons sugar
6 tablespoons shortening

4 packages yeast
4 cups plain flour
1 teaspoon salt

Place in a saucepan and heat until warm, milk, sugar, and shortening. Add yeast to warm milk mixture until dissolved. Add flour and salt and beat with a spoon until batter is very smooth. Cover and let rise for 30 minutes. Punch down and shape or roll into rolls. Place rolls on a buttered pan or in buttered muffin tins and let rise in a warm place for 15 minutes. Bake at 425 degrees for 12-15 minutes.

Mrs. Brenda Powell

YEAST ROLLS

2 packages yeast	1½ teaspoons salt
1 cup lukewarm water	2 eggs
1 cup water, boiling	6 cups plain flour
1 cup shortening	Melted butter
¾ cup sugar	

Dissolve yeast in lukewarm water. Pour 1 cup boiling water over shortening. Add sugar, salt, eggs, and flour. Knead. Cover and leave in refrigerator until ready to use, break off what you want at that time. Leave the rest in the refrigerator to be used at a later time. Knead dough for a few minutes and roll out ½ inch thick. Cut with biscuit cutter. Dip rounds in melted butter and fold in half. Put on greased pan about 1 inch apart. Let rise 2-3 hours. Bake at 425 degrees until brown.

Mrs. Charles Thompson (Cyndy)

SIX WEEK BRAN MUFFINS

10 ounces raisin bran	2 teaspoons salt
4 cups flour	1 quart buttermilk
1 cup wheat germ	1 cup oil or margarine, melted
3 cups sugar	4 eggs, beaten
5 teaspoons soda	

Mix dry ingredients well in bowl. Add buttermilk, oil and eggs, mix well again. Store in refrigerator as long as six weeks. Fill muffin tins ⅔ full and bake at 400 degrees for 15-20 minutes.

Mrs. Kenneth Hutton (Phyllis)

BRAN ROLLS

1 cup shortening	3 packages yeast dissolved in 1 cup
1 cup All-Bran	lukewarm water
1 cup water, boiling	2 eggs, beaten
1½ teaspoons salt	6 cups flour
¾ cup sugar	Melted shortening

Combine shortening, All-Bran and water. Add salt to sugar and mix with shortening mixture. Add yeast, eggs and flour mixing well. Put in refrigerator until ready to use. Break off dough and roll into shape of large marble. Put 2 pieces of marble-shaped dough if using a small greased muffin tin and 3 pieces of dough if using a large greased muffin tin. Brush top with melted shortening and let rise 2 hours. Bake at 325 degrees until brown.

Mrs. W. T. Miars, Jr. (Emma)

BRAN MUFFINS

3 cups sugar
¾ cup butter or margarine,
   softened
4 eggs
4 cups All-Bran
4 cups shredded wheat biscuits
   in 1½ cups boiling water

5 cups flour
1 quart buttermilk
5 teaspoons soda
1 teaspoon salt
1 cup nuts, chopped
1 cup dates, chopped

Mix all ingredients. Put in gallon container. Will keep 4-6 weeks in refrigerator. When ready to use, put into greased muffin tins without stirring batter. Bake at 375 degrees for 20 minutes. May make half recipe.

Makes great gift to take friends. Put in 1 quart cartons with baking directions on top.

Mrs. Samuel D. Bissette (Ruby)

CINNAMON BRAN MUFFINS

3 cups whole bran cereal
1 cup water, boiling
1½ cups flour
¾ cup sugar
2½ teaspoons baking soda
1½ teaspoons cinnamon

½ teaspoon salt
2 eggs
2 cups buttermilk
½ cup oil
½ cup raisins

In a large bowl stir cereal with water to moisten evenly. Let cool. Stir together flour, sugar, baking soda, cinnamon, and salt and set aside. Add eggs, buttermilk, oil and raisins to cereal mixture and mix well. Stir in flour mixture and mix well. Bake or store for future use. Keeps 2 weeks in refrigerator. Fill greased muffin tins ¾ full. Bake in 425 degree oven for 20 minutes or until top springs back when touched. Makes 24 muffins.

Mrs. Robert Poitras (Louise)

COOT'S CORN MEAL MUFFINS

1½ cups corn meal
½ cup flour
1 teaspoon salt
2 teaspoons baking powder
2 eggs, beaten

1¾ cups milk
⅓ cup melted shortening
(a combination of Crisco,
butter and bacon grease is
good)

Sift dry ingredients. Beat eggs, add the milk and melted shortening. Add the dry ingredients. Stir and pour into well greased muffin tins filling tins half full. Bake in preheated 425 degree oven for 20 minutes. Makes 24 muffins.

Estelle Murray Brewington

MEXICAN CORNBREAD

1 cup self-rising cornmeal
¼ cup flour
2 eggs
¾ cup milk
¾ cup Cheddar cheese, grated
⅓ cup cooking oil
1 8¾-ounce can cream style
  corn

½ bell pepper, diced
2 small hot peppers, finely chopped
1 medium onion, chopped
½ teaspoon salt
½ teaspoon baking powder

Mix all ingredients together and bake at 400 degrees for 20-30 minutes. For best results, bake in cast iron skillet.

Mrs. J. E. McTeer, Jr. (Gail)

YELLOW CORNMEAL MUFFINS

1 cup yellow cornmeal
1 cup all-purpose flour, sifted
¼ cup sugar
4 teaspoons baking powder

½ teaspoon salt
1 egg
1 cup milk
¼ cup oil or melted shortening

Mix all dry ingredients. Mix egg, milk, and oil. Add to dry ingredients. Beat by hand for 1-2 minutes. Bake at 425 degrees for 15-20 minutes. Makes 1 dozen.

Secret to good corn muffins is in cooking. Heat small amount of oil in each section of muffin pan until hot. Remove from oven and spoon mixture into sections. Return to oven. These are good frozen. May be warmed in microwave oven or under broiler with butter.

Mrs. J. Lee Bollman (Nancy)

SOUR CREAM CORN BREAD

1½ cups self-rising corn meal
½ cup bell pepper, chopped
½ teaspoon chili powder
½ cup oil

1 cup sour cream
2 eggs
1 cup cheese, grated
Butter

Combine meal, bell pepper, chili powder, oil, sour cream, eggs, and ½ cup cheese. Place in 8 x 8 x 2 pan; put remaining cheese on top of batter. Bake at 350 degrees for 35 minutes. Brush with butter after removing from oven. Yield 6 servings.

Mrs. Bert Parker (Kaye)

HY'S HUSH PUPPIES

1 egg
¾ cup beer
1 cup self-rising cornmeal
2½ cups self-rising flour
¾ cup milk
½ cup Cheddar cheese,
    coarsely grated

1½ cups onion, diced
1 teaspoon salt
1 teaspoon pepper
1 teaspoon seafood seasoning
1 teaspoon baking powder
3 teaspoons sugar
Vegetable oil

Mix all ingredients except oil. Chill. Deep fry in vegetable oil at 350 degrees. Drop with teaspoon, remove when golden brown. Drain on paper towels and serve while hot.

Mrs. William Hyland (Mary)

COFFEE CAN BREAD

½ cup milk
½ cup water
1 teaspoon salt
¼ cup vegetable oil

2-4 tablespoons sugar
3 cups flour, divided
1 envelope yeast
2 eggs

Grease two 1-pound coffee cans and lids. Place milk, water, salt, oil and sugar in saucepan and heat until warm. Place 1½ cups flour in a bowl and sprinkle yeast on top. Add warm milk mixture and mix well. Add eggs and 1½ cups flour. Place mixture in cans and shake down. Put lids on and place in warm oven for 35 minutes. Remove tops and cook 35 minutes at 350 degrees. Let stand for 10 minutes and shake from can.

Mrs. Spencer King (Caroline)

SOUR DOUGH BREAD

1 package yeast
5-6 cups unbleached white
    flour
2 cups warm water

2 tablespoons sugar
1 teaspoon salt
3 tablespoons butter, melted and
    cooled

Place yeast, 2 cups flour and warm water in a large non-metallic bowl. Stir just enough to moisten. Cover and let stand in a warm place overnight or longer if a more sour flavor is desired. The following day, remove ½ cup of yeast mixture and refrigerate in small covered jar for future use. The next time you make bread add the reserved yeast mixture to the new yeast mixture and the bread will have more flavor. To the remaining yeast mixture add sugar, salt, butter, and enough of the remaining flour to make a soft dough. Turn onto a floured board and knead until dough is smooth and satiny, about 15 minutes. Place in greased bowl. Grease the top of the dough and let rise in warm place until doubled in size, about 1½ hours. Punch the dough down, knead briefly, and shape into a loaf. Place in 9 x 5 x 3-inch greased loaf pan. Cover and let rise until doubled, about 1 hour. Bake at 375 degrees for 45 minutes or until done.

Mrs. Peter Neidig (Daune)

EGG BREAD

2 packages yeast
½ cup warm water
⅓ cup sugar
½ cup butter or margarine,
    melted
4 teaspoons salt

2 cups milk, scalded
½ cup cold water
4 eggs, beaten
9-10 cups unbleached flour, sifted
Melted butter

Soften yeast in warm water. Combine sugar, butter, salt, milk, and cold water. Cool to lukewarm. Stir in yeast and eggs. Add flour gradually to form a stiff dough. Knead on floured surface for 10 minutes or until smooth and satiny. (Do not add too much flour during the kneading process. This makes the bread dry and tough. Vigorous kneading helps to make the bread have a nice texture and also helps to relieve the cook's frustrations and tensions.) Place kneaded dough in greased bowl. Turn once to grease top. Cover and let rise in a warm place until doubled, about 1½-2 hours. Punch down dough. Shape into loaves by flattening pieces of dough and rolling jelly-roll fashion, being careful to work out any air bubbles. Place in greased pans. Let rise in warm place until doubled, about 1¼ hours. Bake at 350 degrees for about 35 minutes or until brown. Brush top with melted butter while still hot. This recipe makes five 8 x 4-inch loaves.

Mrs. O. R. Bishop, Jr. (Mary)

CHEESEBREAD

1¾ cups milk, scalded
3 cups sharp cheese, divided
    and grated
5 tablespoons sugar
3 teaspoons salt

2 tablespoons butter
1 package yeast
¼ cup water, warm
5½ cups flour
Melted butter

Combine milk, 2 cups of cheese, sugar, salt and butter. Stir until cheese melts. Cool. Sprinkle yeast in warm water to dissolve. Add to milk mixture and let stand for 3 minutes. Add 5 cups of flour and remaining cheese. Mix well and turn dough onto board that has been sprinkled with flour. Knead until smooth and satin like. Place in large bowl and brush with melted butter, cover, let stand until double; about 1½ hours. Pinch down and divide in half. Knead both sections. Cover and let rest 10 minutes. Shape into loaves and place in greased loaf pans. Cover and let rise in warm spot until double in size. Bake 35-45 minutes at 300 degrees. Remove from pans to cool.

Mrs. J. Howard Stone, Jr. (Sandra)

HONEY WHOLE WHEAT BREAD

2 packages yeast
1½ cups warm water
1 teaspoon honey
⅓ cup honey
⅓ cup molasses

⅓ cup vegetable oil
1 tablespoon salt
¾ cup milk, scalded
4 cups whole wheat flour
2 cups unbleached flour

Sprinkle yeast into 1½ cups warm water in large bowl. Add 1 teaspoon honey and stir until dissolved. Let stand and work for about 5 minutes. Add honey, molasses, vegetable oil and salt to scalded milk after it has cooled slightly. Add this to yeast mixture. Add 2 cups whole wheat flour. Beat well. Add unbleached flour. Beat well. Add more whole wheat flour to make a stiff dough. Turn out on floured board and knead 10 minutes, adding just enough unbleached flour to handle easily. Place dough in a warm, greased bowl turning to coat lightly. Cover and place in warm, draft-free place until doubled in bulk, about 1½ hours. Punch down. Turn out onto board. Cover and let rest 10 minutes. Divide in half and shape into 2 loaves. Place in 2 greased 9 x 5 x 3-inch loaf pans. Cover and let rise until almost doubled in bulk, about 1 hour. Place in a 350 degree preheated oven and cook 35-40 minutes. Turn out on rack as soon as golden brown to cool.

Mrs. James Will Wright (Amy)

OATMEAL BREAD

4 cups prepared non-fat dry
   milk, scalded
2 cups quick oatmeal
¼ cup butter
1 package dry yeast
½ teaspoon sugar

¼ cup warm water
1 teaspoon salt
½ cup molasses
9-10 cups unbleached white flour,
   sifted
Melted butter

Combine milk, oatmeal and butter in large mixing bowl. Let stand ½ hour. Meanwhile, mix yeast and sugar in warm water (body temperature) and let stand. When oatmeal mixture is ready, add yeast, salt, molasses, and 8 or 9 cups of flour making a soft dough. Oil a large bowl and turn dough so it is thoroughly moistened. Cover with towel and place in warm place to rise. Let stand until doubled, about 1½ to 2 hours. This is sponge dough. After doubled, punch down well on floured bread board. Knead about 10 minutes, adding remaining flour as needed until dough is smooth and elastic. Cover with cloth and let proof while 3 loaf pans are greased. Divide dough into thirds, shape into loaves, place in pans. Cover pans, letting rise until level with top of pan, about 1 hour. When they are ready remove cloth and bake 50 minutes at 400 degrees. Five minutes before time is up, brush tops of loaves with melted butter for crispness. Cool on racks. Freezes nicely.

Mrs. Mark Brimijoin (Kay)

RHUBARB BREAD

1 cup rhubarb, finely diced
¼ cup sugar
1 teaspoon salt
3 cups flour, sifted
4½ teaspoons baking powder
1 cup sugar

1 tablespoon orange rind, grated
½ cup walnuts, chopped
¾ cup milk
1 egg, beaten
¼ cup butter, melted
¼ cup orange juice

Mix rhubarb with ¼ cup sugar and salt. Let stand while preparing batter. Sift flour, baking powder and 1 cup sugar. Add orange rind and nuts. Combine milk, egg, butter and orange juice. Mix well. Add to flour mixture. Fold in rhubarb. Turn into greased 9 x 5 x 2 loaf pan. Bake at 350 degrees for 1 hour. Cool. Will slice easier the next day. Makes one loaf.

Mrs. J. P. Dowling (Dee)

BONANZA BREAD

1 cup all-purpose flour, sifted
1 cup whole wheat flour
½ teaspoon salt
½ teaspoon baking soda
2 teaspoons baking powder
⅔ cup nonfat dry milk powder
⅓ cup wheat germ
½ cup brown sugar, firmly
    packed
¼ cup walnuts, chopped

½ cup unsalted dry roasted
    peanuts, chopped
½ cup raisins
3 eggs
½ cup vegetable oil
½ cup molasses
¾ cup orange juice
2 medium size bananas, mashed to
    equal 1 cup
⅓ cup dried apricots, chopped

Combine flours, salt, soda, baking powder, dry milk, wheat germ, sugar, nuts and raisins in a large bowl; blend thoroughly with pastry blender or fork. Whirl eggs in blender until foamy. Add oil, molasses, orange juice, and bananas, whirling after each addition. Add apricots; whirl just to chop coarsely. Pour mixture into bowl with dry ingredients. Stir just until all flour is moistened. Pour into two 7¾ x 3⅝ x2¼-inch greased loaf pans. Bake in a 325 degree oven for 1 hour until center is firm when pressed lightly with fingertip. Cool slightly in pan on wire rack, then remove from pan and cool completely. When cool, wrap tightly and store overnight to mellow flavors.

Mrs. Darwin B. Bashaw (Margaret)

APPLESAUCE BREAD

1½ cups bran
1 cup milk
1 cup applesauce
½ cup sugar
½ cup oil

½ teaspoon baking soda
2 cups self-rising flour
2 eggs
½ cup raisins
½ cup nuts, chopped

Soak bran in milk for five minutes. Add all other ingredients and bake at 350 degrees in greased loaf pan for one hour.

Mrs. John Hryharrow (Dee)

BANANA NUT BREAD

2 cups flour
1 tablespoon baking soda
¼ teaspoon salt
1 cup sugar
½ cup margarine or butter

1 egg
2 large ripe bananas
1 cup nuts, chopped
1 teaspoon vanilla

Sift together once, flour, soda, and salt. Work in sugar and margarine until light and fluffy. Beat in egg well. Add bananas, stir in flour mixture and mix thoroughly. Add nuts and vanilla. Pour into a 9 x 5 x 2-inch loaf pan and bake 50 minutes in a 325 degree oven.

Mrs. Richard W. Whitney (Jessie)

ORANGE BANANA NUT BREAD

1 cup sugar
¼ cup butter, softened
1 egg, beaten
1 cup ripe bananas, mashed
2 tablespoons orange peel, grated

½ cup milk
2½ cups all-purpose flour, sifted
3 teaspoons baking powder
½ teaspoon salt
1 cup walnuts or pecans, coarsely chopped

Beat sugar, butter and egg until smooth; add bananas, orange peel and milk. Mix well. Add dry ingredients that have been sifted together and beat just until smooth. Stir in nuts. Bake in greased 9 x 5 x 2-inch loaf pan at 350 degrees for about 1 hour. Let cool in pan 10 minutes. Serve in thin slices.

Mrs. Gunter van der Heyde (Carole)

DATE NUT LOAF

1 cup dates, chopped
1 cup brown sugar
2 tablespoons butter or margarine
1 cup water, boiling
1 egg, beaten

2¼ cups flour
1 teaspoon soda
2 teaspoons baking powder
½ teaspoon salt
1½ cups nuts, chopped

Place dates, brown sugar, and butter in large bowl and pour over this boiling water. When this mixture cools, add egg and flour sifted with soda, baking powder and salt. Add nuts. Pour into greased and floured loaf pan. Bake 60 minutes in 300 degree oven.

Mrs. W. Burns Jones (Elizabeth)

HONEY WALNUT BREAD

1 cup milk, scalded
1 cup honey
½ cup sugar
¼ cup butter, softened
2 egg yolks

2½ cups flour
1 teaspoon salt
1 teaspoon soda
½ cup nuts, chopped

Beat scalded milk, honey, and sugar together until sugar is dissolved. Beat in butter and egg yolks. Stir in flour, salt, and soda. Mix until smooth. Add chopped nuts. Pour into greased floured loaf pan. Bake 1 hour at 325 degrees. Cool 15 minutes before removing from pan. Delicious served with cream cheese and jam.

Mrs. G. G. Cummings (Carol)

LEMON BREAD

1½ cups flour
1 teaspoon baking powder
1 cup sugar
¼ teaspoon salt
½ cup butter
2 eggs

½ cup milk
Grated rind of 1 lemon
½ cup walnuts, chopped
2 tablespoons lemon juice
¼ cup sugar

Sift flour, baking powder, 1 cup sugar and salt together. Cream butter, eggs and milk and add to flour mixture. Beat until smooth. Fold in lemon rind and walnuts. Bake in a greased loaf pan, 8½ x 4½, at 350 degrees for 1 hour. While bread is baking, mix lemon juice and ¼ cup sugar. When bread is done, remove from oven and pour lemon juice mixture over top. Cool about 1½ hours. Yields 1 loaf.

Battery Creek Catering
Dianne and Debbie TenEyck

POPPY SEED BREAD

3 cups flour, sifted
½ teaspoon salt
3½ teaspoons baking powder
½ cup poppy seeds
¾ cup sugar

¼ cup oil
2 eggs
1 teaspoon lemon peel, grated
1⅓ cups milk

Combine above ingredients and bake 1 hour at 350 degrees in a 9 x 5 x 2 pan. Freezes well. Slightly sweet, great for breakfast with cream cheese.

Dale Hryharrow Friedman

PORTUGESE SWEET BREAD

2 packages yeast
¼ cup lukewarm water
1 cup sugar
1 teaspoon salt

6 cups flour
3 eggs
1 cup milk
½ cup butter, softened

In a small bowl, mix the yeast in lukewarm water with a pinch of sugar. Let stand in a warm place until the mixture doubles in volume and bubbles. Combine the sugar, salt, and 4 cups of flour in a bowl. Make a well in the middle and add the eggs, the yeast mixture and the milk. Mix together. Add the butter and more flour; keep adding flour until the dough can be shaped into a big soft ball. Knead the dough until it looks smooth and has a rubbery feel. Place dough in a bowl greased with a little butter, then turn the dough over so both sides are greased. Cover with a damp towel. Leave the dough in a warm place until doubled in size. After dough has risen, punch so all the air leaves it. Then let it rest for 10 minutes. Shape into any shape you want. Place on cookie sheet or pie pan. Let the dough rise for about 45 minutes. Bake loaves at 350 degrees for about 1 hour. If desired, brush on a little egg yolk and water to make crust pretty.

Miss Cricket Spragins

BLUEBERRY COFFEE CAKE

1 cup butter, softened
2 cups sugar
3 eggs
3 cups all purpose flour
1½ teaspoons baking powder
⅛ teaspoon salt

¼ teaspoon mace
½ cup milk
2 cups blueberries
2 teaspoons sugar
2 teaspoons all purpose flour

Cream butter and 2 cups sugar until light and fluffy. Add eggs, one at a time, beating well after each addition. Combine flour, baking powder, salt and mace; add to creamed mixture alternately with milk, beating well after each addition. Coat blueberries with remaining sugar and flour; fold into batter. Pour into a greased and floured 10-inch tube or bundt pan. Bake at 350 degrees for 70-80 minutes. Yield 1 10-inch cake. Great for breakfast. Freezes well.

Mrs. C. A. Larsen, Jr. (Eleanor)

ZUCCHINI BREAD

2¼ cups sugar
3 eggs, beaten
1 cup oil
2 cups zucchini, grated
1½ teaspoons vanilla
3 cups flour

½ teaspoon baking powder
1 teaspoon salt
1 teaspoon baking soda
3 teaspoons cinnamon
1 cup nuts, chopped

Beat sugar into eggs. Add oil, zucchini and vanilla. Mix flour, baking powder, salt, baking soda, and cinnamon together and stir into egg-zucchini mixture. Blend well. Stir in nuts. Pour into two greased and floured loaf pans. Bake at 350 degrees for 1-1¼ hours.

Linda M. Satterfield

RAISIN NUT BREAD

1 cup raisins
1 cup water
1 egg, beaten
¾ cup sugar
½ teaspoon vanilla

1½ cups flour, sifted
1 teaspoon baking powder
¼ teaspoon baking soda
¼ teaspoon salt
½ cup nuts, chopped

In saucepan, combine raisins and water; bring to boiling point. Remove from heat and cool to room temperature. Mix egg, sugar, and vanilla; stir in raisin mixture. Sift dry ingredients and add to egg and raisin mixture, beating well. Stir in nuts. Pour into two greased and floured 16-ounce fruit or vegetable cans. Bake at 350 degrees for 50-60 minutes.

Mrs. J. W. Logan (Evelyn)

BREAKFAST CINNAMON PUFFS

⅓ cup butter
½ cup sugar
1 egg
1½ cups flour, sifted
1½ teaspoons baking powder
½ teaspoon salt

¼ teaspoon nutmeg
½ cup milk
½ cup butter, melted
½ cup sugar
1 teaspoon cinnamon

Mix butter, sugar and egg in food processor using the steel blade. Sift together flour, baking powder, salt and nutmeg. Add this and milk alternately to mixture in food processor. Fill greased muffin tins ⅔ full. Bake 20-25 minutes in 350 degree oven. Roll hot muffins in melted butter, then in cinnamon-sugar mixture. Serve hot. Makes 1 dozen.

Mrs. Robert Poitras (Louise)

STICKIE BUNS

¾ cup milk
1⅓ cups butter
¼ cup sugar
1 teaspoon salt
2 packages yeast
½ cup warm water
2 eggs

5½ cups unsifted flour
2 tablespoons soft butter
2⅜ cups sugar
1½ teaspoons cinnamon

Scald milk. Remove from heat and add 1⅓ cups butter, sugar and salt. Stir and cool. In a large bowl dissolve the yeast in warm water. Whisk in milk mixture and eggs until blended. Add 3 cups flour and mix until smooth. Then add 2 more cups flour. Dough will be soft. Turn out on lightly floured surface and knead for 5 minutes (use remaining ½ cup of flour to keep dough from sticking). Place in a large greased bowl and turn to grease the top. Cover and let rise until double, about 30 minutes. Divide dough in half and on lightly floured surface, roll out one half to 14 x 10 inches. Spread with 1 tablespoon of butter and sprinkle with sugar and cinnamon. Starting at one end roll up and pinch ends. Slice into ten pieces. Repeat with remaining dough.

TOPPING:
1 cup sugar
1 tablespoon water
½ cup butter

½ cup molasses
2⅜ cups pecans, chopped

Combine all ingredients and stir over low heat until sugar dissolves. Divide topping in bottom of two greased pans. Put dough slices on top and cover. Let rise for 30 minutes. Bake in preheated 350 degree oven for 25-30 minutes. Freezes well.

Mrs. R. C. Harris, Jr. (Rena)

SOUR CREAM COFFEE CAKE

1 cup butter or margarine
2 cups sugar
2 eggs
½ teaspoon vanilla

2 cups flour
1 teaspoon baking powder
½ teaspoon salt
1 cup sour cream

TOPPING MIXTURE:
½ cup pecans
½ teaspoon cinnamon

2 teaspoons sugar

Cream butter, sugar and eggs. Add vanilla, 1 cup flour, baking powder, and salt. Add other cup flour. Beat slowly; add sour cream. Pour half of batter into greased tube pan. Mix the pecans, cinnamon, and sugar. Sprinkle pecan mixture on top. Bake at 350 degrees for 55-60 minutes. Sprinkle powdered sugar over cake when done.

Mrs. A. G. Burris (Gail)

GRANOLA

2 cups rolled oats
2½ cups raw wheat germ
1 cup coarse bran
1 cup rye or wheat flakes
½ cup walnuts, chopped
½ cup cashews, chopped
½ cup sunflower seeds

¼ cup sesame seeds
¼ cup blackstrap molasses
¼ cup honey
½ cup coconut
½ cup liquid lecithin or
    safflower oil

Mix all ingredients until the oil, honey and molasses are sufficiently distributed. Pour into a roasting pan and toast in 350 degree oven for 15 minutes, or until the granola is somewhat dry and crispy. Stir occasionally while baking to produce an evenly toasted mixture. Yield 7 to 8 cups.

Mrs. John Burbage (Helen)

APPLE PANCAKES

2 cups flour, sifted
3 teaspoons baking powder
1 teaspoon salt
1 tablespoon sugar

1 egg, beaten
1½ cups milk
2 tablespoons butter, melted
1 cup apples, finely chopped

Sift together flour, baking powder, salt, and sugar. Stir egg, milk, and butter into flour mixture; beat until smooth. Add apples and mix well. Bake on hot griddle turning only once. Makes 12 3-inch pancakes.

Mrs. MacDonald Dixon (Phyllis)

COTTAGE CHEESE PANCAKES

2 cups cottage cheese
6 eggs
6 tablespoons flour

¼ teaspoon salt
Salad oil sufficient to grease
    griddle or skillet

Blend all ingredients except oil in blender until smooth. Grease griddle or heavy skillet with light coating of salad oil. Bring to moderate temperature. Allow ¼ cup batter per pancake. Cook until entire surface bubbles. Flip and cook until nicely browned. Makes 3 dozen pancakes.

Mrs. Charles D. Ravenel (Mollie)

EMILINE'S FRESH CORN PANCAKES

4-6 ears corn
1 cup milk
2 tablespoons butter
2 eggs, separated

⅔ cup flour, sifted
1 teaspoon sugar
1 teaspoon baking powder
1½ teaspoons salt

Boil corn 1 minute, and cut enough kernels off to make 2 cups. Combine with milk, butter, and egg yolks in bowl. Sift dry ingredients together, then add to liquid mixture and stir well. Beat egg whites until stiff, then fold into mixture. Fry on a well greased hot griddle, turning once. Serve with warm maple syrup and butter. Makes 16 pancakes.

Mrs. Reese Lindsay (Annie Sue)

QUICK SOURDOUGH PANCAKES

½ cup milk
½ cup water
1 tablespoon cooking oil

1 cup pancake mix
1 package yeast
1 egg

Combine milk, water and oil in a saucepan. Heat over low heat until barely warm. In a large bowl thoroughly mix pancake mix and undissolved yeast. Gradually add the warm milk mix to the dry ingredients and beat for 1 minute at low speed. Add egg and continue beating at same speed for 1 minute longer. Cover batter and let stand at room temperature for 30 minutes. Stir batter. Lightly oil a hot griddle. Bake pancakes using about 2 tablespoons batter per cake. Stir down batter occasionally as it is used.

Mrs. George Eidson (Jeanne)

WAFFLES

2 eggs, separated
1½ cups flour
2 teaspoons baking powder
½ teaspoon salt

4 tablespoons butter, melted
1 tablespoon sugar
1 cup milk

Add beaten egg yolks to flour, baking powder, salt, butter, sugar and milk. Add stiffly beaten whites last. Bake in waffle iron until golden brown.

Fannie Van Sant

SPOON BREAD I

2 cups milk, boiling
½ cup white cornmeal
2 tablespoons butter

¼ teaspoon salt
4 egg yolks, beaten
4 egg whites, stiffly beaten

Slowly stir cornmeal into milk. Let simmer 5 minutes and stir well to prevent lumps. Add butter and salt. Remove from fire and cool. Stir in egg yolks and fold in egg whites. Turn into deep well greased 1-quart casserole that has been heated. Bake 25 minutes at 350 degrees.

Mrs. Leon Stansell (Frances)

SPOON BREAD II

1 cup cornmeal, sifted
1 cup water, boiling
1 cup milk
2 eggs

1 teaspoon salt
1 teaspoon sugar
⅓ cup butter, melted and cooled
2 teaspoons baking powder

Scald cornmeal with water. Add milk, mix well. Add salt, sugar, butter and baking powder. Pour into well greased 1-quart baking dish and bake about 45 minutes in 350 degree oven.

Mrs. Arthur A. Marscher (Gladys)

SALLY LUNN

2 cups milk, scalded
1 package yeast
2 teaspoons sugar
4 tablespoons butter

2 teaspoons salt
3 eggs, beaten until light
4-5 cups flour

Divide milk. Into ¼ cup milk put yeast and set aside. Dissolve sugar, butter and salt in remaining milk. Combine eggs with yeast mixture. Add sugar mixture. Add enough flour to make a stiff batter; at least 4 cups. Let rise until double in bulk. Stir down. Put in oiled tube pan and let rise again until double in bulk. Bake at 375 degrees until brown like a pound cake, about 30-40 minutes.

The Editors

MARTHA HOPKINS' BEATEN BISCUITS

4 cups plain flour
1 teaspoon salt
1 teaspoon sugar

3 heaping tablespoons lard
1¼ cups ice water, or enough to
    make dough stiff

Sift together flour, salt and sugar. Work the lard in perfectly. Add ice water. Flour board and work in as much flour as you can. Put through biscuit brake until it blisters, or divide in 6 parts and use food processor with the steel blade for 2 minutes. Let dough rest. Roll dough one half at a time. Cut out with biscuit cutter and prick top 3 times with a fork. Preheat oven to 400 degrees. Bake 10-15 minutes. Turn heat to 250 degrees. Let stay for 20 minutes.

Mrs. Sam Clark, Jr. (Carolyn)

ANGEL FLAKE BISCUITS

5 cups regular flour
1 teaspoon salt
1 teaspoon soda
1 tablespoon baking powder
¼ cup sugar

1 package dry yeast
¼ cup warm water
⅔ cup shortening
2 cups buttermilk

Sift 4 cups of the flour with the salt, soda, baking powder and sugar into a large bowl. Dissolve the yeast in ¼ cup warm water. Cut shortening into the flour mixture. Stir in buttermilk and yeast. Mix thoroughly. Add the 5th cup of flour only if necessary to make a dough that will mound slightly when stirred to the center of the bowl. The dough should be sticky. Refrigerate dough overnight before rolling out on a well floured surface. Cut into biscuits and bake at once in a 450 degree oven until browned. Dough can be kept 3-4 days in the refrigerator.

Mrs. Dwight A. Dunbar

DORIS' BISCUITS

2 cups self-rising flour
½ cup shortening

¾ cup milk
Flour

Lightly spoon flour into measuring cup. Place flour in a large bowl and cut in shortening with a fork. Stir until moist. Add milk at once. Stir with a fork until mixture leaves the side of the bowl and forms a soft, moist dough. Turn onto floured surface and sprinkle lightly with flour. Knead gently until dough is no longer sticky.

Roll dough out to ½-inch thickness. Cut with a 2-inch floured biscuit cutter. Bake at 450 degrees on ungreased cookie sheet for 12 minutes or until golden brown.

Mrs. James Johnson (Doris)

EASY BISCUITS

1 cup all-purpose flour
½ cup butter

1 8-ounce package cream cheese
½ teaspoon salt

Combine ingredients and pat together. Cut out biscuits and bake at 425 degrees for 15 minutes.

Mrs. Edward Holt (Kitty)

SWEET POTATO BISCUITS

1 cup flour
3 teaspoons baking powder
½ teaspoon salt
4 tablespoons shortening

1 cup sweet potatoes, cooked and
  mashed
½ to ¾ cup milk

Sift together flour, baking powder, and salt. Add shortening and sweet potatoes. Add milk to make stiff enough to roll. Cut and bake in 400 degree oven 20-30 minutes.

Mrs. Hugh O. Pearson (Marie)

WHEAT GERM BISCUITS

1¾ cups flour
¼ cup wheat germ
1 tablespoon baking powder

¾ teaspoon salt
⅓ cup butter
¾ cup milk

In a bowl combine flour, wheat germ, baking powder and salt. Add butter cut into bits and blend with pastry cutter until it resembles meal. Add milk, stir the mixture until it forms a soft dough and turn dough out onto a lightly floured surface. Knead lightly for a few seconds. Roll it into a circle ½-inch thick and cut with biscuit cutter about the size of a 50 cent piece. Arrange rounds in buttered pan barely touching and bake at 400 degrees for 12 minutes or until golden.

Dale Hryharrow Friedman

EGG POPOVERS

2 eggs
1 cup flour

1 cup milk
½ teaspoon salt

Combine eggs, flour, milk and salt. Beat mixture thoroughly with rotary beater. Pour batter into 6 well greased muffin cups ¾ full. Place in *cold* oven. Set temperature at 400 degrees and bake 30 minutes. *Do not* open while baking.

The Editors

Desserts

CRYSTALLIZED MINT LEAVES

1 bunch of mint
3 drops green coloring

½ cup sugar
1 egg white, beaten

Separate the leaves from a bunch of mint and wipe them. In a dish, rub green coloring into sugar with hands. Coat the mint leaves on both sides with the egg white, and put them on a sheet of wax paper. Sift the colored sugar over the leaves, turn the leaves, and sift the sugar over the other sides. Line a jelly roll pan with a sheet of parchment paper, transfer the sugared leaves to the paper, and put them in a preheated 250 degree oven. Turn off the oven and let the leaves stand in the oven for 30 minutes, or until they are hard and dry. The leaves will keep indefinitely stored in an airtight container.

Mrs. Richard G. Price, Jr. (Mary Jo)

BREAD PUDDING

2 cups milk
½ cup sugar
2 tablespoons butter, melted
2 eggs, slightly beaten
4-6 slices bread, crumbled

¼ teaspoon ground cinnamon
¼ teaspoon ground nutmeg
½ cup seedless grapes
½ teaspoon lemon peel
½ cup apple, chopped, optional

Combine milk, sugar, butter, eggs, bread, cinnamon, nutmeg, raisins, lemon peel, and apple and pour into 4 custard cups, set in a pan of water. Bake in 350 degree for 40-45 minutes. Serves 4.

Mrs. T. Miles Burbage (Marion)

BIG MAMMA'S BREAD PUDDING

2 cups bread crumbs
1 quart milk, scalded
½ cup sugar
3 tablespoons butter, melted
2 eggs, separated

½ teaspoon salt
1 teaspoon vanilla
1 cup raisins, optional
2 tablespoons sugar

Soak bread crumbs in scalded milk, cool. Add sugar, butter, egg yolks, salt, vanilla and raisins. Pour into 1½-quart baking dish and bake for 40 minutes in a 325 degree oven. Cover with meringue made of 2 stiffly beaten egg whites and 2 tablespoons sugar. Brown and serve with desired sauce. Serves 8-10.

Miss Madeline Trask

DATE PUDDING

4 eggs, separated
1 cup sugar
⅔ cup flour
1 teaspoon baking powder

Pinch salt
1 8-ounce package dates, finely
   chopped
1 cup pecans, finely chopped

Beat egg yolks, add sugar. Add flour sifted with baking powder and salt. Add stiffly beaten egg whites. Add dates and nuts. Bake in slightly greased muffin tins at 350 degrees. Cool in pans. Serve warm with wine sauce topped with whipped cream.

Mrs. F. W. Scheper, Jr. (Margaret)

WINE SAUCE

1 cup sugar
½ cup water

1 teaspoon flour
½ cup wine

Combine and simmer for 10 minutes. Serve warm over date pudding.

Mrs. F. W. Scheper, Jr. (Margaret)

DATE NUT DESSERT

3 eggs
1 cup sugar
1 cup all-purpose flour
1½ teaspoons baking powder

1 8-ounce package dates, cut up
1 cup nuts, chopped
1 teaspoon vanilla
Sherry sauce

Beat eggs and sugar thoroughly. Fold in flour, baking powder, dates and nuts. Add vanilla. Line muffin tins with paper liners or grease evenly. Spoon batter into muffin cups. Bake 30 minutes at 350 degrees. Remove from oven, cool and remove paper linings. One hour before serving, spoon 1 tablespoon sherry sauce over each muffin and let soak in. Add more sauce and whipped cream just before serving. These freeze well. Do not use sauce until they are defrosted. Serves 12.

Mrs. John Smoak (Norine)

SHERRY SAUCE FOR DATE NUT DESSERT

1 cup sugar
1 cup dry sherry

1 tablespoon flour

Cook sugar, sherry, and flour just long enough to thicken. Do not allow to boil.

Mrs. John Smoak (Norine)

COLD ORANGE SOUFFLÉ

1 tablespoon gelatin
¼ cup cold water
3 eggs, separated
1 cup sugar
1 teaspoon lemon juice

⅓ cup orange juice
Grated rind of 1 orange
1 tablespoon Cointreau
2 cups heavy cream

Soak gelatin in cold water. Melt gelatin mixture over low heat. Beat egg yolks until pale and lemon colored. Add sugar gradually and beat until very light. Beat in juice, grated orange rind and liqueur. Add the hot gelatin in a thin stream beating yolk mixture all the time. Allow mixture to cool until it starts to congeal. Beat egg whites. Add ⅓ whites to mixture. Blend remaining whites with whipped cream and fold into orange mixture. Pour into souffle dish and chill several hours. Serves 6-8.

Mrs. F. T. Davis, Jr. (Winifred)

ORANGE CHARLOTTE

1½ envelopes unflavored
    gelatin
½ cup cold water
½ cup boiling water
1 cup sugar

1 cup orange juice
3 tablespoons lemon juice
1 pint heavy cream, whipped
2 egg whites, beaten

Soften gelatin in cold water. Add ½ cup boiling water and stir until completely dissolved. Add sugar, orange juice, and lemon juice. Let partially congeal in refrigerator. Add cream. Fold in 2 beaten egg whites. Chill. Serves 4-6.

Mrs. James Cook (Cynthia)

WINE JELLY

2½ tablespoons gelatin
½ cup cold water
1½ cups boiling water
1 cup sugar

⅓ cup orange juice, strained
3 tablespoons lemon juice, strained
1 cup sherry wine
3 jiggers whiskey

Dilute gelatin in cold water, add the boiling water and sugar, dissolving thoroughly. Add orange juice and lemon juice. Place in refrigerator until room temperature. Add the sherry and whiskey. Cover tightly and return to refrigerator. Will keep for days. Always be sure it is tightly covered as that keeps the liquor from evaporating.

Mrs. Omar Beasley (Sadie)

LE GÂTEAU MEGEVE

MERINGUE:

3 egg whites

1 cup sugar

CREME PATISSIENE:

1 cup milk, heated

3 egg yolks

3 tablespoons sugar

2 tablespoons cornstarch

GANACHE:

½ cup whipping cream

8 ounces Bakers German sweet
chocolate

½ cup unsalted butter

2 tablespoons water

DECORATIONS:

2 ounces chocolate, bitter or sweet, shaved

Make meringue first. Beat egg whites until stiff; add sugar slowly. Grease and dust with flour 3 cookie sheets. Make circles on cookie sheets 9 inches and fill with meringue. Bake at 225 degrees for 50 minutes.

Make creme. Using mix master, beat egg yolks and sugar until pale yellow (takes several minutes). Add cornstarch. Add hot milk; place in pan and cook, stirring constantly until thickened. Let cool. In a double boiler melt chocolate with 2 tablespoons water, adding whipping cream and reduce heat to medium high and stir. It will thicken in about 10 minutes. Remove from heat, add butter in small pieces, beating all the time.

Mix two creams together and coat one meringue. Cover with another meringue. Cover with more of cream mixture. Add third meringue, and cover with remaining cream. Place shaved chocolate on top and refrigerate.

Mrs. John M. Trask, Jr. (Caroline)

CAPERS ISLAND TRIFLE

5 slices pound or angel food
   cake
2 tablespoons rum
4 cups milk

4 eggs
½ cup sugar
1 teaspoon vanilla

Break cake into pieces in a serving bowl. Sprinkle with rum. Heat milk in a saucepan. Beat eggs and sugar together in a bowl. Stir in a small amount of heated milk into egg mixture, adding more milk until you have used about one cup. Stir egg mixture into remaining milk in saucepan. Cook and stir over medium heat until custard just coats spoon. Pour over cake. Serve warm or cold. Serves 4-6.

Mrs. Jack Chaplin (Sally)

CAROLINA TRIFLE

1 small package vanilla
   INSTANT pudding
½ 9-inch cake layer
¾ cup grated coconut

3 cups milk
1 teaspoon vanilla
8 ounces non-dairy whipped
   topping

Crumble ½ of the cake into a 10 x 6 x 2-inch casserole. Sprinkle with ¼ cup coconut. Make pudding according to directions, using the 3 cups milk and 1 teaspoon vanilla. Pour ½ of the pudding immediately over the crumbled cake and coconut. Quickly crumble remaining cake over the pudding and sprinkle with ¼ cup coconut. Pour remaining pudding over the cake and coconut. Spread whipped topping over pudding; sprinkle with remaining coconut.

Chill at least 2 hours before serving. Serves 8.

Beaufort County Open Land Trust

TRIFLE

2 9-inch layers sponge cake
12 lady fingers, split
1 cup apricot or raspberry jam
1 cup sherry
½ cup brandy
8 egg yolks
½ cup sugar

4 cups half and half, scalded
2 teaspoons almond extract
1 cup heavy cream, whipped
Angelica strips, macaroons,
    chopped nuts or crystallized
    mint leaves garnish

Line a crystal bowl with 1 layer of sponge cake and make a border of lady fingers around the rim. Spread the sponge cake with the jam and sprinkle well with the sherry. Sprinkle the lady fingers with sherry and let dry.

In top of a double boiler, beat egg yolks with sugar until thick. Slowly stir in scalded half and half. Cook over simmering water until thickened. Remove from heat and stir in almond extract. Cool. Place one half of custard into bowl on top of sponge cake. Place the second half of cake on top, spread with jam, sprinkle liberally with sherry and brandy. Pour remaining custard on top of second cake layer.

Whip cream until stiff and spread over the top, allowing the lady fingers to create an edge.

Decorate the top with angelica strips, macaroons, nuts or crystillized mint leaves. Chill well. Serves 12-14.

Mrs. Sam Stafford III (Nancy)

LEMON SPONGE

8 eggs, separated
1½ cups sugar
Juice and rind of 2 lemons
1½ tablespoons gelatin

½ cup orange juice
½ cup boiling water
1½ packages lady fingers
1 cup whipping cream

Beat egg yolks well. Add ½ cup sugar and juice and rind of lemons to egg yolks. Cook in double boiler. Stir. After mixture thickens, remove from stove and cool. Soak gelatin in orange juice. Add boiling water and add to hot lemon mixture. Beat egg whites stiff and add 1 cup sugar. Fold into egg yolk mixture. Line 9-inch spring mold with lady fingers and pour in mixture. Let congeal overnight. Release mold before serving and ice top with whipped cream. Serves 10-12.

Mrs. W. H. Gaither (Louise)

CHOCOLATE ICE BOX DESSERT

1 cup butter
3 cups confectioners' sugar
6 eggs, separated
3 ounces unsweetened
    chocolate, melted
1 teaspoon vanilla

½ teaspoon almond extract
2 dozen lady fingers, split
1 cup almonds, blanched and
    slivered
Whipped cream
Toasted almond slivers, optional

Cream butter and sugar thoroughly in large bowl of mixer. Add egg yolks one at a time, beating well after each addition. Blend in melted chocolate and flavorings. Beat egg whites until stiff and carefully fold in by hand. Line a buttered 9-inch spring form pan with lady fingers. Spoon in some of the chocolate mixture, then sprinkle almonds over this. Continue layering until all ingredients are used. Refrigerate overnight or freeze for later use. Before serving, unmold and frost with whipped cream. Sprinkle with toasted almond slivers, if desired.

Mrs. Peter Fuge (Meredith)

CHOCOLATE ROLL

5 large eggs, separated
½ cup sugar
6 ounces semi-sweet chocolate
3 tablespoons strong coffee

Cocoa
2 cups heavy cream, whipped
    and sweetened

Butter a 10 x 5-inch jelly roll pan, line it with waxed paper and butter the paper. Beat the egg yolks until they are light and lemon colored. Gradually beat in the sugar until the mixture is light and creamy. Melt the chocolate with the coffee in the top of a double boiler over hot water. Let cool slightly, then beat it into the egg-sugar mixture. Beat the egg whites until stiff enough to form peaks when you remove the whisk or beater, but not dry. Fold them into the chocolate mixture. Pour the batter into the greased pan and spread evenly with a spatula. Bake in a 350 degree oven for about 15 minutes, or until a knife inserted into the center comes out clean. Remove from the oven, cover with a slightly damp towel and let stand for about 20 minutes, until cool. Arrange two 18-inch lengths of waxed paper on a work table, side by side and slightly overlapping. Sprinkle with cocoa. Run a spatula around the edges of the cake and invert it onto the waxed paper—it should come out easily. Carefully remove the paper from the bottom of the cake. Spread the cake with the sweetened whipped cream. Then, by lifting the long edge of waxed paper under the side of the cake nearest you, start the cake rolling up like a jelly roll. Continue lifting the waxed paper, gently but quickly, until the cake is completely rolled. If the surface breaks a little, don't worry, you can cover the marks with a light dusting of cocoa. To serve, arrange on a long board or platter and cut in crosswise slices. Makes 8-10 servings.

Mrs. C. A. Larsen, Jr. (Eleanor)

CHOCOLATE MOUSSE CAKE

MOUSSE:

4 cups heavy cream
2 cups unsifted confectioners'
   sugar
1 cup unsifted cocoa

3 teaspoons vanilla
¼ teaspoon salt
1½ teaspoons gelatin
2 tablespoons cold water

Pour cream into large bowl. Refrigerate until very cold (30 minutes). Add sugar, cocoa, vanilla and salt. Beat until stiff enough to hold its shape. Refrigerate. Sprinkle gelatin over 2 tablespoons cold water to soften. Heat over hot water until dissolved. Let gelatin mixture cool completely.

CHIFFON CAKE:

7 egg whites
½ cup unsifted cocoa
¾ cup boiling water
1¾ cups cake flour
1¾ cups sugar
1½ teaspoons baking soda

1 teaspoon salt
½ cup salad oil
7 egg yolks
2 teaspoons vanilla
½ teaspoon cream of tartar

In large bowl of electric mixer let egg whites warm to room temperature (1 hour). Preheat oven to 325 degrees. Place cocoa in small bowl. Add boiling water, stirring until smooth. Let mixture cool about 20 minutes. Into a second large bowl, sift flour with sugar, soda and salt. Make a well in the center, pour in salad oil, egg yolks, vanilla and cooled cocoa mixture. With spoon or mixer beat just until smooth. Sprinkle cream of tartar over egg whites. With mixer at high speed, beat until very stiff peaks are formed. *Do Not Underbeat.* Pour batter over egg whites and with rubber scraper or wire whisk, gently fold until just blended. Turn batter into ungreased 9-inch spring mold. Bake 60 minutes or until cake springs back when pressed. Let cake cool. With sharp knife cut cake into 3 layers. Remove 3½ cups mousse to small bowl. Fold into cooled gelatin. Use for filling. Ice cake with remaining mousse. Refrigerate.

Mrs. Mary L. McDowell

MAPLE MOUSSE

1½ cups maple syrup
2 egg whites

Few grains of salt
2 cups heavy cream

Cook syrup 5 minutes—watch it as it boils over easily. Beat egg whites stiff; add syrup to beaten egg whites in a thin stream, beating constantly. Beat in salt. Cool. Whip cream firm, and fold into maple mixture. Pour into 2 ice trays and freeze 3 hours or overnight. Serves 10.

Mrs. Thomas H. Truslow (Frances)

QUICK CHOCOLATE MOUSSE

2 whole eggs
2 tablespoons rum
1 6-ounce package semi-sweet
   chocolate morsels

3 tablespoons very strong hot
   coffee
¾ cup milk, scalded

In blender combine eggs, rum, and chocolate morsels. Blend until chocolate morsels are in very fine pieces. Add coffee and blend until smooth. Add milk and blend the mixture at very high speed for 2 minutes. Pour the mousse into dessert cups and chill in refrigerator for at least 6 hours. Can be prepared the day before. Serve topped with ice cream or whipped cream. Serves 4.

Mrs. Stoddard Lane, Jr. (Patricia)

BAVARIAN CREME, COINTREAU

1 tablespoon gelatin
¼ cup cold water
½ cup hot milk
⅔ cup sugar

1 pint cream, whipped
1½ ounces Cointreau
Lady fingers

Soak gelatin in water. Scald milk and sugar, and cook together about 5 minutes over low heat. Add gelatin mixture and blend well. Cool until thoroughly cold. Fold in whipped cream, Cointreau, and orange peel. Line an angel cake pan with split lady fingers. Pour in the cream mixture and chill overnight. Turn out onto plate and serve. Serve with chocolate sauce. Serves 10.

Mrs. Lloyd Brown (Nancy)

RASPBERRY CREAM

¾ of a 10-ounce box vanilla
   wafers, crushed and
   divided
½ cup butter
2 cups confectioners' sugar,
   sifted

2 eggs, beaten
1 cup whipping cream
1 teaspoon almond flavoring
1 pint fresh raspberries or 1
   package frozen raspberries,
   drained and juice reserved

Grease an 8 x 8-inch pan and line with vanilla wafer crumbs. Cream butter and sugar until smooth; add eggs. Spoon onto vanilla wafer crumbs and smooth with knife. Whip cream adding almond flavoring. When stiff, add raspberries and smooth over top of butter and sugar mixture. Drizzle some fruit juice over top, if desired; also sprinkle with some vanilla wafer crumbs, if desired. Chill several hours or overnight. Can be made several days ahead and other fruits may be substituted.

Mrs. T. Ladson Webb (Ann)

SNOWFLAKE PUDDING WITH RASPBERRY SAUCE

1 cup sugar
1 tablespoon plain gelatin
½ teaspoon salt
1¼ cups milk
1 teaspoon vanilla

1⅓ cups flaked coconut
2 cups heavy cream, whipped
10 ounces raspberries, crushed
1½ teaspoons cornstarch
½ cup red currant jelly

Mix sugar, gelatin and salt; add milk. Stir over medium heat until dissolved. Chill until partially set. Add vanilla. Fold in coconut and then whipped cream. Place into a 1½ quart mold. Chill until set, about 4 hours. Unmold and serve with Crimson Raspberry Sauce. Serves 8.

SAUCE:
Crush 10 ounces of raspberries. Combine the raspberries, cornstarch, and jelly. Cook and stir until mixture is clear and slightly thickened. Strain and chill. Yields 1½ cups.

Mrs. C. Blackburn Brewer (Frances)

AMBROSIA DELUXE

2 grapefruits, peeled and
    sectioned
6 oranges, peeled and
    sectioned
4 apples, chopped
3 bananas, sliced
1 pound white, seedless grapes,
    sliced

1 16-ounce can crushed pineapple
12 ounces grated coconut
1 cup sugar
1 6-ounce bottle maraschino
    cherries

In a large bowl you can serve from, layer the ingredients (with the exception of the cherries) in the order given. There should be at least three layers. Place the cherries on top. Refrigerate for several hours.

Miss Katherine W. Kroeg

PERFECT APPLE COBBLER

3 cups apples, chopped
1 tablespoon lemon juice
1 cup sugar
1 cup biscuit mix or self-rising
     flour

1 egg
½ cup butter

Put apples in 11 x 7-inch pan. Sprinkle lemon juice over apples. Mix sugar and flour in bowl. Beat egg well, stir into sugar and flour until crumbly. Sprinkle over apples. Pour melted butter on top of this. Bake at 375 degrees for 35 minutes. Serves 6.

Mrs. Anthony Fuller (Rebecca)

BANANAS FOSTER

4 tablespoons butter
¼ cup packed brown sugar
½ teaspoon ground cinnamon
2 tablespoons banana liqueur
4 firm bananas, halved
     lengthwise and crosswise

¼ cup rum
4 scoops vanilla ice cream,
     optional

In flambé pan or skillet, melt butter. Add sugar, cinnamon, and banana liqueur; stir to mix. Bring to boil and simmer 2 minutes. Place bananas in sauce. Cook, stirring occasionally, until bananas are soft, about 4 minutes. Add rum and allow to heat slightly. Ignite and serve. Top with vanilla ice cream, if desired. Serves 4.

Mrs. Wayne Flietner (Jennie)

CRANBERRY CASSEROLE

3 cups apples, diced
2 cups raw cranberries
1 cup sugar
1⅓ cups oatmeal

⅓ cup flour
½ cup brown sugar
½ cup pecans, chopped
½ cup butter or margarine

Mix and spread in 2-quart baking dish apples, cranberries, and sugar. Mix oatmeal, flour, brown sugar, pecans, and margarine and spread over the apple mixture. Bake uncovered at 325 degrees for 1 hour. Serve hot, plain or with cream. Also good cold. Serves 8.

Mrs. Julien K. Taylor (Elizabeth)

FIGS WITH CREAM

1 quart fresh figs (making
    about 2½ cups pulp)
3-4 tablespoons dark rum
Granulated sugar to taste

1 cup whipping cream, chilled
1 cup sour cream, chilled
Confectioners' sugar to taste

Skin figs and mash to pulp in a serving bowl with a fork. Stir in rum and sugar to taste. Beat the cream in a chilled bowl with a chilled beater until beater leaves light traces on the cream. Fold the sour cream into whipped cream, fold in confectioners' sugar to taste, then fold the cream into the fig mixture. Chill until serving time. Serves 12.

Mrs. L. E. Lovette (Louise)

FRUIT COMPOTE DESSERT

3 fresh raw pears, peeled,
    cored, and quartered
1 cup cranberries, uncooked
3 oranges, peeled and
    sectioned

6 whole cloves
1½ sticks cinnamon
1 cup light corn syrup

Put pears, cranberries, oranges, cloves, cinnamon, and syrup in casserole dish. Cover and bake at 350 degrees or until pears are tender. Chill before serving. Serves 6.

Mrs. William Elliott (Martha)

POACHED PEARS IN RED WINE

1 bottle red wine (Beaujolais)
5 ounces sugar
1 stick cinnamon
1 whole clove

2 slices lemon
2 slices orange
1 teaspoon peppercorns
6 firm Basque pears

Peel pears, leaving stem on, and cut bottoms so they will stand in dessert dish. Cook pears for 15 minutes in wine, sugar, cinnamon, clove, lemon, orange, and peppercorns. Serve pears cold in a small bowl in juice. Serves 6.

Mrs. John M. Trask, Jr. (Caroline)

PEACH COBBLER

4 cups peaches
¾ cup sugar, divided
½ cup butter

1 cup self-rising flour
1 cup milk

Toss peaches in ½ cup sugar. Melt butter in 2-quart baking dish. Sift together flour and ½ cup sugar and add milk. Pour into baking dish. Put peaches on top. Bake 45 minutes in 350 degree oven. Serves 6.

Mrs. John Hightower (Lois)

BAKED PINEAPPLE, NATILLAS

1 large fresh pineapple
¼ cup sugar

2-3 tablespoons rum
¼ cup butter

SAUCE:
1 pint light cream
¼ teaspoon salt
¼ cup sugar

1 whole egg plus 2 egg yolks
1 teaspoon cornstarch
1 teaspoon vanilla

Lay pineapple on its side and take off a thick slice that does not include green leaves. Carefully scoop out pineapple and cut into bite-size pieces. Sweeten pineapple with sugar, add rum and return to shell. Dot with butter, cover with foil (including leaves) and bake 30 minutes at 350 degrees. Serve in small bowl with cold sauce over it.
To make sauce, scald the cream and cool slightly. Add salt, sugar beaten with the eggs, cornstarch and vanilla. Cook over hot water, stirring constantly until smooth and slightly thickened. Chill. Serve over hot pineapple. Serves 6-8.

Mrs. William D. Brooks, Jr. (Helen)

GOLD EAGLE BENNE DELIGHT

½ cup butter
1 cup evaporated milk
1 16-ounce box light brown
    sugar

1 cup marshmallows
Benne seed, toasted

Combine butter, evaporated milk, brown sugar and marshmallows in double boiler. Cook until soft and marshmallows are melted. Store in refrigerator in jar and reheat as needed. Serve hot on vanilla ice cream with benne seed sprinkled over the top. Makes 1 quart.

Mrs. S. S. Stokes (Dreka)

OLD-FASHIONED BOILED CUSTARD ICE CREAM

3 quarts milk
6 eggs
2½ cups sugar
1 tablespoon flour or
  cornstarch

1 tablespoon vanilla extract
½ pint whipping cream
Pinch of salt

Put milk in saucepan or double boiler large enough not to boil over. Warm milk and add well beaten eggs, sugar and flour. Stir constantly until milk boils and thickens. Be very careful not to let your milk scorch. Take off and cool. Then add vanilla and cream (not whipped). Churn in ice cream freezer. Makes 1 gallon.

Mrs. Earl Hayes (Hettie)

HOME MADE ICE CREAM

6 eggs
2½ cups sugar
1 teaspoon vanilla
1 13-ounce can evaporated
  milk

Milk
Fresh fruit of choice, mashed

Beat eggs several minutes. Beat in sugar one cup at a time. Add vanilla, evaporated milk, and pour in 4-quart freezer container. Either add fresh milk to full line in freezer container or add sweetened fresh fruit, reducing sugar in ice cream mixture by ½ to 1 cup depending on taste desired. Makes 8-10 servings.

Mrs. Claude E. Surface, Jr. (Page)

PEACH ICE CREAM

24 ounces peach purèe
¼ cup sugar
1 tablespoon lemon juice
6 eggs

2¼ cups sugar
26 ounces evaporated milk
26 ounces water

Put enough fresh or frozen peaches in blender to equal 24 ounces, add ¼ cup sugar and lemon juice. Blend well and put aside. Put the eggs and 2¼ cups sugar in blender mixing until sugar has dissolved. Meanwhile, heat the milk and the water until hot; do not boil. Add the sugar-egg mixture. Cook 5 minutes stirring constantly. Add to peach mixture and cool in refrigerator. Freeze in 4-quart ice cream freezer. Makes 4 full quarts.

Mrs. Ted Ledford (Suzi)

WEST INDIAN CHOCOLATE ICE CREAM

2 quarts milk, divided	4 teaspoons vanilla
5 ounces unsweetened	¼ cup dark rum
chocolate	¾ teaspoon Angostura bitters
2 cups sugar, divided	2 cups half and half cream
2 tablespoons flour	2 cups whipping cream
¾ teaspoon salt	Ice
2 teaspoons cinnamon	Rock salt
4 eggs	

Pour half of milk into top of a large double boiler. Add chocolate, and heat, stirring occasionally, until chocolate is melted and well combined with milk. Combine half of sugar with flour, salt, and cinnamon. Add hot milk slowly and stir until well mixed. Return to double boiler and cook for 10 minutes, stirring frequently. Combine remaining sugar with eggs; add to hot milk mixture; cook until custard coats a silver spoon. Add remaining milk, vanilla, rum and bitters. Chill, preferably overnight. Add the two types of cream, and pour into chilled container of your ice cream freezer. Pack in ice and salt, using 8 parts chopped ice to 1 part rock salt. Freeze, pack, and allow to mellow 2-3 hours. Makes 1 gallon.

Mrs. N. R. Hower (Mary)

SHERRIED ICE CREAM

2 egg whites	½ cup pecans, chopped
½ teaspoon cream of tartar	1 cup shredded coconut
1 cup confectioners' sugar	½ gallon vanilla ice cream,
½ teaspoon vanilla	softened
Dash of salt	½ cup sherry

Beat egg whites and cream of tartar. Add sugar, vanilla, salt, nuts and coconut. Spread on greased foil on baking sheet. Bake in 350 degree oven for 20-30 minutes. Crumble and mix with vanilla ice cream and sherry.

Mrs. Mary L. McDowell

CANTALOUPE ICE

1 3-pound cantaloupe	½ cup dry sherry
¼ cup sugar	1 tablespoon lime juice

In a blender combine the cantaloupe meat with sugar, sherry, and lime juice. Blend until smooth. Freeze. Serves 6-8.

Mrs. George G. Trask (Connie)

CRANBERRY SHERBET

1 tablespoon gelatin
½ cup cold water
4 cups cranberries
2½ cups water

2 cups sugar
⅓ cup lemon juice
⅓ cup orange juice

Turn refrigerator to coldest setting. Sprinkle gelatin over ½ cup cold water to soften. Cook cranberries in 2½ cups water, covered until skins pop open. Force through colander or sieve. Add sugar and gelatin mixture and heat until dissolved. Cool. Add lemon juice and orange juice. Turn into two ice trays (without dividers). Freeze until firm. Take out of trays and beat mixture until thick and mushy. Return to trays and freeze. Especially good with turkey dinners at Thanksgiving and Christmas.

Mrs. Gene Grace (Beth)

FROZEN CHOCOLATE CHARLOTTE

2 packages lady fingers
½ cup white crème de menthe
1 8-ounce package semi-sweet
    chocolate
6 egg yolks, beaten
½ cup sugar

3 tablespoons instant coffee
½ cup boiling water
1 teaspoon vanilla
6 egg whites, beaten
1½ cups whipped cream

Brush surface of 9-inch spring mold with crème de menthe and then line mold with lady fingers. Melt chocolate in top of double boiler. Beat egg yolks in bowl until foamy. Beat in sugar gradually and beat until thick. Dissolve coffee in boiling water. Add coffee, vanilla, and chocolate to egg yolks and sugar. Beat egg whites until stiff. Stir 1 cup egg whites into chocolate to lighten it. Fold in whipped cream which has been blended with rest of egg whites. Serves 12.

Mrs. Sam Clark, Jr. (Carolyn)

LEMON MILK SHERBET

Juice of 10 lemons
Juice of 2 limes
4½ cups sugar

2½ quarts milk
Few grains of salt

Mix juice and sugar. Add gradually to milk and salt, beating with a rotary beater. Curdled appearance will disappear in freezing. Freeze in ice cream churn. Makes 1 gallon.

Mrs. Neil Trask, Jr. (Rebecca)

BISCUIT TORTONI

½ cup confectioners' sugar
1 teaspoon vanilla
3 tablespoons sherry
¼ teaspoon salt
1 pint heavy cream, whipped

2 egg whites
2 tablespoons sugar
1 cup macaroon crumbs
½ cup toasted almonds, sliced

Fold confectioners' sugar, vanilla, and salt into whipped cream. Whip egg whites until foamy; add 2 tablespoons granulated sugar, a tablespoon at a time, whipping until the mixture is stiff. Fold beaten egg whites and macaroon crumbs into cream mixture. Spoon into small paper souffle cups. Sprinkle tops with almonds. Freeze until firm. Serves 6-8.

Mrs. William C. Pitt, Jr. (Alta)

PECAN TORTONI

2 cups Cool Whip
¾ cup macaroons, crushed
½ cup pecans, finely chopped

2 tablespoons confectioners' sugar
4 tablespoons light rum
Maraschino cherries

In large bowl put one half Cool Whip and add macaroons and pecans (reserve 2 or 3 teaspoons pecans for garnish). To other half of Cool Whip add confectioners' sugar and rum, then fold the two mixtures together. Spoon into aluminum muffin cups or freezer-proof dessert cups. Sprinkle with remaining pecans and top with cherries. Freeze until ready to serve. Serves 6.

Mrs. William Firth (Louise)

Pies and Pastry

CHOCOLATE ANGEL PIE

2 egg whites
¼ teaspoon salt
¼ teaspoon cream of tartar

½ cup sugar
1 teaspoon vanilla
½ cup nuts, chopped

FILLING:
1 4-ounce bar German
    chocolate

3 tablespoons water
½ pint heavy cream, whipped

Beat egg whites with salt and cream of tartar until stiff. Beat in sugar a spoonful at a time. Beat in vanilla drop by drop. Fold in nuts. Spread meringue mixture in a buttered 8-inch pie plate, having mixture higher around edge. Bake 1 hour at 300 degrees. Prepare the filling by placing water and chocolate, broken into pieces, in a saucepan over low heat. Melt the chocolate and blend with water. Cool this chocolate mixture and then blend this into the whipped cream. Place the filling in the meringue shell after it has been allowed to cool. Refrigerate 2 hours or more before serving. Serves 6.

Mrs. Colum J. Boyland (Deo)

CHOCOLATE MOCHA PIE

2 squares baking chocolate
½ cup coffee, very strong
    and hot
1 envelope plain gelatin
½ cup water, cold
4 egg yolks
½ cup sugar
½ teaspoon salt

1 teaspoon vanilla
½ cup sugar
4 egg whites, stiffly beaten
1 10-inch pie shell, baked
½ pint heavy cream
3 tablespoons sugar
Chocolate, grated

Melt the chocolate in the coffee over low heat. Soften the gelatin in the cold water and add to the chocolate/coffee mixture. Stir until gelatin dissolves. Add egg yolks beaten lightly with ½ cup sugar. Add salt and vanilla. Cool. Beat remaining ½ cup sugar into egg whites. Fold into chocolate mixture and pour into pie shell. Chill. Top with whipped cream that has been sweetened with 3 tablespoons sugar. Garnish with grated chocolate. Serves 8 to 10.

Mrs. Timothy Doughtie (Betsy)

FRENCH CHOCOLATE PIE

3 egg whites
½ teaspoon cream of tartar
1 cup sugar
1 tablespoon cocoa
12 Ritz crackers, crushed

½ cup pecans or walnuts, chopped
1 teaspoon vanilla
1 cup cream, whipped
1 tablespoon powdered sugar
1 teaspoon cocoa

Beat egg whites until frothy. Add cream of tartar. Gradually add sugar mixed with the 1 tablespoon cocoa. Beat until stiff. Fold in crackers, nuts and vanilla. Bake in a well greased pie plate in 325 degree oven for 25 to 30 minutes or until done. After pie has cooled thoroughly, cover with whipped cream which has been flavored with powdered sugar and cocoa.

Miss Caroline Trask

FRENCH SILK PIE

1 9-inch pie shell, baked and
    cooled
½ cup butter
¾ cup sugar
2 eggs

1 square unsweetened chocolate,
    melted and cooled
1 teaspoon vanilla
½ pint heavy cream, whipped
½ cup pecans, finely chopped

Cream butter until smooth. Gradually add sugar. Add eggs one at a time, beating 3 minutes after each with electric mixer at highest speed. Add chocolate and vanilla. Beat well. Pour into pie shell. Chill for 2 hours. Top with cream. Sprinkle with chopped pecans. Serves 6.

Mrs. James A. Trumps (Blanche)

RICHMOND PIE

1 pie shell, baked
½ cup butter
¾ cup sugar, extra fine
3 ounces semi-sweet chocolate
    bits, melted and cooled

1 teaspoon vanilla
2 eggs
½ pint whipping cream, whipped
1 tablespoon unsweetened
    chocolate shavings

Cream the butter with the sugar. Add the chocolate bits, vanilla and 1 egg. Beat 5 minutes. Add the second egg and beat another 5 minutes. Pour into pie shell and refrigerate 4 to 5 hours. Before serving top with whipped cream and chocolate shavings.

Mrs. Matthew Merrens (Roberta)

MAMIE EISENHOWER PIE

MERINGUE:

2 egg whites
⅛ teaspoon cream of tartar

½ cup sugar
½ cup nuts, chopped

Beat egg whites until foamy (cream of tartar added) and add 1 tablespoon of sugar at a time, beating well after each addition. Spread meringue over bottom and sides of buttered 9-inch pie plate, preferably tin, making meringue slightly higher around edge; sprinkle with nuts and bake at 275 degrees for 50 to 60 minutes or until crisp. Let cool while making filling.

FILLING:

1 cup semi-sweet chocolate
  pieces
3 tablespoons coffee, strong
1 teaspoon vanilla

1 cup heavy cream, whipped
Sugar
Vanilla

Melt chocolate in top of double boiler over hot, not boiling water. Stir in coffee; cook, stirring constantly until thick. Stir in vanilla. Whip cream until stiff, and fold into chocolate mixture. Pour into meringue shell; chill 2 or 3 hours or until filling is set enough to cut. Garnish with lightly sweetened whipped cream with small amount of vanilla added. Delicious!

Mrs. Stan Hurt (Gray)

MOTHER'S CHOCOLATE PIE

FILLING:

1 pastry shell, partially baked
2 egg yolks
1 cup milk
1 cup sugar

2 tablespoons cocoa
2 tablespoons flour
2 tablespoons butter
½ teaspoon vanilla

MERINGUE:

3 egg whites
3 tablespoons sugar, optional

½ teaspoon vanilla, optional

Beat egg yolks with milk. Set aside. Mix sugar, cocoa and flour. Set aside. Melt butter in a large iron skillet over medium heat. Add sugar-cocoa-butter mixture. Mix well. Add egg-milk mixture, stirring constantly. Increase heat until filling begins to thicken, then decrease heat. Continue to cook until very thick, stirring constantly. Add vanilla. Pour into partially baked pie shell. For meringue, beat egg whites until stiff. Sugar and vanilla may be added to stiff whites, if desired. Beat again. Spread over pie. Brown in 350 oven. Variation: Line dish with lady fingers. Sprinkle generously with cream sherry or Cognac. Use same filling with meringue on top. Serves 6.

Mrs. J. R. Lentz (Virginia)

KEY LIME PIE

FILLING:

4 eggs, separated
1 14-ounce can sweetened
   condensed milk
Green food coloring

½ cup lime juice
2 teaspoons lime peel, grated
1 9-inch graham cracker pie shell

MERINGUE:

3 egg whites
½ teaspoon cream of tartar

½ cup sugar

Beat egg yolks. Stir in milk, lime juice, peel and a few drops of food coloring. Beat 1 egg white until stiff. Fold into milk mixture. Turn into pie shell. Beat egg whites with cream of tartar until foamy. Gradually add sugar beating until stiff. Spread meringue on top of pie sealing edges to crust. Bake at 350 degrees for 15 minutes or until brown. Cool and then chill in refrigerator. Serves 6.

Mrs. H. Patrick Cotton (Jean)

LEMON ANGEL PIE

CRUST:

4 egg whites, stiffly beaten
¼ teaspoon cream of tartar

1 cup sugar
½ teaspoon vanilla

Beat egg whites until stiff. Beat cream of tartar and sugar into egg whites a spoonful at a time. Beat in vanilla drop by drop and continue beating for a few minutes. Spread in 9-inch buttered pie pan, having mixture higher about edges. Bake 10 minutes in 275 degree oven and then 30 minutes at 250 degrees.

FILLING:

4 egg yolks
4 tablespoons sugar

4 tablespoons lemon juice
½ pint heavy cream, whipped

Beat yolks until thick and light with sugar and lemon juice. Cook over hot water until slightly thickened. Cool. Spread on meringue shell. Cover with thin layer unsweetened whipped cream. Put in refrigerator for several hours. Serves 6 to 8.

Mrs. Richard G. Price, Jr. (Mary Jo)

LEMON PIE

1 cup sugar
1½ tablespoons flour
½ cup butter, melted

2 eggs, beaten
2 lemons, juice and grated rind
1 9-inch pie shell, partially baked

Mix sugar and flour. Add this to melted butter. Add beaten eggs, lemon juice and rind. Pour into partially baked pie shell. Bake at 350 degrees for 25 to 30 minutes. Serves 6.

Miss Lois Fuller

LEMON CHESS PIE

2 pie shells, partially baked
2 cups sugar
2 tablespoons flour
2 tablespoons corn meal
4 eggs

4 tablespoons butter, melted
¼ cup milk
¼ cup lemon juice
1 tablespoon lemon rind

Mix sugar, flour and corn meal. Add eggs one at a time, beating thoroughly after each addition. Gradually add the 3 liquids. Add lemon rind. Pour into pie shells. Bake at 350 degrees for 35 minutes or until set.

Mrs. James O. Cook (Cynthia)

LEMON MERINGUE PIE

FILLING:
1 cup sugar
5 tablespoons plain flour
1 cup water, boiling
2 egg yolks

Pinch of salt
1 tablespoon butter
2 lemons, juice and grated rinds
1 pie crust, baked

MERINGUE:
2 egg whites

2 tablespoons sugar

In a double boiler, combine sugar and flour and stir in boiling water. Cook until clear. Beat yolks. Stir slowly into clear mixture cooking until thick. Remove from fire and add salt, butter, lemon juice and grated rinds. Pour into cooled crust and top with egg whites and sugar which have been beaten until stiff. Place in 350 degree oven and brown meringue.

Mrs. I. T. Matthews (Mae)

PECAN PIE I

½ cup butter
¾ cup sugar
2 eggs
1 teaspoon vanilla

1 cup dark Karo syrup
1 cup nuts, chopped
1 pie shell, unbaked

Cream butter and sugar. Beat in eggs and add the vanilla, syrup and nuts. Pour into pie shell and bake at 350 degrees for 40 to 45 minutes. Place on a rack to cool before cutting. Serves 6-8.

Mrs. Paul M. Cooper (Melba)

PECAN PIE II

½ cup butter
1 16-ounce box light brown sugar
2 tablespoons corn meal
2 tablespoons water

4 eggs, lightly beaten
1 teaspoon vanilla
2 cups pecans
2 pie shells

Melt butter in saucepan. Remove from heat and add all other ingredients. Stir well. Pour into pie shells. Bake at 300 degrees for 1 hour. Cool before slicing.

Mrs. Russell A. Harley (Kitty)

ORANGE PECAN PIE

1 cup light Karo syrup
4 tablespoons butter, melted
4 tablespoons sugar
¼ teaspoon salt
2 tablespoons orange juice

1 teaspoon orange rind, grated
3 eggs, slightly beaten
¾ cup whole pecans
1 9-inch pastry shell, unbaked

Mix syrup, butter and sugar. Add salt, orange juice, orange rind, eggs and pecans, stirring carefully. Pour mixture into pie shell. Bake 15 minutes in 400 degree oven. Lower temperature to 350 degrees and bake 30 minutes more. Serves 6.

Mrs. S. W. Koller (Paulette)

SOUTHERN NUT PIE

20 Ritz crackers, finely crushed
½ cup sugar
¾ cup nuts, chopped
3 egg whites
¼ teaspoon cream of tartar

½ cup sugar
1 teaspoon vanilla
Whipped cream
Chocolate, grated

Mix crackers with sugar and nuts. Fold in egg whites, stiffly beaten with cream of tartar, sugar and vanilla. Pour mixture into a 9-inch pie pan. This pie makes its own crust. Bake 20 minutes at 350 degrees. Allow to cool and top with whipped cream and grated chocolate. Refrigerate 3 to 4 hours before serving.

Mrs. W. K. Pillow, Jr. (Anne)

DEEP DISH APPLE PIE

6 tart apples, peeled and
    chopped
½ cup sugar
½ cup brown sugar
½ teaspoon cinnamon or
    nutmeg

1 lemon rind, grated
1 orange rind, grated
4 tablespoons butter
Pie pastry, rolled thin
    to fit baking dish

Place apples in bottom of baking dish. Combine sugar, brown sugar, cinnamon or nutmeg, lemon rind and orange rind and sprinkle over apples. Dot with butter. Top with pastry. Bake at 425 degrees for 40 to 45 minutes. Serves 6.

Mrs. Ray Williams (Hedy)

SWEDISH APPLE CRUMBLE

5 to 7 apples, peeled and sliced
¾ cup sugar, divided into
    fourths

1 teaspoon cinnamon
¾ teaspoon flour
4 tablespoons butter

Place half of apples into shallow 1½-quart baking dish. Combine ¼ cup sugar and all of cinnamon and sprinkle half of this mixture over apples. Repeat process until all apples and mixture are used up. Combine flour and remaining ½ cup of sugar. Cut in butter with 2 knives or whisk until the mixture resembles coarse meal. Bake at 425 degrees until top is brown (about 15 minutes). Serve hot with ice cream or custard. Serves 6 to 8.

Mrs. Claude N. Dinkins (Cathy)

ST. LOUIS APPLE PIE

1 egg, beaten
¾ cup sugar
½ cup flour
1 teaspoon baking powder
¼ teaspoon salt

½ teaspoon vanilla
1 cup apple, diced
½ cup nuts, chopped
Whipped cream or vanilla ice
   cream

Mix together and bake in a buttered 8-inch pie plate for 25 minutes at 375 degrees. Top with whipped cream or vanilla ice cream. Serves 6.

Mrs. Edward M. Dooley (Martha)

PEACH ANGEL PIE

Graham cracker crust
3 egg whites
¼ teaspoon cream of tartar
¼ teaspoon salt
½ teaspoon vinegar

1 cup granulated sugar
2 cups fresh peaches, peeled and
   sliced
1 cup heavy cream, whipped
1 cup shredded coconut

Beat egg whites until frothy with cream of tartar, vinegar and salt. Add sugar gradually and beat until stiff peaks form. Spread over graham cracker crust. Bake at 300 degrees for 40 minutes. When cool, spread peaches over meringue. Toast ¼ cup of coconut until brown in oven (325 degrees for 10 minutes). Whip the cream and add the remaining ¾ cup coconut to cream. Spread on top of peaches. Sprinkle toasted coconut on top. Chill in refrigerator for at least 12 hours. Serves 6 to 8.

Mrs. David McEwan (Alice)

PEACH PIE-FRENCH GALETTE STYLE

This version of French Galette has a rich crust that is the perfect setting for ripe peaches.

1 cup flour
½ cup brown sugar
½ cup white sugar
5½ tablespoons butter

5 cups peaches, sliced
2 tablespoons brandy
Sour cream
Brown sugar

Mix flour and sugars and then cream with butter. Line a pie tin with this mixture. Bake at 400 degrees for 5 minutes and then reduce heat to 325 degrees and bake 10 minutes longer. Fill crust with peaches which have been sprinkled with brandy. Cover lightly with sour cream and sprinkle with brown sugar. Serves 6.

Mrs. Edward F. Brewster (Jane)

FRESH PEACH PIE

¼ cup sugar
1 tablespoon lemon juice
2 cups peaches, peeled and
  sliced
3 tablespoons corn starch

2 teaspoons butter
¼ teaspoon almond extract
1 9-inch pie shell, baked
½ pint heavy cream, whipped

Add sugar and lemon juice to peaches and let sit about 1 hour as juice forms. Measure. If there is not enough juice to make 1 cup, add enough water to the juice to make 1 cup. Cook with the corn starch until thick and clear. Add the butter and almond extract. Cool slightly and add sliced peaches. Serve in a baked pie shell with whipped cream. Serves 6.

Mrs. William S. Tilley (Mary Ann)

RUTHIE'S OLD FASHIONED PEACH PIE

1 9-inch pastry shell
6 to 8 peaches, peeled and
  halved
½ cup sugar

2 tablespoons flour
1 egg yolk
3 tablespoons light cream

Line pie pan with pastry. Arrange peach halves, cut side up, close together over pastry. Mix sugar and flour and sprinkle over fruit. Mix egg yolk and cream and drizzle over fruit. Bake on lower shelf of a hot oven (450 degrees) about 25 minutes. Serve plain, with cream or ice cream. Serves 6.

Mrs. John Morrison (Marion)

PEACH COBBLER WITH SAUCE

½ cup butter
1 cup flour
1 cup sugar
2 teaspoons baking powder

¾ cup milk
7 to 9 fresh peaches, sliced
4 tablespoons sugar
½ cup water

SAUCE:
Butter, melted
Confectioners' sugar

Sherry, to taste

Melt butter in 13 x 9-inch (or smaller) baking dish. In mixing bowl, combine flour, sugar and baking powder. Add milk and pour over melted butter. Place peaches on top of mixture and sprinkle in 4 tablespoons sugar. Over this pour ½ cup of water. Bake 1 hour at 325 degrees or until brown crust forms. Serves 6.

Mrs. F. William Scheper III (Jean)

FRESH PEACH COBBLER

FILLING:

6 large ripe peaches, peeled
and sliced
½ cup sugar (If peaches are
not very sweet, add a little
additional sugar)

3 tablespoons tapioca or corn
starch
Dash of nutmeg
Dash of salt
2 tablespoons butter

CRUST:

¼ cup shortening
1 cup self-rising flour

2 tablespoons sugar
¼ cup milk

To peaches add sugar, tapioca, nutmeg and salt. Stir lightly and set aside. Cut shortening into flour and sugar. Add milk and mix until flour is just dampened. Pat out to ¼-inch on floured surface. Cut into strips about 2 inches wide and line sides of 1-quart baking dish. Add peach mixture. Dot with butter. Cut remaining dough with biscuit cutter and place rounds close together on top of peaches. Sprinkle with a little sugar and nutmeg. Bake at 400 degrees for 10 minutes. Reduce heat to 325° and bake for 25 minutes. Serve warm. Serves 6.

Mrs. Stanley Waskiewicz (Betty)

STRAWBERRY MERINGUE TARTS

3 egg whites
½ teaspoon almond extract
½ teaspoon cream of tartar
Dash of salt

1 cup sugar, sifted
1 cup sour cream
40 fresh strawberries

Let egg whites stand at room temperature for approximately 1 hour before beating. Combine egg whites, almond extract, cream of tartar, and salt and with electric beater on high, beat mixture until frothy. Gradually add sugar, 1 tablespoon at a time, beating until glossy and stiff peaks form. Do not under-beat. Drop meringue by tablespoons onto a cookie sheet which has been covered with heavy brown paper or a parchment sheet. Using back of small spoon, make a depression in top of each meringue. This depression will hold strawberries and sour cream after baked. Bake meringues at 250 degrees for about 30 minutes. Turn off oven; leave meringues in oven with door closed for 1 hour. Cool meringues away from draft. These may be covered with wax paper and kept in a cool place for at least 24 hours. When ready to serve, place 1 teaspoon sour cream in each meringue. Top each with a whole strawberry. Since these meringues are small, they may be served as refreshments for a party. Yields 40.

Mrs. Temple R. Harris

STRAWBERRY PIE

1 8-inch pie shell, baked
1 quart strawberries
1 cup sugar

3 tablespoons cornstarch
Heavy cream, whipped

Place half of the strawberries in shell. Cook the remaining half with sugar and cornstarch until thick. Pour this mixture over raw strawberries. Put in refrigerator. Serve with whipped cream. Serves 6.

Mrs. Harold E. Trask (Margaret)

MILE HIGH PIE

1 pint heavy cream
1 teaspoon vanilla
1 10-ounce package
   strawberries, frozen
1 10-ounce package
   raspberries, frozen

3/4 cup sugar
3 egg whites
1 tablespoon lemon juice
Dash of salt
2 9-inch pie shells, baked

Whip cream, adding vanilla. Place remaining ingredients in another large mixing bowl and beat at high speed until mixture remains in stiff peaks (about 10 to 15 minutes). Fold in whipped cream. Place in pie shells. Place in freezer for at least 4 hours. Remove about 15 minutes before serving and place in refrigerator. Serves 12.

Mrs. William R. Satterfield (Lorna)

ANGEL FOOD PIE

1 9 inch pie shell, baked
1 cup crushed pineapple,
   drained
1 cup sugar
5 tablespoons cornstarch
1 cup water, cold

1/2 teaspoon salt
4 egg whites, stiffly beaten
1/2 pint heavy cream, whipped
1 tablespoon confectioners' sugar
1/4 cup walnuts, finely chopped

Cook together in the top of a double boiler the pineapple, sugar, water, cornstarch and salt. When mixture is thick remove from heat and cool in refrigerator until completely chilled. This portion can be made the day before. Fold egg whites into the chilled pineapple mixture. Mix thoroughly. Pour this mixture into the baked pie shell. Add the confectioners' sugar to the cream. Spoon the whipped cream over the pineapple mixture and sprinkle with walnuts. Chill about 1 hour before serving.

Mrs. Paul Thomas (Dorothy)

BUTTERMILK PIE

2 9-inch pie shells
2 cups sugar
½ cup butter, melted
3 eggs, beaten

1 cup buttermilk
2 tablespoons flour
1 tablespoon lemon extract
1 tablespoon lemon juice

Mix all together and pour in pie shells. Bake 30 minutes at 350 degrees. Let stay in oven until cool. Makes 2 pies. Freezes well.

Mrs. Mary L. McDowell

CHEESE KUCHEN

DOUGH:
1½ cups self-rising flour
¾ cup sugar
½ cup butter

2 eggs, beaten
1 teaspoon vanilla

CHEESE FILLING:
1½ pounds cottage cheese
8 tablespoons cornstarch
¼ teaspoon salt
12 ounces of sour cream

3 lemons, rind and juice
1¾ cups sugar
5 eggs, separated

Dough: Sift flour. Add sugar. Work in butter with fingers. Add eggs and vanilla. Mix well. Put in bottom and sides of casserole (13½ x 8¾ x 1¾-inch). Filling: Press cheese through ricer. Add cornstarch and salt. Add sour cream. Add juice and grated rind of lemons. Add sugar. Mix well. Add beaten egg yolks. Beat egg whites and fold into mixture. Pour mixture on top of the dough and bake in 350 degree oven for 1 hour or until well set and browned at bottom.

Mrs. Herbert Keyserling (Harriet)

COCONUT PIE

4 eggs
1½ cups sugar
½ cup self-rising flour
4 tablespoons butter, melted

1 teaspoon vanilla
2 cups milk
1 7-ounce can coconut

Mix all ingredients together. Pour into two 8-inch greased pie pans. Bake at 350 degrees for 30 to 40 minutes.

Mrs. Jim Chassereau (Belinda)

CRÈME DE MÊNTHE ICE CREAM PIE

5½ tablespoons butter,
    softened
2 cups chocolate wafer crumbs

3 pints vanilla ice cream
5 tablespoons green crème de
    mênthe

Combine crumbs with butter and press into 10-inch spring form pan or pie plate. Chill 1 hour. Place ice cream in large bowl to soften. Pour crème de mênthe over it. Swirl it through the ice cream. Pour into pie shell. Freeze. Serves 8 to 10.

FUDGE SAUCE:

3 ounces unsweetened
    chocolate
½ cup water
¾ cup sugar

¼ teaspoon salt
4½ tablespoons butter
¾ teaspoon vanilla

Combine chocolate with water. Cook over low heat. Stir occasionally until chocolate is melted. Add sugar and salt. Cook, stirring constantly until sugar is melted and mixture thickens (about 5 minutes). Remove from heat. Stir in butter and vanilla. Cool. Drizzle over top of pie and return pie to freezer until firm. Serve remaining sauce hot with pie.

Mrs. C. Blackburn Brewer (Frances)

ICE CREAM PIE

1 graham cracker pie shell
1 cup semi-sweet chocolate
   pieces
½ cup whipping cream

½ teaspoon vanilla
½ pint chocolate ice cream
1 quart vanilla ice cream

Chill crust in freezer. In a small saucepan melt chocolate pieces in whipping cream over low heat, stirring constantly; stir in vanilla, chill until thickened. Soften ice cream. Spoon chocolate ice cream into crust; spread ¾ of the chocolate sauce over ice cream. Return to freezer to harden. Spoon vanilla ice cream over chocolate sauce; drizzle remaining chocolate sauce over top of pie. Freeze.

Mrs. Henry Chambers (Betty)

GLENWOOD PLANTATION SHERRY PIE

CRUST:
Almond macaroons

Sherry

Line bottom and sides of pie plate with macaroons which have been soaked in sherry wine.

FILLING:
¾ cup sugar
1 tablespoon flour
Pinch salt
¾ cup sherry

4 egg yolks
4 egg whites, stiffly beaten
Heavy cream, whipped
Almonds, toasted

In top of double boiler, cook sugar, flour, salt, sherry and egg yolks until thickened. Cool mixture. Fold in egg whites. Pour over pie crust. Spread with whipped cream, and garnish with toasted almonds. Serves 6.

Mrs. Richard G. Price, Jr. (Mary Jo)

SWEET POTATO PIE I

3 cups sweet potatoes, cooked
1 cup butter
3 cups sugar
4 egg yolks

1 cup milk or cream
1 teaspoon vanilla
1 9-inch pie shell, unbaked

Mash hot potatoes in mixer. Add butter. When butter has melted, add sugar and egg yolks one at a time. Beat thoroughly after each addition. Add milk and vanilla. When thoroughly mixed, pour into pie shell. Bake 10 minutes at 400 degrees, then 35 minutes at 375 degrees. Serves 6 to 8.

Mrs. W. R. Von Harten (Jean)

SWEET POTATO PIE II

3 9-inch pie crusts, uncooked
7 large sweet potatoes boiled,
   peeled and put through
   ricer
1 cup butter
2 cups sugar

6½ ounces evaporated milk,
   enough to soften
Vanilla to taste
Nutmeg to taste
Meringue

Mix hot riced sweet potatoes with butter, sugar, and evaporated milk. Add vanilla and nutmeg to taste. Bake at 350 degrees until done, cover with meringue and brown. Makes 3 9-inch pies if topped with meringue.

Mrs. J. D. Lockwood (Josephine)

SAPPHIRE VALLEY CHEESE PIE

PIE CRUST:

1½ cups fine graham cracker
   crumbs
½ cup butter, melted
½ cup pecans, chopped

2 tablespoons white sugar
1 tablespoon brown sugar

Mix all ingredients well. Press into pie plate and chill.

FILLING:

1 8-ounce package cream
   cheese
2 tablespoons lemon juice

½ cup sugar
2 eggs

Beat cheese, lemon juice and sugar until creamy. Add eggs, 1 at a time, beating well after each addition. Pour into pie shell. Bake 20 minutes at 350 degrees. Cool.

TOPPING:

1 pint sour cream
1 teaspoon vanilla

3 tablespoons sugar
¼ teaspoon mace

Mix all ingredients and spread over pie. Bake 10 minutes at 325 degrees. Chill. Serves 8.

Mrs. C. Blackburn Brewer (Frances)

SOUR CREAM RAISIN PIE

1 cup raisins
Water
1 cup sugar
1 cup sour cream
3 egg yolks

3 tablespoons cornstarch
Pinch of salt
1 teaspoon vanilla
1 pie shell, cooked

MERINGUE:
3 egg whites

3 tablespoons sugar

Cover raisins with water and cook until water is almost evaporated. Set aside. Mix together sugar, sour cream, egg yolks, cornstarch and salt. Stir constantly over medium heat until thickened. Add vanilla and raisins. Pour into cooked pie shell. Beat egg whites until stiff. Add sugar. Top with meringue and bake at 350 degrees until lightly browned. Serves 6 to 8.

Mrs. J. E. McTeer, Jr. (Gail)

EASY NO-FAIL PIE CRUST

¾ cup Crisco shortening
¼ cup water, boiling
1 tablespoon milk

2 cups flour
1 teaspoon salt

In a deep bowl whip shortening into boiling water until fluffy. Whip in milk. Add flour and salt, blending until moistened. Form into a ball. Divide in half. Roll out dough on floured wax paper ⅛-inch thick. Peel crust from wax paper onto 9-inch pan. Pierce crust with fork before baking. Bake at 350 degrees for about 10 minutes or until golden brown. Makes 2 pie shells.

Mrs. Ted Ledford (Suzi)

NEVER FAIL MERINGUE PIE CRUST

5 egg whites
¼ tablespoon salt
½ tablespoon cream of tartar

1½ cups sugar
1 teaspoon vanilla

Beat egg whites until foamy. Add salt and cream of tartar. Now beat until egg whites stand in soft peaks. Add sugar gradually and continue beating until very stiff. Add vanilla. Grease a 9-inch pie pan and flour it. Spread meringue over pie plate and put into a preheated 400 degree oven. Turn off immediately and leave for 4 hours. Do not open oven. This takes 10 minutes to prepare and if done at night can be ready in the morning. Use any desired fruit, ice cream, etc., for filling.

Mrs. Barney Rickenbacker (Florence)

PIPSISSEWA

Cakes and Frostings

CHEESE CAKE

7 double graham crackers,
   crushed
4 8-ounce packages cream
   cheese
1½ cups sugar

¾ cup milk
4 eggs
1 pint sour cream
1 tablespoon vanilla

Butter sides of 9-inch spring pan lightly. Line bottom of pan with graham cracker crumbs. Mix cream cheese, sugar, and milk. Add remaining ingredients, adding eggs one at a time. Bake 1 hour in preheated 375 degree oven. When done, let cake stand in oven 30 minutes with oven door open. Remove from oven and let cool to touch. DO NOT remove sides from pan. When cool, put in refrigerator and let chill, preferably overnight. Cake is liquid until thoroughly chilled. Remove from pan and serve.

Mrs. Ray DeCastro (June)

CRUSTLESS CHEESE CAKE

1 pound cottage cheese
1 pound cream cheese
1 cup sugar
4 eggs, slightly beaten
1½ tablespoons lemon juice
1 teaspoon vanilla

½ cup sugar
3 tablespoons cornstarch
3 tablespoons flour
½ cup butter, melted
1 pint sour cream

Press cottage cheese and cream cheese through sieve into bowl. Stir in 1 cup of sugar. Add eggs, lemon juice, and vanilla. Sift ½ cup sugar with cornstarch and flour. Gradually add to cheese mixture. Add butter and sour cream. Blend thoroughly. Pour into 9-inch greased spring form pan. Bake at 300 degrees for 2 hours; should be firm. Turn off heat. Open oven door. Cool cake in oven. (It takes several hours.) Chill.

Mrs. Frederick Guile (Allie)

SPECIAL CHEESE CAKE

½ cup butter, room
    temperature
1½ cups graham cracker
    crumbs
⅓ cup sugar
2¼ pounds cream cheese,
    room temperature

1½ cups sugar
4 eggs
2 teaspoons vanilla
2 teaspoons lemon juice

Combine the butter, crumbs, and ⅓ cup sugar to make crust and line a 9-inch spring form pan. Refrigerate while making cheese cake. Put the cream cheese, 1½ cups sugar, eggs and flavorings in a large bowl. Beat for 30-45 minutes and pour over crust. Bake at 375 degrees for 35-45 minutes.

Mrs. Peter Fuge (Meredith)

AUNT FANNIE'S JAPANESE FRUIT CAKE

1 cup butter
2 cups sugar
6 eggs, separated
3½ cups flour
1 teaspoon baking powder
1 cup water (if batter is stiff,
    add a little more water)
1 tablespoon cinnamon

1 tablespoon cloves
1 tablespoon allspice
1 tablespoon nutmeg
1 cup raisins
1½ cups citron, chopped
1 small wine glass of brandy
Flour

Cream butter and sugar together. Add one egg yolk at a time, beating after each addition. Sift dry ingredients and add alternating with water. Beat egg whites until stiff and fold into mixture. Fill two 9-inch layer cake pans with about ½ of the batter. To the remaining batter, add the other ingredients dusting the raisins and citron with flour first. Pour into two additional 9-inch layer pans. Bake at 350 degrees for 30 minutes.

JAPANESE FRUIT CAKE FILLING:

1 cup coconut, grated
2 cups sugar
1 cup boiling water

1 tablespoon cornstarch
Juice and rind of 1 lemon

Mix all ingredients together and boil for about 20 minutes. Spread between layers.

Mrs. Jack D. Pollitzer (Toni)

LEARMONT'S FRUIT CAKE

¼ pound candied orange peel, finely chopped
¼ pound candied lemon peel, finely chopped
1 pound citron, finely chopped
1 pound candied red cherries
1 pound candied green cherries
¾ pound candied red pineapple
¾ pound candied green pineapple
1 pound white raisins
1 pound flour, divided
1 pound whole pecans
1 pound butter
1 pound sugar
12 eggs, separated
1 teaspoon baking powder
1 4-ounce jar of jelly (any flavor)
2 ounces bourbon
1 teaspoon lemon extract
1 teaspoon vanilla extract
1 teaspoon mace

Cut fruit with ¼ of the flour. Mix fruits and nuts together well. Cream butter and sugar well, then add egg yolks one at a time. Add flour and baking powder, jelly, whiskey and flavorings. Fold in stiffly beaten egg whites. Pour batter over fruit and carefully fold batter into fruit until well mixed. Grease and flour three tube pans and carefully pour cake batter into them. Put pans of hot water large enough to hold cake pans into oven, cover loosely with foil and bake at 300 degrees for 2-3 hours until firm. Remove foil and bake until brown.

Mrs. O. Stanley Smith (Connie)

ORANGE FRUIT CAKE

2 oranges, rind and juice
2 cups sugar, divided
2 cups raisins
3 cups pecans
1 cup butter, softened
4 eggs
4 cups flour
2 teaspoons soda
1 teaspoon salt
1⅓ cups sour milk*
2 teaspoons vanilla

Combine orange juice and 1 cup sugar. Stir several times while cake is cooking. Put orange rinds, raisins, and pecans through food grinder. Cream butter and 1 cup sugar well. Add eggs to butter mixture and beat until fluffy. Sift flour, soda, and salt together. Add flour mixture to butter mixture alternately with sour milk. Mix well and fold in fruit and nuts. Lastly add flavoring. Turn batter into a greased and floured tube pan. Bake 1½ hours in 325 degree oven. Pour juice mixture over hot cake and let remain in tube pan until all juice is absorbed and partially cooled.

*To make sour milk, place 5 teaspoons vinegar in measuring cup and add enough milk to measure 1⅓ cups.

Mrs. Laurance Davis (Sarah)

WEIHNACHTSKUCKEN (NUT AND FRUIT CAKE)

1 pound pitted dates
1 pound pecans, shelled
½ pound candied cherries
½ pound candied pineapple
1 cup sugar

1 cup flour
2 teaspoons baking powder
4 eggs, beaten
2 teaspoons vanilla

Leave dates, nuts and cherries whole. Cut pineapple rings in pieces. Mix and sift dry ingredients over fruit and nuts. Pour beaten eggs over the fruit and nuts. Mix well. Add vanilla and mix well. Line loaf pan with wax paper. Put mixture in pan and bake at 275 degrees for 1½ hours. Let stand 2-3 days before cutting.

Mrs. B. D. Kitchings, Jr. (Kitty)

OLD FASHIONED POUND CAKE

2 cups cake flour
½ teaspoon baking powder
1 cup butter, at room
   temperature

1¾ cups sugar
5 large eggs, at room temperature
1½ teaspoons vanilla

Grease and flour a tube cake pan (about 3-inch deep). Sift the flour before measuring. Put the flour into a sifter along with the baking powder. Sift 3 more times. In large bowl of electric mixer, cream butter slightly on low speed. Slowly add sugar and beat until light and fluffy. On very low speed, add eggs one at a time, alternating with flour mixture, beating 1 minute after each addition. Blend thoroughly but do not over beat. Add vanilla and beat until batter is smooth and creamy. Spoon batter into pan and place pan in center of 300 degree oven. Bake for 1 hour and 15 minutes minimum. Do not open oven door for at least 1 hour as cake will fall. Remove from oven and let cool in pan on rack for 5 minutes. Carefully remove from pan and let cool completely on rack. Wrap well in waxed paper and foil. Store in covered tin. Keeps well.

Mrs. Arthur Marscher (Gladys)

SOUR CREAM POUND CAKE

1 cup butter	¼ teaspoon salt
3 cups sugar	¼ teaspoon soda
6 eggs, separated	¼ teaspoon baking powder
8 ounces sour cream	¼ teaspoon mace
3 cups flour	

Cream butter and sugar. Add egg yolks one at a time and beat until lemon colored. Sift flour with salt, soda and baking powder. Add flour mixture and sour cream alternately to butter mixture. Beat egg whites stiff and fold into mixture. Season with mace. Bake in greased tube pan at 300 degrees for 1½ hours.

Mrs. W. Brantley Harvey (Thelma)

GERMAN CHOCOLATE POUND CAKE

1 4-ounce bar German chocolate	½ teaspoon salt
1 cup butter	1 teaspoon baking powder
½ cup shortening	1 cup milk
3 cups sugar	1 teaspoon vanilla flavoring
5 eggs	1 teaspoon lemon flavoring
3 cups flour	1 teaspoon almond flavoring

Melt chocolate in small pan over low heat. Cream butter, shortening, and sugar until fluffy. Add melted chocolate to creamed mixture. Beat eggs and add to mixture. Sift flour, salt and baking powder together. Add milk and flour mixture alternately to batter. Add flavorings. Bake in a greased and floured tube pan at 325 degrees for 1 hour and 45 minutes.

Jane Dowling Fender

DEVIL'S FOOD CAKE

1 teaspoon salt	2 squares chocolate, unsweetened, melted
½ cup shortening	1 teaspoon vanilla
2¼ cups flour, sifted	1½ cups buttermilk
1¾ cups sugar	3 eggs
1½ teaspoons soda	

Place shortening in mixing bowl. Sift flour, sugar, soda, and salt into bowl with shortening. Add vanilla and one cup milk. Beat 2 minutes. Add eggs, melted chocolate and remaining ½ cup milk. Beat 2 minutes. Pour into two greased 9-inch cake pans and bake at 350 degrees for about 30 minutes.

Mrs. George E. Baucom, Jr. (Martha)

MARGARET'S CHOCOLATE CAKE WITH CHOCOLATE ICING

½ cup butter, softened
1¼ cups sugar
2 yolks plus one whole egg
1¾ cups plain flour
1 cup milk

1 teaspoon soda
1 teaspoon salt
2 squares chocolate, unsweetened,
    melted
1 teaspoon vanilla

Preheat oven to 350 degrees. Cream butter and sugar. Add eggs. Add all dry ingredients alternating with milk. Add melted chocolate and vanilla. Grease two cake pans with shortening and lightly flour them. Bake for 20-25 minutes (cake will begin to leave side of cake pans). Cool in cake pans, right sides up on racks. In warm weather, freeze briefly before frosting. The frosting stays where you put it for a beautiful cake.

CHOCOLATE ICING:

3 squares bitter chocolate
⅓ cup butter
1 16-ounce package confectioners'
    sugar

7 tablespoons milk
1 teaspoon vanilla

Melt chocolate and butter in top of double boiler. Combine sugar and milk with electric beater. To this add melted ingredients and vanilla. Beat until mixed. Frost cake.

Mrs. H. E. Trask (Margaret)

PICNIC CHOCOLATE CAKE

2 cups flour
2 cups sugar
1 cup margarine or butter
4 tablespoons cocoa
1 cup water

½ teaspoon salt
2 eggs
½ cup buttermilk
1 teaspoon vanilla
1 teaspoon soda

Mix flour and sugar in bowl. In saucepan put margarine, cocoa, and water. Bring to a boil. Pour this mixture over flour and sugar. Add remaining ingredients, soda last. Bake for approximately 20 minutes at 400 degrees in a 9 x 13-inch pan. Ice immediately with chocolate sauce.

CHOCOLATE ICING:

½ cup margarine or butter
6 tablespoons milk
4 tablespoons cocoa

1 1-pound box confectioners' sugar
1 teaspoon vanilla
1 cup nuts, chopped

Put margarine, milk, and cocoa in a saucepan and bring to a boil. Take off heat and add remaining ingredients. Stir well. Put icing on warm chocolate cake.

Mrs. James M. Gray (Doris)

FILLED DEVIL'S FOOD CAKE

2½ cups cake flour, sifted
1 teaspoon soda
¼ teaspoon salt
1 cup butter
2 cups sugar
5 eggs

3 ounces unsweetened chocolate,
   melted
1 cup sour cream or buttermilk
2 teaspoons vanilla
2 teaspoons rum flavoring

Sift flour once. Add soda and salt and sift three times. Cream butter thoroughly. Add sugar gradually and cream together until light and fluffy. Add eggs and beat mixture well. Add chocolate and blend. Add flour alternately with cream to butter mixture, a small amount at a time. Beat after each addition until smooth. Add flavorings. Bake in three greased 9-inch layer pans at 350 degrees for 25 minutes or until done. Use Raisin and Pecan Filling for this cake and Cream Cheese Icing.

RAISIN AND PECAN FILLING:
½ cup sugar
3 tablespoons flour
1 tablespoon orange rind
½ cup orange juice

¾ cup water
2 cups raisins, ground
⅔ cup toasted pecans, chopped

Cook all of the ingredients except pecans gently for 5 minutes or until thick, stirring constantly. Add pecans, cool to lukewarm before spreading.

CREAM CHEESE ICING:
1 8-ounce package cream
   cheese
2 teaspoons milk
2 cups confectioners' sugar,
   sifted

Grated rind of 1 orange
1 teaspoon orange juice
1 teaspoon lemon juice

Soften cream cheese with milk. Add the confectioners' sugar, one cup at a time; add the orange rind, orange juice and lemon juice. If the mixture is too thin, add more sugar; if too thick, more orange juice.

Fannie Van Sant

CHOCOLATE WHIPPED CREAM CAKE

¾ cup butter or margarine
1¾ cups sugar
1 teaspoon vanilla
3 eggs
1 cup semi-sweet chocolate
   chips

¼ cup water
2¼ cups cake flour
¼ teaspoon salt
1 cup buttermilk
1 teaspoon baking soda

Cream butter, sugar and vanilla until fluffy. Add eggs, one at a time. Add chocolate which has been melted in ¼ cup water. Add flour sifted with salt and buttermilk to which soda has been added. Divide into three 3 x 9-inch pans that have been greased and lined with wax paper. Bake at 375 degrees for 25-30 minutes. When cake is cool, frost with chocolate whipped cream frosting.

CHOCOLATE WHIPPED CREAM FROSTING:
1 pint whipping cream
1 cup semi-sweet chocolate
   chips

2 tablespoons water
¼ cup honey
½ cup almonds, slivered

Whip cream until fluffy. Melt chocolate with water and honey. Cool and fold into cream. Frost cake layers and top and sides of cake. Press slivered almonds over the top of cake. Refrigerate cake. This cake freezes well.

Mrs. Mark Fordham (Virginia)

DATE-COCONUT CAKE

1 pound pitted dates
¼ pound grated coconut
1 cup broken pecans or
   walnuts

1 14-ounce can condensed milk
Pinch salt

Cut dates into 3 or 4 pieces each and put into mixing bowl. Add coconut, nuts, condensed milk and salt. Mix thoroughly but lightly. Line 6 inch square pan with wax paper and pack cake into pan. Bake at 350 degrees about 35 minutes or until golden brown. Remove from pan and *immediately* remove wax paper. If you wish to slice this cake thin, chill before slicing. You may cut this cake into squares and serve with a hard sauce or whipped cream. Keeps if stored in air tight container.

Martha O. Wallbank

FRESH COCONUT CAKE

FILLING:

1 fresh coconut, grated and   Milk
   milk reserved   3 cups sugar

Combine the coconut milk with milk to make 1½ cups liquid. Combine milk and sugar in a saucepan and bring to a boil. Cook until slightly thickened, stirring constantly. Remove from heat and add 2 cups grated coconut. Cool completely.

CAKE:

1 cup butter, softened
2 cups sugar
4 eggs
3 cups plain flour
2 teaspoons baking powder

1 teaspoon salt
1 cup milk
½ teaspoon lemon extract
½ teaspoon vanilla extract

Cream butter and sugar until light and fluffy. Add eggs one at a time, beating well after each addition. Combine flour, baking powder and salt. Add to butter mixture alternately with milk, beating well after each addition. Blend in flavorings. Pour batter into five greased and floured 9-inch cake pans. Bake at 350 degrees for 18 minutes or until done. Cool completely and spread cooled filling between layers. Frost with Seven Minute Frosting and garnish with grated coconut.

SEVEN MINUTE FROSTING:

3 egg whites
¾ cup sugar
¾ cup light corn syrup

1 tablespoon water
½ teaspoon vanilla extract

Combine all ingredients except vanilla in top of double boiler. Place over boiling water and beat constantly with electric beater. Cook about 7 minutes. Remove from heat and stir in vanilla.

Ms. Paula Battey

ITALIAN CREAM CAKE

½ cup butter or margarine
½ cup Crisco
2 cups sugar
5 egg yolks
2 cups cake flour

1 teaspoon soda
1 cup buttermilk
1 teaspoon vanilla
5 egg whites

Cream butter and Crisco. Add sugar gradually and beat. Add egg yolks one at a time beating thoroughly after each addition. Combine flour and soda and add alternately with buttermilk. Add vanilla and beat. Fold in stiffly beaten egg whites. Grease and flour four 9-inch cake pans. Bake 20-25 minutes in 350 degree oven.

ICING:

8 ounces cream cheese
¼ cup butter or margarine
1 16-ounce box confectioners'
    sugar

1 teaspoon vanilla
1 cup coconut
1 cup pecans

Cream cream cheese and butter. Add sugar and vanilla and beat. Spread on cooled cake layers and sprinkle each layer with coconut and nuts. Spread icing on top and sides of cake and sprinkle with coconut and nuts. Keep in refrigerator. Serves 20.

Mrs. Preston W. McElveen (Madlyn)

MRS. RANEY'S YELLOW CAKE

1 cup butter
2 cups sugar
5 eggs
3 cups plain flour

3 teaspoons baking powder
1 cup milk
1 teaspoon vanilla

Cream butter and sugar thoroughly. Add eggs one by one. Add dry ingredients alternately with milk. Add vanilla. Bake in two greased 8-inch cake pans in preheated 350 degree oven. Cook until lightly brown, approximately 30 minutes.

Mrs. H. E. Trask (Margaret)

SUNSHINE CAKE

12 large eggs, separated   1 cup sugar
1 teaspoon salt   1 cup cake flour
1 tablespoon lemon juice   1 teaspoon cream of tartar

Beat egg whites until stiff and peaks form. Set aside. In another bowl beat egg yolks until frothy; add salt, lemon juice and sugar and beat well to blend. Pour the egg yolk mixture into the stiffly beaten egg whites, fold lightly. Sift cake flour and cream of tartar three times and sift from sifter into mixture, stirring lightly to blend. Bake in an ungreased tube pan 45 minutes in a 350 degree oven.

FROSTING:
¾ cup softened butter   Confectioners' sugar
1 egg   Black walnuts, chopped
1 teaspoon vanilla

Combine butter and egg beating until well mixed. Add vanilla and mix. Beat in enough confectioners' sugar to make a stiff but pliable paste. Spread over cooled cake and sprinkle liberally with chopped black walnuts if desired.

Mrs. Stoddard Lane, Jr. (Patricia)

YELLOW CAKE AND CARAMEL ICING

1 cup butter   3 teaspoons baking powder
2 cups sugar   ¾ teaspoon salt
4 eggs, separated   2 teaspoons vanilla
2¾ cups all purpose flour   1 cup milk

Cream butter and sugar. Add egg yolks, one at a time. Sift flour and baking powder together, then add salt. Add flour mixture and milk alternately. Add vanilla. Beat egg whites until stiff. Fold into batter. Bake in preheated 350 degree oven for about 35 minutes. Makes 2 large or 3 small layers.

CARAMEL ICING:
2 cups sugar, divided   1 cup butter
1 cup milk   Pinch of salt

Mix 1½ cups sugar, milk, butter and salt and bring to a boil. Melt ½ cup sugar in small, heavy frying pan stirring constantly. When melted, add to boiling mixture. Stir until candy thermometer rises to soft boil. Remove from heat and beat until slightly cool. Will make enough for filling and icing.

Mrs. DeAlton Ridings (Jane)

BLACK WALNUT CAKE

3 cups plain flour, divided
1 cup black walnuts, finely
  ground
1 cup butter
½ cup shortening
3 cups sugar

5 eggs
1 teaspoon baking powder
1 cup heavy cream (may use half
  and half)
1 teaspoon vanilla
½ teaspoon rum flavoring

Sprinkle ½ cup of the flour over finely ground nuts. Cream butter and shortening well; add sugar and mix thoroughly. Add eggs one at a time, beating about 2 minutes after each addition. Add remaining flour with baking powder alternately with cream, ending with flour. Add flavorings. Fold in nuts and mix well. Preheat oven to 325 degrees and bake 1 hour and 30 minutes. You may use either a well greased and floured large tube pan or two loaf pans, 9¼ x 5¼ x 2¾-inch. Do not open oven door during first hour of baking. Let cake cool in pan on rack before removing.

Mrs. Walter Ioor Rodgers (Edie)

APPLE NUT CAKE

3 cups flour, sifted
3 eggs
2 cups sugar
1 teaspoon soda
1 teaspoon salt

1½ cups salad oil, minus 1
  tablespoon
2 teaspoons vanilla
1 cup pecans, chopped
3 cups apples, finely chopped

Beat all ingredients except pecans and apples until well blended. Fold in pecans and apples and pour into greased and floured 9 x 13-inch pan. Bake at 350 degrees for 45 minutes.

TOPPING:
½ cup butter
1 cup brown sugar

¼ cup evaporated milk, undiluted
1 teaspoon vanilla

Melt butter and add brown sugar and milk. Bring to boiling point. Remove from heat and add vanilla. Cool and pour over cake.

Mrs. F. William Scheper III (Jean)

SPICY JAM CAKE

3 cups all purpose flour,
  divided
1 teaspoon ground cinnamon
1 teaspoon ground cloves
1 teaspoon ground allspice
1 teaspoon soda
¼ teaspoon salt

1 cup citron, diced
1 cup pecans, chopped
½ cup shortening
1 cup sugar
3 eggs
1 cup blackberry jam
¾ cup buttermilk

Combine flour, spices, soda, and salt. Combine citron and pecans and dredge with ½ cup flour mixture. Set aside. Cream sugar and shortening until light and fluffy. Add eggs, one at a time, beating well after each addition. Stir in jam, buttermilk, and remaining flour mixture. Fold in fruit and nut mixture. Spoon batter into two greased and floured 9-inch cake pans. Bake at 350 degrees for 35 minutes or until cake tests done. Cool on wire racks. Spread caramel frosting between layers and on top of cake.

CARAMEL FROSTING:

1½ cups firmly packed brown
  sugar
⅔ cup milk

⅛ teaspoon salt
3 tablespoons butter or margarine
1 teaspoon vanilla

Combine sugar, milk and salt in saucepan. Place over low heat and cook to soft ball stage, stir frequently to prevent scorching. Remove from heat. Add butter and vanilla. Beat until frosting begins to thicken. When frosting is of spreading consistency, frost the cake quickly.

Mrs. A. M. McCormick (Roberta)

GINGERBREAD

2 eggs
¾ cup sugar
¾ cup molasses
1 cup boiling water
¾ cup shortening

2½ cups flour
2 teaspoons soda
1½ teaspoons cinnamon
1½ teaspoons ginger

Beat eggs; add sugar, molasses, boiling water and shortening. Sift all dry ingredients and add to molasses mixture. Mix together and bake in a 12 x 8 x 2-inch greased and floured pan at 350 degrees for 30 minutes. Serve with whipped cream or hard sauce.

Miss Madeline Trask

PRUNE CAKE

3 eggs
1½ cups sugar
1 cup salad oil
2 cups all purpose flour
1 teaspoon baking soda
1 teaspoon cinnamon

1 teaspoon allspice
1 teaspoon nutmeg
½ cup buttermilk
1 cup pecans, chopped
1 cup cooked prunes, chopped

SAUCE:
½ cup butter
1 cup sugar

½ teaspoon baking soda
½ cup buttermilk

Mix eggs, sugar and oil. Sift together flour, baking soda and spices and add alternately with buttermilk. Stir in nuts and prunes. Bake in a 9 x 12-inch pan in a 350 degree oven for 40 minutes. Bring sauce ingredients to a boil. Pour over cake which should still be warm. Cut cake into squares.

Mrs. Mikell Harper (Madeline)

UPSIDE DOWN CAKE

¼ cup butter
1 cup brown sugar
Pineapple slices or peeled
   apricot halves
1 cup flour
1 teaspoon baking powder

4 eggs
1 cup white sugar
Heavy cream, whipped
Sugar, to taste
Vanilla, to taste

Melt the butter in a 10-inch iron skillet on top of the stove. Add the brown sugar and mix well. Place the pineapple or apricots in a single layer in the skillet, making a pleasing design. Sift flour and baking powder. To flour mixture, add eggs and white sugar. Pour over pineapple slices in skillet. Place in 350 degree oven on lower middle shelf. Bake for 30 minutes or until brown. Let cool in skillet and turn onto serving plate. To serve, cut into wedges and garnish with whipped cream which has been flavored with sugar and vanilla.

Mrs. Arthur Marscher (Gladys)

HUMMINGBIRD CAKE

3 cups all-purpose flour
2 cups sugar
1 teaspoon salt
1 teaspoon soda
1 teaspoon ground cinnamon
3 eggs, beaten

1½ cups oil
1½ teaspoons vanilla
8 ounces crushed pineapple, undrained
1 cup bananas, diced
1 cup pecans, chopped

Combine dry ingredients in large mixing bowl. Add eggs and oil. Stir until dry ingredients are moistened. Do not beat. Stir in vanilla, pineapple, bananas, and pecans. Spoon batter into three greased and floured 9-inch pans. Bake at 350 degrees for 30 minutes or until done. Cool and frost with Cream Cheese Frosting.

CREAM CHEESE FROSTING:

½ cup butter
8 ounces cream cheese
1 16 oz. box 10-X powdered sugar

1 teaspoon vanilla
1 cup bananas, diced
1 cup pecans, chopped

Cream butter, cream cheese, and sugar in mixing bowl until smooth. Add vanilla and bananas and mix well. Fold in pecans. Spread between layers and on top and sides of cake.

Mrs. Ed Thames (Verna)

NEW ZEALAND WATERMELON CAKE
Children's Favorite

½ cup butter
¾ cup sugar
1¾ cups flour
½ teaspoon salt
½ teaspoon soda
¾ cup milk

3 egg whites, stiffly beaten
½ teaspoon lemon juice
½ teaspoon red coloring
½ cup raisins
½ teaspoon green coloring
Basic white frosting

Cream butter and sugar. Sift flour, soda, and cream of tartar together. Add flour mixture to butter mixture alternately with milk. Add lemon juice. Fold in egg whites. Take ¾ of mixture and add red coloring and raisins. Put pink mixture in bottom of greased and floured tube pan and remaining uncolored cake mixture on top. Bake in 350 degree oven for 50-60 minutes. Frost with white icing to which has been added green food coloring.

Mrs. Tom Story (Heather)

PINEAPPLE CAKE

½ cup butter
½ cup Crisco
2 cups sugar
4 eggs, separated
3 cups cake flour, sifted

¼ teaspoon salt
3 teaspoons baking powder
1 cup milk
1 teaspoon vanilla

Cream shortening and sugar; then add egg yolks one at a time. Sift dry ingredients together three times; add alternately with milk and vanilla to sugar, beating until smooth each time. Fold in stiff egg whites, pour into three 9-inch pans lined with waxed paper. Bake at 350 degrees for 25 minutes.

FILLING:

1 20-ounce can crushed
    pineapple, drained
¼ cup sugar

2 tablespoons cornstarch
4 tablespoons orange juice

Mix pineapple, sugar, cornstarch, and cook over medium heat until thick and shiny. Remove and add orange juice. Put layers together with filling and ice with seven minute frosting.

FROSTING:

3 egg whites
2 teaspoons light corn syrup
2¼ cups sugar

7½ tablespoons water
1 teaspoon vanilla

Combine egg whites, corn syrup, sugar and water in double boiler. Beat with rotary egg beater until mixed well. Place over boiling water, beating constantly until it stands in peaks, about 7 minutes. Remove. Add vanilla and beat until thick enough to spread on cake.

Mrs. Eugene Spears (Lillian)

ZWIEBACK CAKE

5 eggs, beaten separately
1 cup sugar
1 cup Zwieback toast, finely
    crumbled
1 cup nuts (pecans or walnuts),
    finely chopped

1 teaspoon vanilla
1 teaspoon baking powder
Whipped cream

Beat yolks and sugar. Add Zwieback, nuts, vanilla and baking powder. Fold in beaten egg whites. Bake in two 8-inch layer pans at 350 degrees for 25 minutes. Put together with whipped cream.

Mrs. Spencer Hart (Dee)

DOMINOS

1 cup butter
1½ teaspoons vanilla
2 cups sugar
4 eggs
2 cups sifted flour

½ teaspoon salt
2 cups nuts, chopped
2 squares unsweetened chocolate,
    melted and cooled
Velvety Chocolate Frosting

Cream butter, vanilla and sugar until light and fluffy. Add eggs, one at a time, beating well after each addition. Add flour and salt and mix until well blended. Stir in nuts. Divide batter in half. Add chocolate to one half. Drop batter alternately by teaspoonsful onto greased waxed-paper lined 9 x 13 x 2-inch pan. Run knife through batter a few times to marbleize. Bake in 350 degree oven about 45 minutes. Turn on rack to cool. Remove paper. Frost with the following frosting. Cut into 3 x 1½-inch bars to serve.

VELVETY CHOCOLATE FROSTING:

¼ cup hot water
2¼ cups confectioners' sugar,
    sifted
4 squares unsweetened
    chocolate, melted

4 egg yolks
¼ cup butter, melted
1 teaspoon vanilla

Add hot water and sugar to chocolate; mix well. Add egg yolks one at a time, beating well. Add butter slowly. Add vanilla and beat until smooth.

Mrs. Neil W. Trask, Jr. (Becky)

CARAMEL ICING

4 cups light brown sugar
1 cup milk

1 cup butter, melted
1 teaspoon vanilla

Let sugar and milk come to boiling point, stirring vigorously all the time. Let boil 5 minutes without stirring. Remove from heat and let cool. Add melted butter and vanilla and beat until right consistency.

Mrs. Neil Trask, Jr. (Rebecca)

MIMI'S BUTTER ICING

2 cups sugar
½ cup milk

⅓ cup butter
1 teaspoon vanilla

Cook in saucepan 3-5 minutes until soft ball forms; 238 degrees on candy thermometer. Beat until icing is thick enough to spread. Will ice one layer.

Mrs. Marvin Dukes (Cilla)

WHITE ICING

2¼ cups sugar
½ cup water
3 tablespoons white Karo
3 egg whites, stiffly beaten

⅓ cup confectioners' sugar, scant
1 teaspoon vanilla, or flavoring of
   choice

Mix sugar, water, and Karo and cook to 238 degrees (soft boil) on candy thermometer. Add slowly to egg whites, which have been beaten stiff but not dry. Beat until the icing is like cream. Add confectioners' sugar and flavoring. This icing is soft on the inside and crusty on the outside. This will ice a two layer cake.

The Editors

CHOCOLATE FUDGE FROSTING

2 cups sugar
½ cup cocoa
⅔ cup milk

½ cup vegetable shortening
¼ teaspoon salt
1½ teaspoons vanilla

Mix sugar and cocoa. Add milk, shortening and salt. Bring to a slow boil and cook until firm ball forms when dropped into cold water. Add vanilla and beat until thickened. Spread on cake.

Mrs. John S. Woods (Jane)

CHOCOLATE FUDGE ICING

2 squares unsweetened
   chocolate
2 cups sugar
2 tablespoons Karo, white or
   dark

¾ cup milk
¼ teaspoon salt
2 tablespoons butter
1 teaspoon vanilla

Mix all ingredients together except butter and vanilla. Stir over medium heat until sugar and chocolate melt. Stir gently. Allow to come to soft ball stage. Remove from heat. Cool pot in cool water until mixture is just warm; add butter and vanilla. Beat until creamy. Spread on cake.

Miss Madeline Trask

PASSION-FLOWER

Cookies and Candy

BESSIE BELL'S COOKIES

1 cup butter
2 cups brown sugar
2 unbeaten eggs
3½ cups flour, sifted

1 teaspoon soda
¼ teaspoon salt
1 cup pecans, chopped

Cream butter and sugar and add eggs one at a time, beating after each. Add flour, soda and salt sifted together 3 times. Add nuts. Roll in waxed paper in 2 inch diameter. Refrigerate for 24 hours. Slice thin and bake on greased sheet at 400 degrees for 8-9 minutes. Yields 50 cookies.

Mrs. Emil Klatt (Alice)

SNICKERDOODLES

1 cup margarine
1½ cups sugar
2¾ cups flour
2 teaspoons cream of tartar
1 teaspoon soda

½ teaspoon salt
2 eggs
2 tablespoons sugar
2 tablespoons cinnamon

Cream margarine and sugar. Sift flour, cream of tartar, soda, and salt. Add flour mixture to margarine and sugar. Add eggs. Chill dough. Roll into balls the size of a small walnut and roll into mixture of sugar and cinnamon. Place on ungreased cookie sheet 2 inches apart. Cook at 400 degrees for 8-10 minutes.

Mrs. F. W. Scheper, Jr. (Margaret)

SUGAR COOKIES—CHILDREN'S CHOICE

½ cup butter
¾ cup brown sugar
¼ cup white sugar
1 egg, beaten

2 cups sifted flour
½ teaspoon salt
1 teaspoon vanilla

Cream butter and sugar. Add egg. Beat until fluffy. Mix in flour, a little at a time and add salt and vanilla. Drop onto greased cookie sheet, ½ teaspoon of dough and flatten slightly with a floured fork. Bake at 350 degrees for 8 to 10 minutes. Makes 3 to 4 dozen cookies.

Mrs. James Warwick (Betty)

SUGAR COOKIES

¾ cup butter
4 tablespoons margarine
2 cups sugar
2 eggs
3 cups flour

1½ teaspoons salt
3 teaspoons baking powder
2 teaspoons vanilla
Mace to taste
1 cup nuts, optional

Cream butter, margarine and sugar. Add eggs one at a time. Beat well. Add flour to which salt and baking powder have been added. Add vanilla and mace. Chill dough until firm enough to handle. Roll into balls about the size of a large marble. Roll in granulated sugar. Place balls on greased sheet about 1 inch apart. Bake at 350 degrees until slightly brown on top. This dough freezes well. Yields about 8 dozen cookies.

Mrs. Jack Bond (Elizabeth)

DATE PASTRIES

½ cup butter
¼ pound Cheddar cheese,
    grated
1 cup flour, sifted

1 8-ounce package dates, chopped
½ cup brown sugar
¼ cup water

Cream butter and cheese with an electric mixer. Blend in flour and chill for at least 1 hour. Cook the dates, brown sugar and water until soft. Cool. Roll out dough and cut with biscuit cutter. Place 1 teaspoon of date mixture on a piece of dough. Place another piece of dough on top and join edges with fork. Bake on a greased cookie sheet 15 minutes in a 350 degree oven. Yields approximately 2 dozen.

Mrs. Louis J. Roempke (Marijo)

BENNE COOKIES

¾ cup butter
1½ cups brown sugar
1 egg
¾ cup plain flour, sifted

¼ teaspoon baking powder
1 teaspoon vanilla
1 cup benne seed, parched

Blend butter and brown sugar, add egg, flour and baking powder. Add vanilla and benne seed. Drop from teaspoon on lightly buttered tinfoil—mixture will spread. Preheat oven to 325 degrees and bake for 10 minutes. Remove from oven and allow a few minutes to cool before removing from pan. Seal tightly. Makes 5 dozen.

Mrs. Alfred Lengnick (Georgie)

BUTTERSCOTCH COOKIES

¾ cup butter
2 cups brown sugar
2 eggs
1 cup flour

1 teaspoon baking powder
1 cup pecans or walnuts, chopped
1 teaspoon vanilla
Powdered sugar

Melt butter, add sugar and eggs, one at a time, beating well. Add flour that has been sifted with baking powder. Add nuts and vanilla. Place in 9 x 14-inch pan and cook in preheated 325 degree oven for 30 minutes. Let cool in pan. Cut in squares and sprinkle with powdered sugar, if desired.

Mrs. F. W. Scheper, Jr. (Margaret)

BLOND BROWNIES

1 16-ounce box light brown
    sugar
½ cup butter, melted
3 eggs
2 cups all-purpose flour, sifted

2 teaspoons baking powder
1 teaspoon vanilla
Pinch of salt
1 cup nuts, chopped

In a medium size bowl, combine sugar with butter and stir. Beat in eggs one at a time. Don't overbeat. Fold in flour that has been sifted with baking powder and a pinch of salt. Add vanilla and nuts. Put in a 9 x 13-inch greased pan. Bake at 325 degrees for about 25 minutes. When done it will shrink from sides of pan and the top will be brown but still soft. Cut into squares. Yields 4 dozen.

Miss Bessie Levin

CHOCOLATE BARS

CAKE:

1½ cups sugar
3 tablespoons cocoa
¾ cup butter
3 eggs

1½ cups self-rising flour
1½ cups pecans, chopped
1 teaspoon vanilla

Mix sugar and cocoa; then cream with butter. Add eggs one at a time, beating well after each addition. Add flour, pecans, and vanilla. Mix well. Pour into greased and floured 9 x 13-inch pan. Bake 40 minutes in 325 degree oven. Remove from oven and cool. Ice while still warm.

ICING:

1 pound box 10-X powdered
    sugar
4 tablespoons cocoa

4 tablespoons butter
1 teaspoon vanilla
⅓ cup evaporated milk

Cream powdered sugar, cocoa and butter. Add vanilla and milk and beat. Spread over warm cake and cool completely. Yields 16 pieces.

Carroll Smith

CHOCOLATE BROWNERS

4 squares unsweetened
    chocolate
1 cup butter
¾ cup nuts, chopped
2 cups sugar

1 cup flour
¼ teaspoon salt
4 eggs, beaten
2 teaspoons vanilla

Melt chocolate and butter in double boiler and cool. Mix nuts, sugar, flour and salt. Add eggs. Pour mixture into chocolate and butter. Stir until blended. Add vanilla and pour into 10 x 14-inch greased pan. Bake in 350 degree preheated oven for 30 minutes. Cut into squares and let stand until cool. Browners will be soft, but will harden when cool.

Mrs. DeAlton Ridings (Jane)

CHOCOLATE MACAROONS

½ cup vegetable shortening
4 squares unsweetened
    chocolate
2 cups sugar
4 eggs, unbeaten

2 teaspoons vanilla
2 cups flour, sifted
2 teaspoons baking powder
½ teaspoon salt
Confectioners' sugar

Melt together shortening and chocolate. Add sugar to chocolate, stirring until smooth. Add eggs one by one, beating well after each addition. Add vanilla. Sift together flour, baking powder and salt. Add flour mixture to chocolate mixture and blend thoroughly. Chill dough 2 or 3 hours. Dip out rounded teaspoons of dough. Form into small balls. Roll each in confectioners' sugar. Place on cookie sheet. Bake in 375 degree oven for about 10 minutes. Do not overbake. Cookies should be soft when taken from oven. Yields 6 dozen.

Mrs. Ken Stalter (Lois)

FORGOTTEN COOKIES

2 egg whites
⅔ cup sugar
1 teaspoon vanilla

1 6-ounce package chocolate chips
½ cup pecans, chopped

Beat egg whites until stiff. Add sugar and vanilla until stiff, then stir in chocolate chips and pecans. Drop on greased cookie sheet. Preheat oven to 350 degrees. Place cookies in oven and turn off oven. Leave cookies in oven overnight and do not open oven until the next morning. Yields approximately 2 dozen.

Mrs. Hunter Wyatt-Brown (Nancy)

COWBOY COOKIES

1 cup shortening
1 cup white sugar
1 cup brown sugar
2 eggs
2 cups flour
1 teaspoon baking soda

½ teaspoon salt
½ teaspoon baking powder
2 cups rolled oats
1 teaspoon vanilla
6 ounces chocolate chips

Blend shortening and sugars until fluffy. Add eggs and beat well. Sift flour, soda, salt and baking powder together, then add to egg mixture. Mix. Add oats, vanilla and chocolate chips. Mix with spoon. Drop by teaspoonful on to greased cookie sheet. Bake 15 minutes in 350 degree oven. Remove from pan and let cool.

Miss Margaret Gray

FUDGE BROWNIE DELIGHT

½ cup butter
2 squares unsweetened chocolate
1 cup sugar
2 eggs
¾ cup flour

½ teaspoon salt
½ teaspoon baking powder
½ cup nuts, chopped
1 scant tablespoon cocoa for
   sprinkling pan

Melt butter and chocolate together over hot (not boiling) water. Add sugar and mix well. Add eggs separately and beat well after each addition. Sift dry ingredients together, add nuts and combine with chocolate mixture. Pour into greased shallow 9 x 12-inch pan which has been sprinkled with cocoa. Bake 20 minutes at 350 degrees. Cool thoroughly in pan. Makes 3½ dozen.

BUTTER FROSTING:
2 tablespoons butter, softened
2 cups sifted confectioners'
   sugar
1-2 tablespoons cream

¼ tablespoon vanilla or ½
   teaspoon peppermint flavoring
1-2 drops pink or green food
   coloring

Combine all ingredients and spread over cooled brownies.

CHOCOLATE TOPPING:
1 square unsweetened chocolate
¼ cup water
3 teaspoons butter

1 teaspoon vanilla
½ cup brown sugar
1½ cups confectioners' sugar

Combine chocolate, water, butter, vanilla and brown sugar. Place over medium heat and bring to a boil and boil for 1 minute. Cool slightly. Add confectioners' sugar. Spread over butter frosting. Allow to set before cutting into squares. Freeze if desired. Makes 3½ dozen.

Battery Creek Catering
Dianne and Debbie TenEyck

CHOCOLATE MERINGUES

2 egg whites
⅛ teaspoon cream of tartar
⅛ teaspoon salt

1 teaspoon vanilla
¾ cup sugar
3 ounces chocolate chips

Beat egg whites and cream of tartar until stiff. Add salt, vanilla and sugar until egg whites are stiff and peak. Add chocolate chips. Drop by teaspoonful on brown paper and bake 25 minutes at 300 degrees. Makes 2 dozen.

Mrs. Patrick Cotton (Jean)

MINT MERINGUE COOKIES

2 egg whites, at room
   temperature
½ teaspoon mint or
   peppermint extract
¼ teaspoon cream of tartar

½ cup sugar
6 drops green food coloring,
   optional
1 6-ounce package semisweet
   chocolate morsels

Combine egg whites, mint extract and cream of tartar. Beat until frothy. Gradually add sugar, 1 tablespoon at a time, beating until glossy and stiff peaks form. Beat in food coloring, if desired. Do not underbeat. Fold chocolate morsels into meringue. Drop meringue by rounded teaspoonfuls onto cookie sheets covered with wax paper. Bake at 225 degrees for 1 hour or until dry and set. Cookies should not brown. Transfer to wire racks to cool. Yields 2 dozen cookies.

Mrs. Charles V. Wilson (Jean)

THREE LAYER COOKIES

17½ tablespoons margarine,
   divided
¼ cup sugar
⅓ cup cocoa
1 teaspoon vanilla
1 egg
2 cups graham cracker crumbs

½ cup chopped pecans
½ cup flaked coconut
3 tablespoons milk
2 tablespoons vanilla pudding mix
2 cups powdered sugar
4 ounces semi-sweet chocolate
   squares

First Layer:
In top of double boiler, cook slowly until blended: 8 tablespoons of margarine, ¼ cup sugar, cocoa and vanilla. Stirring constantly, add egg and cook 5 minutes longer. Add cracker crumbs, pecans and coconut. Press firmly into a 9 x 9 x 2-inch pan and let stand 15 minutes.

Second Layer:
Cream 8 tablespoons of margarine until light and fluffy. Mix together milk and pudding mix and add to margarine. Blend well. Add powdered sugar *gradually* and beat until smooth. Spread *over* first layer and let stand in refrigerator 15 minutes until set.

Third Layer:
Melt on *low* heat, semi-sweet chocolate and 1½ tablespoons margarine. Cool. Spread on second layer. When cool, cut into squares or bars.

Mrs. Rivers Varn (Eleanor)

GERMAN COOKIES

1 cup honey
¾ cup sugar
1 egg
1 teaspoon lemon rind, grated
1 tablespoon lemon juice
2¾ cups flour, sifted
½ teaspoon soda
½ teaspoon allspice
1 teaspoon cinnamon

½ teaspoon nutmeg
¼ teaspoon cloves
⅓ cup citron, diced
⅓ cup nuts, chopped
½ cup blanched almond halves
½ cup candied cherries
Almonds
Cherries

Heat honey and cool. Stir in sugar, egg, lemon rind and juice. Add flour, spices, citron and nuts to honey mixture. Mix dough well and chill 8 hours. Roll ¼ of dough at a time ¼ inch thick. Keep remainder of dough chilled. Cut rolled dough into 2 inch rounds. Place on greased cookie sheet and bake at 400 degrees for 10 minutes. Decorate with almonds and cherries. Cookies can be decorated with following icing:

1 cup sugar
½ cup hot water

1 cup powdered sugar

Combine sugar and water and cook to 230 degrees on candy thermometer. Add powdered sugar. Mix and spread on cookies. Yields 40 cookies.

Mrs. Malcolm Goodwin (Barbara)

FILLED CHRISTMAS COOKIES

DOUGH:

1 cup butter
2 cups sugar
2 eggs
2 teaspoons vanilla
½ cup buttermilk

½ teaspoon salt
1 teaspoon baking powder
1 teaspoon soda
9 cups flour, approximately

FILLING:

½ pound raisins
1 small orange, with seeds
    removed and chopped
½ cup sugar

½ cup water
Pinch of salt
1 teaspoon cornstarch
1 teaspoon vanilla

Heat oven to 350 degrees. Cream butter, sugar and eggs. Add vanilla and milk. Mix salt, baking powder and soda with 2 cups flour. Add this to egg mixture. Keep adding flour until mixture can be rolled out. Chill. Grind raisins and orange, with peel, in a blender. Place raisins and orange in saucepan with sugar, water and salt and bring to a boil. Thicken mixture with cornstarch, dissolved in a little water. Add vanilla. Roll out cookie dough, using pastry cloth. Use large round cookie cutter to cut out rounds. Add 1 teaspoon filling to first round, cover with second round of dough. Crimp with fork, being sure filling is entirely covered. Lift with spatula onto cookie sheet. Bake at 350 degrees for 10 minutes. Makes 5 dozen cookies.

Mrs. Hugh O. Pearson (Marie)

FRENCH BUTTER CREAM COOKIES

½ cup butter
½ cup shortening
1½ cups confectioners' sugar
1 egg, beaten
1 teaspoon vanilla

2 cups flour, sifted
1 teaspoon baking soda
1 teaspoon cream of tartar
½ teaspoon salt

Cream butter and shortening together. Add confectioners' sugar, egg and vanilla. Add flour, soda, cream of tartar and salt, which have been mixed together. Mix well. Chill at least 10 minutes. Form into small balls and flatten with fork on cookie sheet. Dip fork into flour each time to prevent sticking. Bake at 350 degrees for 10 to 12 minutes. You can use a greased pan or an ungreased pan for baking. These cookies may be a little brown around the edges. Makes about 4 dozen.

Mrs. Edward Webb (Margaret)

CREAM CHEESE GEMS

24 ounces cream cheese
¾ cup sugar

3 eggs, separated
¾ cup graham cracker crumbs

FROSTING:
¾ cup sour cream
2½ teaspoons sugar

1 teaspoon vanilla
Graham cracker crumbs

Mix cream cheese, sugar and egg yolks well. Beat egg whites until stiff and fold into first mixture. Pour into miniature muffin tins that have been buttered and lightly coated with graham cracker crumbs. Bake in 350 degree oven for 15 minutes or until set and lightly brown around edges. Cool in pans 5 minutes. Loosen edges by running a knife around sides and turn out of pans. Mix frosting ingredients well. Frost tops and dust with more graham cracker crumbs. Refrigerate or freeze. Serve cold. Yields 6 dozen.

Mrs. Owen Hand (Patsy)

MELTAWAYS

8 ounces creamed cottage
   cheese
1 cup butter
2 cups all purpose flour, sifted
¾ cup light brown sugar
¾ cup walnuts or pecans, finely
   chopped

1 teaspoon cinnamon
¼ cup butter, melted
1 egg yolk
2 tablespoons water

Grease 3 cookie sheets. Blend cottage cheese with 1 cup butter. Add flour and blend until dough forms a soft ball. In a separate bowl, mix brown sugar, nuts and cinnamon. Divide dough into thirds. On a lightly, floured cloth covered board roll out one-third of dough to ⅛ inch thickness and circular in shape. Brush with melted butter and sprinkle one-third of sugar, nut, cinnamon mixture on rolled out dough. Cut circle into 16 pie shaped pieces. Beginning at outer edge, roll up each piece tightly and place point side down on cookie sheet. Repeat with other two-thirds of dough. Beat egg yolk with water and brush top of cookies. Bake in preheated 400 degree oven for 20 minutes or until golden. Yields 4 dozen.

Mrs. Joseph Sedlak (Ruth)

APPLESAUCERS

2 cups sifted all-purpose flour
1 teaspoon baking powder
1 teaspoon pumpkin pie spice
½ teaspoon baking soda
½ teaspoon salt
½ cup butter

1 cup firmly packed brown sugar
1 egg
1 teaspoon vanilla
1 cup applesauce
1 cup golden raisins
1 cup walnuts, coarsely chopped
Confectioners' sugar

Sift together flour, baking powder, spice, baking soda and salt. Cream butter with brown sugar until fluffy in a large bowl; beat in egg and vanilla. Sift in flour mixture, adding alternately with applesauce; blend well; stir in raisins and nuts. Drop dough ¼ cup at a time, 6 inches apart, on greased cookie sheet; spread into 3-inch rounds. Bake at 350 degrees for 15 minutes or until lightly browned around edges. Remove cookies to wire racks to cool. Dust with confectioners' sugar. Yields approximately 3 dozen.

Mrs. Ed Sutton (Jean)

NUT KISSES

3 egg whites
1½ cups light brown sugar
3 cups nuts, chopped

1 teaspoon vanilla
Speck of salt

Beat egg whites until stiff but not dry. Add sugar gradually, beating until very stiff. Fold in nuts, vanilla and salt. Drop by teaspoons on a greased cookie sheet. Bake at 275 degrees for about 45 minutes.

Miss Bessie Levin

GINGER WAFERS

1 cup molasses
½ cup butter
½ cup brown sugar
3¾ cups flour
¾ teaspoon ginger

¾ teaspoon clove, ground
¾ teaspoon cinnamon, ground
¼ teaspoon nutmeg, ground
¼ teaspoon allspice, ground
¾ teaspoon soda

Preheat oven to 375 degrees. Heat molasses and butter. Stir until they are well mixed. Add sugar to molasses mixture. Sift flour, add remaining dry ingredients and sift again. Beat them into the first mixture. Put in refrigerator overnight; the next day roll very thin and cut out. Bake at 375 degrees for 6-8 minutes on cookie sheet. Yields approximately 2 dozen cookies.

Fannie Van Sant

OATMEAL COOKIES

1 cup light brown sugar	1 teaspoon salt
1 cup dark brown sugar	2 teaspoons baking powder
1 cup shortening	1 teaspoon soda
2 eggs, beaten	2 cups oatmeal
1 teaspoon vanilla	½ cup walnuts, chopped
2 cups whole wheat flour	¾ cup raisins

Cream sugars and shortening. Add eggs and vanilla. Beat. Add flour, salt, baking powder, soda, oatmeal, nuts and raisins. Mix. Bake in 350 degree oven on ungreased cookie sheet for 10 or 15 minutes. Can add one or two tablespoons warm water if dough is too stiff. Bake only a few at a time when constraint is needed.

Mrs. Frank A. Osmanski (Edith)

OATMEAL SHORTBREADS

1 cup butter	1½ cups plain flour
⅔ cup brown sugar, packed	⅔ cup rolled oats, uncooked

Blend together butter and sugar. Add flour gradually. Stir in oats. Spread batter into a greased 15 x 10 x 1-inch pan. Use knife to make a thin layer covering the pan. Bake at 350 degrees for approximately 30 minutes. Cut while hot and let cool in pan on rack.

Mrs. Julian Levin (Renee)

SCOTCH SHORTBREAD I

½ cup butter	2 cups plain flour
½ cup margarine	½ cup rice flour
1 cup sugar	

Cream butter, margarine and sugar. Sift flours separately, measure and sift together into mixture. Divide dough into 3 balls. Press each ball into strips about 12 x 3 inches. Arrange in ungreased baking pan (approximately 13 x 9-inches) and press strips together at sides. Prick top with floured fork. Mark into half-inch bars. Bake at 250 to 275 degrees until lightly browned or about 1 hour. Cut through marks. Cool before removing from pan.

Mrs. James D. Caldwell (Elizabeth)

SCOTCH SHORTBREAD II

½ cup butter
¼ cup sugar
2 tablespoons rice flour,
    optional

1¼ cups flour (put rice flour in
    measuring cup and make total
    flour equal 1¼ cups)
⅛ teaspoon salt

With fingers, cream butter and sugar well. Add flour and salt and mix well. Put into heavy 8-inch pan. A skillet works well; do not use glass. Prick entire surface thoroughly with fork. Bake in oven at 350 degrees for 30 minutes or until delicately brown. Cut in 12 small pie-shaped wedges while hot. Allow to cool several hours before using. Keeps for several weeks in tightly closed tin.

Mrs. Charles D. Ravenel (Mollie)

SPRINGERLE COOKIES

½ cup butter
3 pounds confectioners' sugar
12 eggs
1 teaspoon ammonium
    carbonate, crushed
    (available at your
    pharmacy)

Anise oil to taste
Pinch of salt
1 32-ounce box cake flour
All-purpose flour

Cream butter until light and fluffy. Add powdered sugar then the eggs, one at a time. Beat well after each egg. Add the ammonium carbonate, anise oil and salt. Blend in cake flour, ¼ of a box at a time, mixing well after each addition. Shape into a ball and roll out dough in a floured surface. Knead in enough all-purpose flour to make the dough very stiff. Roll dough ¼ inch thick. Press lightly floured springerle rolling pin into dough to make a clear design. Cut frames apart and cover with cloth. Let stand 24 hours. Bake at 325 degrees for 8-12 minutes. Cookie will be very thick. When cool, store in tightly covered container. May be made 1-2 weeks before serving. If softer cookie is preferred, add an apple to cookie container several days before serving. Makes 12 dozen.

Mrs. Ted Ledford (Suzi)

THINSIES

1 cup butter
1 cup sugar
1 egg
2 cups flour

1 teaspoon vanilla
1 egg white
1 cup pecans, finely chopped

Cream butter and sugar. Add egg, flour, and vanilla. Divide in half and spread very thin on two cookie sheets. Spread unbeaten white of one egg on top. Sprinkle with chopped pecans. Bake at 350 degrees for 20 minutes. Cut into squares while hot. Yields approximately four dozen.

Mrs. Meyer Schein (Lois)

CANDIED CITRUS PEEL

1 cup sugar
½ cup water

1 pound prepared peel, orange or
grapefruit

To prepare peel:
Cut peel from fruit in sections. Cover peel with cold water and bring to a boil. Cook 20 minutes, then cool and scrape off white membrane. Julienne peel in ⅛ inch strips.

To candy peel:
Cook water and sugar to boiling point. Add prepared peel and cook slowly until it tests 232 degrees on candy thermometer. Place on paper to cool. Roll in granulated sugar. Let dry and store in an air-tight tin.

Mrs. Sam Stafford, III (Nancy)

SPICED NUTS

1 cup sugar
2 teaspoons ground cinnamon
½ teaspoon salt

¼ cup water
2 cups pecan halves

Cook sugar, cinnamon, salt and water until it spins a thread or about 5 minutes from the time it begins to boil. Stir in nuts quickly and pour out on a buttered platter. Cool. Break into pieces.

Mrs. Eugene Spears (Lillian)

BUTTERMILK CANDY

2 cups sugar
1 cup buttermilk
¼ cup butter
½ teaspoon soda

2 tablespoons white corn syrup
1 teaspoon vanilla
1 cup pecans, chopped

Mix sugar, buttermilk, butter, soda and corn syrup and heat over medium heat in saucepan until mixture comes to a boil and thickens. It should cook to a firm ball stage like boiled fudge and will turn brown as it cooks. Take off heat and add vanilla. When lukewarm, beat until thick and add nuts. Pour onto a buttered plate. Yields 2 dozen pieces.

Mrs. Emil Klatt (Alice)

BUTTER CREAM FONDANT

2 cups sugar
½ cup butter
½ cup white Karo

½ cup water
Chocolate, melted
Peppermint flavoring, optional

Combine sugar, butter, Karo and water and cook to soft ball stage, 236 degrees on candy thermometer. Cool to lukewarm and beat until creamy. Pour on plate and knead. Roll fondant in small balls, chill, and dip in melted chocolate. Top with pecan half. To make mint flavor fondant add a few drops of peppermint, or wintergreen, and color pink or green.

Mrs. Howard Walker (Murray)

DIVINITY

3 cups sugar
⅓ cup white Karo syrup
½ cup water
1 cup pecans, chopped

¼ teaspoon salt
1 tablespoon vanilla
3 egg whites
Whole pecans, garnish

Mix in a saucepan sugar, Karo, water, salt, and vanilla and place mixture on stove to cook. Beat egg whites until stiff. Check mixture to see if it is ready—after candy mixture has come to a rolling boil, drop small amount in cup of water from tap; if it forms a hard brittle ball that clangs when side of cup is struck, candy mixture is ready to pour over egg whites. Pour hot mixture over egg whites and continue to beat rapidly until egg whites and mixture are thoroughly mixed, add nutmeats, and continue to beat until mixture becomes slightly thickened, pour into buttered square pan and then place whole nuts over top of candy. Let set for about 30 minutes and then cut into squares.

Mrs. Bob Chipps (Carolyn)

CHOCOLATE FUDGE

2 cups sugar
¾ cup milk
2 tablespoons Karo syrup
2 squares unsweetened baking
   chocolate, cut up

¼ teaspoon salt
¼ cup butter
1 teaspoon vanilla
½ cup nuts, coarsely chopped

Combine sugar, milk, syrup, chocolate and salt in a medium size saucepan. Set candy thermometer in pan and leave it in during the cooking time. Place pan over low heat and cook, stirring constantly, until mixture comes to a boil. Continue cooking without stirring until candy thermometer reads 238 degrees. Move spoon across bottom of pan occasionally to prevent scorching, but do not stir. Remove from heat and add butter. Let the mixture cool until thermometer reads 110 degrees or until bottom of pan is comfortable to the palm of the hand. Add vanilla and beat the mixture until thick and creamy. Stir in nuts. Pour into a buttered pan or on buttered marble slab. Cut into squares. Makes about 1 pound.

Mrs. John Trask (Flora)

FANNY'S FUDGE

4 squares unsweetened
   chocolate
1 13-ounce can evaporated
   milk
4 cups sugar

3 tablespoons dark Karo syrup
2 tablespoons butter
Pinch salt
1 cup nuts, chopped

Melt chocolate in milk and stir. Add sugar, syrup, butter, and salt. Boil slowly for 45 minutes to 1 hour or to soft ball stage. Beat in nuts and pour onto buttered plates. Yields 2 pounds of fudge.

Mrs. Helen Frances Stokes

BURNT SUGAR FUDGE

3 cups sugar, divided
1 cup evaporated milk

2 or 3 tablespoons butter
1 cup nuts, chopped

Combine 2 cups sugar, milk and butter in heavy deep saucepan and stir until sugar is dissolved and mixture is bubbling softly. Remove from fire. Melt 1 cup of sugar in heavy iron skillet until it turns a deep caramel color. Add to original mixture over low heat, taking care not to bring to a boil. Mix well, then stir no more. Cook slowly until drops form a soft ball. Cool to lukewarm or until it loses gloss. Add nuts and drop by spoon onto wax paper.

Mrs. Howard Walker (Murray)

MEMA'S CARAMEL FUDGE

3 cups white sugar, divided
⅔ cup milk
2 tablespoons butter

¼ teaspoon vanilla
1 cup nuts, chopped

Cook 2 cups sugar, milk and butter to a soft boil (234-238 degrees); remove from heat but keep warm. Brown remaining 1 cup of sugar in a heavy frying pan, being careful not to burn sugar. When sugar is melted and lightly browned, pour slowly into cooked mixture stirring constantly. Add vanilla and nuts, and stir until the fudge begins to get firm. Pour into well buttered 8 x 12-inch pan, cool and cut into squares. Makes 36 pieces.

Lyn Waskiewicz

KENTUCKY COLONELS

2 16-ounce boxes confectioners' (XXXX) sugar
½ cup butter
1 cup bourbon

1 cup pecans, chopped
1 8-ounce box unsweetened chocolate
1 teaspoon paraffin

Cream one box of sugar with butter. In separate bowl mix box of sugar, bourbon and pecans. Combine with first mixture, mix well, refrigerate overnight. Make into small balls. Melt chocolate and paraffin together. Dip balls into chocolate mixture using toothpicks. Put on wax paper to cool.

Mrs. Harold C. Danielson (Mary)

LOLLYPOPS

2 cups sugar
⅔ cup light corn syrup
1 cup water

Few grains of salt
¼ teaspoon flavoring
Few drops food coloring

In a saucepan combine sugar, syrup, water and salt. Stir until the mixture boils. Then cook without stirring until mixture reaches 310 degrees or until syrup spins a brittle thread when dropped from spoon. Quickly stir in flavoring and food coloring. Working very quickly, drop mixture by tablespoonfuls on a greased cookie sheet and press in a stick or toothpick about ⅓ of the way to each lollypop while still hot. Loosen as soon as they are firm.

Miss Caroline Trask

MOTHER'S PULLED MINTS

1 cup water
4 tablespoons butter
1 pound or 2 full cups sugar

6 drops oil of peppermint
½ teaspoon food coloring

Bring water to a boil and add butter. Gradually add sugar and stir until dissolved. Cook rapidly until it spins a thread (261 degrees). Remove from heat and pour on buttered marble slab. Add peppermint and coloring. As soon as candy stiffens around edges, fold to center and pull. Pull until pliable but not stiff. Cut into desired size mints with scissors. Store in tins to cream with waxed paper between layers.

Mrs. Jack Pollitzer (Toni)

PARTY MINTS

1 cup butter
2 pounds confectioners' sugar
1 tablespoon evaporated milk
4 drops oil of peppermint

2-3 drops food coloring: green,
   yellow or pink
50 pecans, halved

Cream butter. Fold in 1½ pounds of sugar. Add milk and oil of peppermint. Blend well. If mixture is sticky, add balance of sugar. Add food coloring. Pinch off piece size of large nutmeg, roll in palm, place on wax paper, and place ½ of pecan on top. Yields 80-100 mints.

Mrs. Malcolm Goodwin (Barbara)

PRALINES

2 cups granulated sugar
1 cup light brown sugar
1 cup water
1 tablespoon butter

1 teaspoon vanilla
Pinch of salt
2 cups nutmeats, unbroken

Boil sugar and water slowly together until it forms a soft ball in cold water. Take off stove and add butter, vanilla and salt. Beat until it thickens slightly. Add nutmeats. Drop by spoonfuls onto buttered wax paper. Do not double. Makes 25 pralines.

Mrs. Ted Marks (Mildred)

THISTLE

Pickles and Preserves

SWEET PICKLED PEACHES

12 pounds peaches	1 quart cider vinegar
6 pounds sugar	2 tablespoons whole cloves

Let vinegar, sugar and cloves come to a boil. Drop peeled peaches in mixture and cook until soft. Seal in hot sterile jars. Four times this recipe for 1 bushel peaches.

Mrs. S. N. Clark, Jr. (Carolyn)

CANTALOUPE PICKLES

3 quarts cantaloupe cubes	3 tablespoons whole cloves
(4 medium cantaloupes)	9 3-inch pieces stick cinnamon
¼ ounce powdered lime	1 lemon, thinly sliced
5 pounds sugar	1 lime, thinly sliced
2 quarts white vinegar	

Cut cantaloupes into quarters and remove seeds and pare. Cut cantaloupe into 1½ inch cubes. Cover with water in which ¼ ounce of lime has been dissolved. Soak overnight. Drain and cover with fresh water. Bring to the boiling point. Drain again. Cook 5 pounds sugar and vinegar with cloves and cinnamon (tied in a cheesecloth bag) for about 15 minutes. Remove spice bag. Cook melon in syrup until tender and transparent looking, about one hour. Add lemon and lime slices to syrup mixture. Boil 1 minute. Pack into hot sterile jars. Yield 8 to 10 pints.

Mrs. Julian K. Taylor (Elizabeth)

PICKLED FIGS
This is a sweet-sour taste, and delicious with meat!

6 quarts figs or about 8 pounds	1 quart vinegar
Water, salted	7 sticks cinnamon
8 cups brown sugar, firmly packed	1-2 teaspoons whole cloves

Cover figs with salted water (1 tablespoon salt to 1 gallon water). Bring to boil and simmer for 15 minutes. Combine sugar and vinegar, bringing to a boil. Add the spices to sugar mixture. Drain figs and add the boiling syrup mixture. Simmer 1 hour. Be sure figs are covered with syrup. Pack into hot sterilized jars. Makes 7 to 8 pints.

Mrs. Stephen Marsh (Donna)

WATERMELON RIND PICKLE

4 quarts prepared watermelon
    rind (use only Stoney
    Mountain melon)
1 small bottle Lilly's Lime
5 pounds sugar (10 cups)

1 quart white vinegar
2 pieces ginger root
2 tablespoons whole cloves
½ box stick cinnamon
1 lemon, thinly sliced

Use rind from Stoney Mountain melon as this is the only rind thick enough to pickle. Buy seeds from Hastings Seed Company, Atlanta, Georgia and plant your own melons!

Prepare watermelon rind by trimming dark skin and pink flesh from rind; cut in 1-inch pieces or as wanted. Dissolve lime in 1 gallon cold water and agitate by directions. Mix thoroughly and pour over rind to cover and soak overnight. If needed, add more water to cover rind. Turn rind several times while soaking. Always soak rind in an enamel pan or stainless steel pot. Lift rind out of pot and rinse thoroughly in cold water. Drain in colanders. Put in uncovered enamel pot and cover with cold water; add 2 pieces ginger root and let come to a boil and boil until thoroughly tender or about 30 minutes. Drain well in colanders using hand, if necessary to gently release more water. Tie cinnamon and cloves in a cheesecloth bag. Combine spice mixture with sugar, vinegar, lemon and simmer 10 minutes or until sugar is thoroughly dissolved. Add watermelon rind. Bring back to a boil and simmer uncovered until clear and until there is no woody residue when you test it for doneness. If syrup becomes too thick before rind is clear, cook ½ pint vinegar, ½ pint water and 1 pound sugar and add to pickles. Remove spice bag. Pack into boiling hot sterilized jars, leaving ⅛ inch head space. Adjust caps. One melon which is very large is enough to put up at 1 time. It takes at least a double recipe of syrup for 1 large melon. Yields about 7 to 9 pints for an average melon or 10 to 11 pints for a large melon.

Mrs. John M. Trask (Flora)

DILLY BEANS

Fresh green beans, small snaps
   are best
¼ teaspoon red pepper
   (for each pint)
½ garlic clove (for each pint)

½ teaspoon dill seed (for each pint)
Pint jars
1 cup vinegar
1 to 2 cups water
¼ cup salt

Wash beans and snap the ends. Tilting the jars, fill with beans so beans remain upright. To each jar add red pepper, garlic and dill seed. Heat together vinegar, water and salt. Pour into jars, seal and let stand for 4 weeks. Good served with pickled Polish sausage as an hors d'oeuvre.

Mrs. John W. Gray III (Molly)

SQUASH PICKLES

4 quarts small yellow squash,
   thinly sliced
2 quarts onions, thinly sliced
½ cup salt
2 quarts crushed ice

5 cups sugar
5 cups vinegar
1½ teaspoons turmeric
1 tablespoon mustard seed
1 tablespoon celery seed

Mix squash, onion, salt and ice. Let stand 3 hours. Drain and wash in cold water. Drain again. Mix sugar, vinegar, turmeric, mustard and celery seeds. Heat to boiling point, but do not boil. Stir constantly. Put squash and onion mixture into sterilized jars. Cover with hot syrup. Adjust lids. Immerse jars in simmering water. Process 10 minutes. Makes 8 to 10 pints.

Mrs. Charles Thompson (Cyndy)

ARTICHOKE PICKLE

1 peck Jerusalem artichokes,
   scrubbed and cut up in 1
   inch pieces
1 gallon vinegar
5 pounds sugar
3 pounds onions, peeled and
   sliced

1 1¼-ounce box dry mustard
3 tablespoons turmeric
1 cup salt
1 small piece of red pepper in
   each jar

Bring vinegar to a boil with sugar, onions, mustard, turmeric and salt. Pour over artichokes that have been placed in jars with red pepper. Yields 8 to 10 quarts.

Mrs. S. N. Clark, Jr. (Carolyn)

HELEN'S ARTICHOKE PICKLE

4 to 6 quarts artichokes, sliced
    and scrubbed
1 quart onions, sliced
6 green peppers, sliced
3 pounds cabbage, sliced
1 gallon water
1 cup salt
½ gallon cider vinegar

3 pounds sugar
1 tablespoon turmeric
1 tablespoon black pepper
3 tablespoons white mustard seed
1 9 to 12-ounce jar prepared
    mustard
1 cup flour

Soak vegetables overnight in 1 gallon water and 1 scant cup salt. Drain the next day. Mix vinegar, sugar, turmeric, pepper and mustard seed. Add to vegetables and boil 10 minutes. Add mustard and flour made into paste to hot vinegar mixture. Boil 5 minutes, stirring constantly. Seal in hot sterilized pint jars. Makes 12 to 14 pints.

Mrs. F. Bethea Rogers (Flora Kate)

BREAD AND BUTTER PICKLE

1 gallon small cucumbers
    (36 pickle size)
8 small white onions
2-3 green peppers
½ cup salt
1 quart ice

5 cups sugar
1½ teaspoons turmeric
½ teaspoon ground cloves
1 teaspoon celery seeds
2-3 tablespoons mustard seeds
5 cups vinegar

Wash and slice cucumbers and onions paper thin. Cut peppers in fine shreds. Mix salt with vegetables and bury pieces of ice in mixture. Cover with lid and let stand for 3 hours. Drain well. Combine sugar, spices, and vinegar and boil 10 minutes. Add drained vegetables. Place over low heat and stir occasionally with a wooden spoon. Heat mixture to scalding but don't boil. Do not over-cook. Place into hot jars and seal. Yields 6-8 pints.

Mrs. John M. Trask (Flora)

TERRY'S BREAD & BUTTER PICKLE

1 gallon medium cucumbers
6 large onions
¼ cup salt
5 cups sugar
5 cups cider vinegar

1½ teaspoons turmeric
½ teaspoon ground cloves
2 tablespoons whole mustard seed
1 teaspoon celery seed

Slice cucumbers just less than ¼ inch thick. Slice onions in rings. Alternate layers in large pan or crock and sprinkle layers with salt. Let stand 3 hours. Drain. Combine in kettle sugar, vinegar and all spices. Heat to boiling. Add vegetables and heat to boiling again. Pack in sterilized jars filling to top with the hot liquid. Seal at once.

Mrs. L. Brent Kuhnle (Terry)

KOSHER DILL PICKLES

20 to 25 pickling cucumbers
⅛ teaspoon powdered alum
    (for each quart jar)
2 heads of dill or 2 tablespoons
    dried dill seed (for each
    quart jar)
1 clove garlic (for each quart
    jar)

1 hot red pepper (for each quart
    jar)
1 grape leaf (for each quart jar)
1 quart vinegar
1 cup salt
3 quarts water

Wash cucumbers. Let stand in cold water overnight. Next day pack in sterilized jars. To each quart add alum, dill, garlic, red pepper and grape leaf on top. Combine vinegar, salt and water. Bring to boil. Fill jars and seal. Yields 6 to 8 quarts.

Mrs. Paul Neel (Nida)

FRESH KOSHER DILL PICKLES

3 or 4 medium size, firm
    cucumbers
1 clove garlic
1 slice medium size white
    onion

1 head fresh dill weed
1 tablespoon rock salt
¼ teaspoon ground turmeric
¼ cup white vinegar

Wash cucumbers well. Put ½ of the garlic, onion and dill in bottom of clean 1 quart jar. Cut cucumbers into quarters length ways and pack into jar. Top with remaining garlic, onion, dill weed. Add salt, turmeric and vinegar and fill with cold water. Screw on lid and let stand at room temperature for 2 or 3 days. Then place in refrigerator. These will keep in refrigerator for about 2 weeks. Yields 1 quart.

Mrs. Stanley Waskiewicz (Betty)

CABBAGE CHOW-CHOW

1 large cabbage, finely
   chopped
1 quart onions, chopped
1 quart green tomatoes,
   chopped (optional)
4 pods green or red peppers,
   chopped
1 quart vinegar

1 teaspoon whole cloves
6 leaves of mace
2 teaspoons white mustard seed
1½ pounds sugar
2 teaspoons ground mustard
1 tablespoon turmeric
Hot vinegar

Put first 4 ingredients in cold, slightly salted water and when it comes to a boiling point, let boil 1 minute. Drain and cover with cold water. Let stand 5 minutes. Drain well. While the cabbage mixture is draining, heat 1 quart vinegar with whole cloves, mace, white mustard seed and sugar. Mix in an earthen bowl the ground mustard and turmeric. Make this into a paste with a little hot vinegar. Add to vegetables and let stand a few minutes. Put in jars and seal.

Miss Fannie Van Sant

PICCALILLI

1 peck green tomatoes
8 large onions
1 head cabbage
3 red or green sweet peppers
1 cup salt
2 quarts vinegar
8 tablespoons mustard seed

1¼ pounds brown sugar
2 tablespoons cinnamon
¼ teaspoon cayenne pepper
2 tablespoons ground black pepper
2 tablespoons ginger
1 tablespoon cloves
1 tablespoon allspice

Grind or chop tomatoes, onions, cabbage, and peppers. Add 1 cup salt. Let stand overnight and drain. Add vinegar, brown sugar, mustard seed, cinnamon, black pepper and cayenne pepper. In a cheesecloth bag put cloves, allspice and ginger. Boil for 30 minutes stirring to keep from scorching. Seal in sterilized jars.

Mrs. Talbird Sams (Therese)

ZUCCHINI RELISH

10 cups zucchini, chopped
4 cups onion, chopped
5 tablespoons salt
1 green pepper, chopped
1 sweet red pepper, chopped
2¼ cups vinegar
6 cups sugar

1 teaspoon dry mustard
1 teaspoon turmeric
2 tablespoons cornstarch
2 teaspoons celery seed
2 teaspoons mustard seed
½ teaspoon black pepper

Mix onions and zucchini with salt and let stand overnight. Rinse well with cold water. Add peppers to squash. Simmer remaining ingredients for 10 minutes then add to vegetables. Heat to a full boil and cook 20 minutes. Seal in jars. Yields 8-10 pints.

Mrs. Mac Donald Dixon (Phyllis)

GREEN TOMATO RELISH

20 green tomatoes, ground
6 onions, ground
¼ cup salt
1 quart vinegar

4 cups sugar
2 tablespoons mustard seed
2 tablespoons celery seed
1 teaspoon salt

Add salt to tomatoes and onions. Let stand for 3 hours and then drain. Boil the remaining ingredients together for 2 minutes. Add tomatoes and onions to the boiling liquid mixture. Bring back to a boil. Pack in sterile jars. Seal.

Mrs. William J. Robicheau (Mary)

SAUERKRAUT RELISH

2 cups sugar
1 cup water
1 red pepper
1 green pepper, finely cut

2 cups celery, finely cut
1 16-ounce can sauerkraut,
    finely cut

Dissolve the sugar in water and bring to a boil. Add the green peppers, red pepper and celery to sauerkraut. Add sugar syrup to sauerkraut mixture. Let stand for 24 hours. Serve as salad or relish.

Mrs. John W. Leslie (Elizabeth)

PEAR RELISH

1 peck pears, ground
6 medium bell peppers, ground
5 large onions, ground
3 hot red peppers, ground
5 cups sugar

4 cups vinegar
2 teaspoons turmeric
2 tablespoons pickling spice (tied in cloth)
Salt to taste, about 2 tablespoons

Boil all ingredients for 30 minutes. Remove spice bag and seal in sterilized jars. Yields 14 pints.

Mrs. Stanley Waskiewicz (Betty)

TOMATO CATSUP
Excellent with black eyed peas.

1 peck tomatoes, peeled
10 large onions, chopped
6 tablespoons salt
4 tablespoons black pepper
1 teaspoon red pepper
2 teaspoons ground cloves
6 tablespoons ground mustard

6 tablespoons mustard seed
2 tablespoons celery seed
½ pound horseradish
2 teaspoons ground mace
2 teaspoons cinnamon
1 quart vinegar
1½ pounds white sugar

Cook all spices with tomatoes and onions until tomatoes are soft. Strain through sieve and add sugar and vinegar. Continue to cook until thick. Cooking may take 5 or 6 hours. Yields 8 pints.

Mrs. Sam Clark, Jr. (Carolyn)

CHILI SAUCE

24 large ripe tomatoes
10 to 12 medium size onions
8 green peppers
4 red peppers
3 cups celery, finely diced
2 tablespoons salt

⅛ teaspoon cayenne
2 cups white vinegar
3 cups sugar
½ teaspoon ground cloves
1 teaspoon allspice
2 teaspoons cinnamon

Put tomatoes, onions and peppers through the food grinder using coarse blade. Mix with celery. Bring to a boil. Cook 1 hour stirring frequently. Add rest of ingredients. Cook over low heat, stirring often for 45 minutes or until thickened. Place in sterilized jars and seal. Makes 12 pints.

Mrs. Henry Merriman (Marge)

TOMATO MARMALADE

2½ pounds ripe tomatoes,
   peeled and coarsely
   chopped

1 lemon, thinly sliced
1 teaspoon ground ginger
2 pounds sugar

Place tomatoes in a 3 quart saucepan for cooking. Add lemon and ginger. Bring to boiling point and simmer for 1 hour uncovered. Stir in sugar and boil uncovered for 30 minutes, stirring frequently until thickened. Ladle marmalade into hot jars. Cover immediately with ⅛ inch of hot, melted paraffin. Makes 5 8-ounce jars.

Mrs. MacDonald Dixon (Phyllis)

PUMPKIN CHIP MARMALADE

6 pounds pumpkin rind, cut
   1″ thick and thinly sliced
6 pounds sugar
1 ounce ginger root

1 tablespoon ground ginger
8 ounces crystallized ginger, cut up
3 lemons, thinly sliced and
   quartered

Use large, tender pumpkins. Mix pumpkin rind and sugar and let stand overnight. Add remaining ingredients and boil until pumpkin is clear in color. Put in jars and seal. Yields 15 pints.

Mrs. MacDonald Dixon (Phyllis)

WHOLE CRANBERRY JELLY

1 pound or 4 cups fresh
   cranberries, washed and
   picked over

2 cups water, hot, or enough to
   cover berries
2 cups sugar

In a saucepan combine berries and water. Cook on high heat, and when they begin to boil, stir with a wooden spoon up from bottom so they won't burn. Knock the berries back. As they boil, foam will appear and skim it off from time to time. Boil about 5 to 10 minutes. After all the berries have popped and after you have skimmed the foam off (be careful not to get juice), add sugar all at once. Stir thoroughly, but carefully so as not to crush the berries. They should be done in about 5 to 10 minutes after you add the sugar. Cranberries are done when the juice begins to gel. You can test by putting a little juice in a saucer. Don't cook too long as it will be candied. Seal in hot jars immediately. Recipe is easily doubled or tripled. Great to have after holiday season is over. Yields 2 pints.

Mrs. John M. Trask (Flora)

RED BEET JUICE JELLY

1½ pounds raw red beets,
　　peeled or scrubbed well
Water to cover
½ cup lemon juice

5 ounces powdered pectin
8 cups sugar
1 6-ounce package raspberry
　　gelatin

Combine beets and water. Boil until tender. Discard beets and reserve juice. Bring 6 cups of beet juice, lemon juice and pectin to a hard boil. Add sugar and gelatin all at once. Boil 6 to 8 minutes. Skim off foam. Pour into glasses and seal.

Mrs. Frank J. Kobes (Lydia)

HOT PEPPER JELLY

¾ to 1 cup hot pepper, seeded
　　and chopped
¾ cup bell pepper, seeded and
　　chopped

1¼ cups cider vinegar, divided
6 cups sugar
1 6-ounce bottle Certo
3 drops red or green food coloring

Put hot peppers, bell peppers and ¼ cup vinegar in blender and liquefy. Add mixture to 6 cups sugar and 1 cup vinegar in a large pot and bring to a boil. Remove from heat and skim foam. Add Certo and food coloring. Return to heat and boil hard 1 minute. Fill sterilized jars and seal. Yields 6 8-ounce jars.

Mrs. Wyatt Pringle (Sally)

PEPPER JELLY

1½ cups vinegar
4 medium green peppers, finely
　　chopped
4 medium hot peppers, finely
　　chopped

6½ cups sugar
1 6-ounce bottle of Certo
Green food coloring

Put vinegar and peppers into a saucepan and bring to a rolling boil. Stir in sugar until it dissolves.

Remove from heat. If you want clear jelly, strain through fine wire strainer. Wait 5 minutes and add Certo and food coloring.

Seal in canning jars. Makes 7 half pints.

Mrs. Henry Jackson (Peggy)

BENGAL CHUTNEY
Serve with all types of curry dishes.

8 pounds sour green apples,
   peeled, cored and sliced
2 pounds dark brown sugar
2 pounds Sultana raisins
8 ounces ginger root, peeled
   and finely chopped

1 quart vinegar
½ teaspoon salt
2 ounces fresh garlic, peeled and
   minced

Boil sliced apples to a pulp. Add all other ingredients and bring to rolling boil. Continue boiling for 1 minute. Seal in jars. Yields approximately 1½ quarts.

Mrs. R. B. Cumming (Barbara)

MOTHER'S CHUTNEY

1 cup raisins, chopped
1 cup currants, chopped
1 cup onions, chopped
1 quart white vinegar
5 cloves garlic, minced
1 cup green ginger, chopped
   or 3 tablespoons ground ginger

7 cups sugar
3 very small red peppers
3 tablespoons salt
10 cups green mangoes or pears,
   chopped
1 cup nuts, chopped

Put all ingredients except mangoes or pears and nuts together in saucepan. Cook slowly, about 2 hours or until somewhat thick and preserve-like. Add the mangoes or pears about 20 to 30 minutes before it is done. Yields 5 pints.

Mrs. Frank Osmanski (Edith)

GODMOTHER'S CHUTNEY

5 pounds pears or peaches,
   chopped
1 green pepper, chopped
1½ cups dark raisins
4 cups sugar
1 cup crystallized ginger,
   chopped
3 cups cider vinegar

½ teaspoon salt
1 cup water
¼ teaspoon powdered cloves
½ teaspoon cinnamon
¼ teaspoon nutmeg
¼ teaspoon allspice
6 bay leaves
1 6-ounce bottle Certo

Mix pears, pepper, raisins, sugar, ginger, vinegar, salt, water, spices and bay leaves. Simmer 6 to 8 hours at a very low heat. Bring to a boil and add Certo. Boil for 1 minute and remove bay leaves. Set aside, skim off foam and pour into sterilized jars and seal at once. Yields 8 8-ounce jars.

Mrs. Sam Stafford III (Nancy)

COCONUT CONDIMENT FOR CURRY

1 tablespoon butter
1 small onion, finely shredded
2 small cloves of garlic, minced
¼ bay leaf
1½ teaspoons ground
    coriander
3 tablespoons undiluted canned
    beef consommé

1 tablespoon lemon juice
6 ounces canned shredded coconut
3 tablespoons peanut oil
2 ounces broken dry roasted
    peanuts, optional
¼ teaspoon salt to taste

In heavy saucepan melt butter. Then add onion, garlic, bay leaf and coriander. Saute a few minutes or until butter is absorbed. Add the consommé and lemon juice with onion mixture to coconut in bowl. Mix thoroughly using clean hands. Spread out on cookie sheet. Sprinkle with peanut oil and roast uncovered in preheated oven until golden, stirring every 5 minutes. Cool; mix in peanuts and salt. Refrigerate airtight. Makes 1 to 2 cups. Serve at room temperature.

Mrs. Hugh O. Pearson (Nancy)

BLUEBERRY CONSERVE

1 cup orange (1 large), thinly
    sliced
½ cup lemon (1 medium),
    thinly sliced

2 cups water
2 cups blueberries, crushed
2½ ounces powdered pectin
6 cups sugar

Boil orange, lemon and water for 30 minutes or until rind is tender. Add blueberries and pectin, stir until it boils hard. Add sugar and stir constantly to full rolling boil. Boil 1 minute. Remove from heat. Skim and stir for 7 minutes. Ladle into sterilized jars and cover with melted paraffin. Yields 9 8-ounce glasses.

Mrs. Harold O. Danielson (Mary)

ORANGE BUTTER

8 oranges, seeded and ground
5 pounds sugar
1 20-ounce can crushed
    pineapple, undrained

½ cup butter

Combine all ingredients in a Dutch oven. Cook, stirring constantly, until mixture is thick or about 40 minutes. Pour into sterilized jars, adjust lids and process in boiling water bath for 10 minutes. Yields 5 pints.

Mrs. Bruce Whitney (Mary Olive)

FRESH PEACH CONSERVE

4 cups fresh peaches, peeled
    and crushed
1 2½-ounce box powdered
    pectin
5 cups sugar

½ cup maraschino cherries
1 cup nuts, chopped
1½ teaspoons vanilla extract
2 teaspoons orange rind, grated
½ teaspoon lemon rind, grated

Mix together peaches and powdered pectin. Bring to a full rolling boil over high heat. Boil 1 minute; stir constantly. Add sugar. Bring to a full rolling boil again. Boil 1 minute and remove from heat. Add cherries, nuts, vanilla extract, orange rind and lemon rind. Skim off foam. Stir with a metal spoon 5 minutes to prevent fruit from floating. Ladle quickly into hot sterilized jars, filling to within ½ inch of top. Seal at once. Makes 6 8-ounce jars.

Mrs. Bert Parker (Kaye)

PEAR HONEY

6 pounds pears, ground and
    drained
4½ pounds sugar
4 oranges, ground with peel
    (less 1 peel)

1 lemon, ground with peel
3 sticks or 1 teaspoon ginger may
    be added if desired

Combine all ingredients and cook until thick over medium heat. Seal in jars while hot. Yields 12 6-ounce glasses.

Mrs. Bruce Whitney (Mary Olive)

PEAR PRESERVES

7 or 8 large hard pears, peeled,
    cored and quartered
1 medium orange, seeded and
    quartered with rind
1 lemon, seeded and quartered
    with rind

4 cups sugar
1 cup crushed pineapple
¼ cup fruit liqueur, optional

Put pears, orange, and lemon in food mill or food processor and chop coarsely. Place sugar in a mound in the center of a heavy pot and pour fruit and pineapple on top. Cook 30 minutes stirring occasionally. Before placing in jars, fruit liqueur may be added if desired. Place in sterilized jars and seal.

Mrs. John H. Chiles (Lucy)

Men

BUD'S CRAB IMPERIAL

⅓ cup onion, finely chopped
⅓ cup green pepper, finely
   chopped
¼ cup butter
⅓ cup pimento, chopped
½ cup mayonnaise
2 teaspoons capers

3 tablespoons parsley, chopped
2 teaspoons Worcestershire sauce
2 teaspoons prepared mustard
½ teaspoon salt
Freshly ground black pepper
Paprika
2 pounds back fin crabmeat

Sauté onions and green pepper in butter until tender. Remove from stove and combine with pimento, mayonnaise, capers, parsley, Worcestershire sauce, mustard, salt, and black pepper. When well mixed, gently fold in crabmeat, avoiding breaking up the large lumps. Place mixture in crab shells greased with butter or in individual ramekins. Dot with butter, sprinkle with paprika and bake in 350 degree oven for about twenty minutes. Serves 10.

John H. Masters

SHRIMP AND CRAB CASSEROLE

4¼ tablespoons butter
1½ medium onions, chopped
1 large green pepper, chopped
2 cups milk
5 tablespoons flour

¾ teaspoon salt
½ pound sharp Cheddar cheese,
   grated
1 pound crabmeat
2 pounds boiled shrimp, chopped

In 3 quart saucepan melt butter. Sauté onion and green pepper for 10 minutes over medium heat. Add milk and stir until thoroughly heated. Add flour and stir until mixture thickens. Add salt, stir in Cheddar cheese until melted. Stir in crabmeat and shrimp. Pour into 2 quart casserole and heat in 425 degree oven until hot and bubbly. Serves 6 to 8.

Henry V. Boyce, Jr.

SHRIMP-STUFFED FLOUNDER

4 medium or 2 large flounder,
   filleted
½ cup butter or margarine,
   softened

Salt and pepper to taste
Lemon juice
1½ pounds shrimp, cleaned,
   deveined and split

Put half of the fillets in a shallow, aluminum foil-lined pan. Spread with ¼ cup butter, then sprinkle on salt, pepper and lemon juice. Place shrimp on fish, then cover with the other half of the flounder. Sprinkle with salt, pepper and lemon juice and spread with remaining butter. Cover tightly with aluminum foil and bake 40 minutes at 400 degrees. Serves 6.

Jack Chaplin

SHRIMP AND VEGETABLES IN WOK

1 tablespoon cornstarch
½ cup soup stock or canned
    bouillon or consommé
1 pound shrimp, uncooked,
    shelled and cleaned
2 tablespoons soy sauce
¼ teaspoon salt
1 teaspoon fresh ginger,
    chopped

1 tablespoon sherry
4 tablespoons cooking oil, divided
1½ cups onions, sliced lengthwise
1 cup celery, sliced diagonally
12 water chestnuts, sliced
    lengthwise
3 cups snow peas, partially thawed
    if frozen

Mix cornstarch and soup stock; reserve. Dredge shrimp with mixture of soy sauce, salt, ginger, and sherry. Heat wok, add 2 tablespoons cooking oil, stir in dredged shrimp. Work fast over a hot fire and when cooked, remove and reserve. Reheat wok and add 2 tablespoons cooking oil. Stir in onions and celery until partially sautéed; work fast over hot fire. When about one half cooked, add water chestnuts and snow peas. Continue cooking for 2-3 minutes. Add shrimp, cornstarch and soup mixture. Cook until thickened stirring constantly. Serve at once. Serves 8.

H. M. Hoyler

BACALAO A LA RIOJANA
(SALT COD, RIOJA STYLE)

½ pound salt codfish
Water
Flour
4 tablespoons olive oil

2 cloves garlic
1 large onion, sliced in rings
1 16-ounce can tomatoes
Salt and pepper to taste

Slice codfish one inch wide, two inches long. Soak in cold water for one hour. Rinse under cold water and replace in container with fresh water. Repeat this three times on hourly basis. Drain fish and dry on paper towels. Dust with flour. Heat oil in large cast iron skillet. Add garlic and remove when brown. Place codfish in oil and brown on all sides. Cook until done. Add onion rings to oil and sauté. Add tomatoes and salt and pepper. When a rich sauce has been obtained, return codfish to skillet. Serve at once. Serves 2.

George M. Potter

SHRIMP CURRY ANCHORAGE

½ cup butter
3 medium onions, finely
   chopped
2 cloves garlic, finely chopped
4 stalks celery, finely chopped
2 medium carrots, finely
   chopped
1 large apple, peeled and finely
   chopped
2 tablespoons curry powder
1 15 ounce can tomato purée
2 tablespoons flour

3-4 cups water
1½ teaspoons salt
¼ teaspoon fresh ground pepper
3 tablespoons mango chutney,
   chopped
1 cup heavy cream
3 tablespoons almonds, toasted
   and slivered
3 tablespoons soaked raisins
3 pounds cooked shrimp, shelled
   and deveined
White rice

In a large skillet heat the butter and all chopped ingredients until onions are transparent (about 5-10 minutes). Add the curry, tomato purée, and flour, cook at low heat for ten minutes. Stir in water, salt, pepper, and mango chutney, let cook for thirty to forty-five minutes. Add the cream and bring to a boil. Correct the consistency of sauce by adding water if it is too thick; if sauce is too thin, thicken by adding a little cornstarch diluted in water. Add shrimp. Pour curry into a hot serving dish, sprinkle with almonds and raisins. Serve with white rice. Serves six.

Edward Jaggi

TROUT AMANDINE

6 fillets of trout
1 cup milk
½ cup flour, sifted
1 teaspoon salt

¼ teaspoon black pepper
¼ cup butter
½ cup almonds, chopped
Parsley as garnish

Dip fillet in milk, then into flour seasoned with salt and pepper. Melt butter in skillet and cook fillets, browning on both sides. Remove fish from skillet, then add almonds and sauté. Pour over fish. Sprinkle with parsley. Tartar sauce adds good flavor. Serves 6.

Jim Warwick

SOUTHERN CATFISH STEW

4 medium catfish, cleaned and
    dressed
4 cups boiling water
4 cups potatoes, diced
2 cups onions, diced

2 cups fresh corn
2 tablespoons butter
2 cups milk
Salt and pepper to taste

Simmer catfish in water until fish flakes from bone. Remove fish from liquid, reserving broth. Remove bones from fish and set aside. Add potatoes and onions to fish broth, cook until tender, about 10 to 15 minutes. Add corn and cook until tender, about 10 minutes. Stir in butter, milk, salt and pepper to taste and reserved fish. Heat thoroughly. Serves 6 to 8.

J. A. Fuller

UNCLE JACK'S MEAT LOAF

3 pounds lean ground chuck
1 pound sausage meat
2 cups Pepperidge Farm
    stuffing

2 tablespoons onion, minced
¼ teaspoon salt
2 eggs
½ cup milk

Mix together ground chuck, sausage meat, stuffing, onion and salt. Beat together eggs and milk. Add to first mixture. Put into loaf pan and bake at 350 degrees for one hour. Serves 8.

John J. Lincoln, Jr.

SPAGHETTI SAUCE

¼ cup olive oil
2 medium onions, chopped
1 small bell pepper, chopped
3 cloves garlic, crushed
2 14-ounce cans Italian style
    tomatoes
1 12-ounce can tomato paste
1 teaspoon salt

1 teaspoon dried basil leaves
1 teaspoon sugar
2 tablespoons chopped parsley
½ teaspoon dried oregano leaves
⅛ teaspoon black pepper
1 cup red wine
½ pound hot sausage, crumbled
1 pound ground chuck

In hot oil sauté onion, bell pepper and garlic. Add tomatoes, tomato paste, salt, basil, sugar, parsley, oregano leaves, pepper and red wine. Mix well. Bring to a boil, reduce heat, simmer covered for at least two hours. Stir occasionally. Sauté sausage and then ground chuck, drain well and add to the above mixture. Simmer additional 30 minutes. Serves 6 to 8.

George L. Tucker

SUMMER SAUSAGE

2 pounds ground chuck
1 cup water
½ teaspoon black pepper
¼ teaspoon garlic powder

1 teaspoon peppercorns
2 tablespoons mustard seed
3 tablespoons Morton quick cure
  salt

Mix all ingredients together. Portion out onto sheets of aluminum foil. Roll into logs. Wrap tight and refrigerate overnight. Place logs into simmering water and simmer for 1 hour. Unwrap, drain and cool. Slice for sandwiches.

Michael V. Fell

HAM-AND-POTATO CASSEROLE

4 cups raw white potatoes,
  ¼ inch slices
1 pound baked ham, sliced
1 cup mild onion, sliced

1 10-ounce can cream of celery
  soup, undiluted
½ cup milk
½ teaspoon salt

In 2-quart buttered casserole, alternate layers of potato, ham and onion. In small bowl, mix together soup, milk, and salt. Pour over casserole. Cover and bake for 1 hour in preheated 350 degree oven. Serves 4.

Kenneth W. Olson

GODLOCK'S GOOSE

1 goose, cleaned and dressed
1 cup salt
4 cups water
Parsley
Chives
Garlic
Sage
Thyme
Basil

Nutmeg
Salt and pepper
4 bacon strips
12 roasted chestnuts, peeled
2 carrots, diced
1 medium onion, diced
1 medium apple, diced
1 cup chicken stock
1 cup white wine

Soak goose overnight in salt water mixture. Rub goose with herbs. Coat bacon strips on both sides with herb mixture. Stuff goose with chestnuts, carrots, onion, and apple. Lay bacon over the top of the goose. Add chicken stock and wine to pan. Bake at 325 degrees for three hours. Remove bacon and skim off fat.

Robert L. Huffines, Jr.

SMOKED VENISON

3 cups hickory blocks or chips,
    soaked in water overnight
Charcoal

1 venison loin, boned
Salt and pepper

Make a fire in a hooded charcoal smoker. When fire is going well, place drained hickory on top of coals. Salt and pepper venison, roll and tie. Place venison on center of rack and cover with hood. Cook 5-7 hours.

Arthur S. Jenkins

SCALLION, CLAM AND GARLIC PASTA

4 6½-ounce cans minced
    clams, reserve liquid
3 large garlic cloves, minced
6 tablespoons butter, divided
¼ cup parsley, minced

8 scallions, cut in ¼" slices,
    including tops
¾ pound homemade or Italian
    pasta, cooked al denté, drained
Lemon wedges

Combine clam liquid and two-thirds of the garlic in pan over medium high heat. Cook until liquid is reduced to 1¼ cups. Combine remaining garlic with 4 tablespoons butter and parsley. Blend until smooth. Put aside. Add clams to reduced clam liquid, lower heat, and simmer 5 minutes. Whisk in remaining butter, 1 tablespoon at a time. Remove from heat and add scallions. Toss cooked pasta with reserved garlic-parsley butter. Turn into shallow bowl. Spoon clam sauce over pasta, toss gently. Garnish with lemon wedges and serve at once. Serves 4-6.

Robert Holmes

NOODLES AU TIM

8 ounces long, medium egg
    noodles
2 cups sour cream
2 cups cottage cheese
1 clove garlic, minced
1 teaspoon Worcestershire
    sauce

Dash of Tabasco
¼ cup onion, chopped
¼ cup butter, melted
Salt and pepper to taste
Grated Parmesan cheese

Cook egg noodles in boiling, salted water for 10 minutes. Rinse in cold water. Combine sour cream, cottage cheese, garlic, Worcestershire sauce, dash of Tabasco, onion, butter and salt and pepper. Combine sour cream mixture with noodles and pour into greased 2 quart casserole. Bake covered at 350 degrees for 35 minutes, remove cover and bake 10 minutes more. Serve with grated Parmesan cheese. Serves 8.

Peter Neidig

GOLDEN EMBER SAUCE FOR CHICKEN

¾ cup cooking oil
¼ cup margarine or butter,
   melted
¼ cup lemon juice
1 tablespoon prepared mustard
2 tablespoons brown sugar
1 tablespoon salt

1 teaspoon paprika
¼ teaspoon pepper
2 teaspoons grated onion
2 cloves garlic, halved
½ teaspoon Worcestershire sauce
¼ teaspoon Tabasco sauce
¼ cup catsup

Combine all ingredients in a jar or bottle. Shake thoroughly. Let stand several hours before using. Stir well before brushing on chicken.

This is enough sauce to bar-b-que two 3 pound broilers. About two hours before cooking, brush chickens with sauce and let stand until ready to cook. Chicken should be removed from refrigerator and allowed to stand at room temperature for a few minutes before cooking. Place on grill as far from heat as possible, turn often basting with sauce each time. Takes about 2 hours.

This is also good for spare ribs, takes about half the cooking time.

Stanley Waskiewicz

OMELET YERBA BUENA

3 eggs
⅓ cup heavy cream
Salt and pepper
4 scallions, chopped
½ pound mushrooms, sliced
Pinch of thyme

2 tablespoons olive oil
Salt and pepper
1 ripe tomato, peeled and wedged
1 6-ounce Monterey Jack cheese,
   grated
1½ tablespoons butter

Beat eggs, cream, salt and pepper together with wire whisk. Sauté the scallions, mushrooms and thyme in olive oil until soft. Add salt and pepper. Add the tomato. Immediately add cheese, stir until melted and remove from heat. Heat butter in omelet pan or deep skillet (9 to 10-inch). Whip egg and cream mixture again with a wire whisk and pour into hot pan. Let it cook until set, then place filling mixture over ½ of the egg. Flip the other side over, cook until barely browned and until filling is hot. Serve at once. Serves 2 to 3.

Sam Stafford, III

CHEESE FILLING AND WINE SAUCE FOR CREPES

CHEESE FILLING:

6 tablespoons butter
½ cup all-purpose flour
2 cups milk
3-4 ounces Gruyére cheese,
    shredded

2 ounces sapsago cheese, shredded
2 egg yolks, beaten
Pepper and nutmeg to taste

Melt butter in heavy saucepan over low heat. Add flour and cook, stirring, for 1 minute. Add milk and cook stirring until thickened. Add Gruyere and sapsago cheese and stir until cheese melts.

Stir 2-3 tablespoons of cheese mixture into egg yolks. Gradually add egg mixture to remaining cheese mixture and mix well. Add pepper and nutmeg. Pour into a 9-inch square pan to cool. Chill 3-4 hours before using. Yields enough to fill 12 crepes.

WINE SAUCE:

3 tablespoons butter
3 tablespoons all-purpose flour
1 cup chicken broth
1 cup dry white wine
2 tablespoons whipping cream
1 egg yolk

Salt and pepper
2 tablespoons parsley, finely
    chopped
½ cup fresh mushrooms, sliced
    and sautéed

Melt butter in a heavy saucepan. Add flour and blend until smooth. Stir in chicken broth and stir constantly until smooth and thickened. Remove from heat and add wine. Combine cream and egg yolk, mix well, and stir in small amount wine sauce. Add egg mixture to remaining wine sauce. Cook stirring until thick and smooth. Season with salt and pepper. Add parsley and mushrooms. Cook 1 minute. Spoon over filled crepes. Yields 2½ cups.

Charles Beck

PANCAKES

3 eggs
1-1½ cups buttermilk
2 cups flour

1½ teaspoons salt
2 teaspoons baking soda
2-3 tablespoons butter, melted

Beat eggs and buttermilk together. Add dry ingredients and mix well. Add butter. Add more buttermilk if necessary until batter is thin enough to pour. Heat frying pan to 360-375 degrees. Cook until batter bubbles up, turn and cook other side until brown.

Edward Webb

OEUF NOËL

2 tablespoons light cream
1 dash Worcestershire sauce
1 dash salt and pepper
1 tablespoon chili sauce
1 drop Tabasco
1 2-inch square Cheddar cheese
1 egg

3 2-inch strips green pepper
3 2-inch strips bacon, partially
   cooked
Paprika
Tarragon

Rub a custard cup with waxed paper greased with butter. Add to the custard cup in the order given: light cream, Worcestershire sauce, salt and pepper, chili sauce, Tabasco. Swirl with fork to mix. Add Cheddar cheese, break in egg. Stick around edges so as not to break yolk. Alternate strips of green pepper and medium cooked bacon. Sprinkle top with paprika and tarragon. Place custard cup in a baking pan containing ¼ inch water. Bake at 325 degrees for 20 minutes or until egg sets. Serves one.

Noël Seeburg

HOT APPLE JUICE

1 quart apple juice
2 pieces of stick cinnamon
6 whole cloves

2 slices lemon, ⅛ inch wide
3 jiggers rum, optional
3 pieces of stick cinnamon, garnish

Heat apple juice, cinnamon, cloves and lemon to just under boiling point. Simmer five minutes. Pour into mugs with or without rum. Garnish each mug with a piece of stick cinnamon.

Louis Roempke

GREEK SALAD

1 head lettuce, cut in medium
   slices
1 cucumber, peeled and cubed
2 firm ripe tomatoes, cut in
   pieces
1 medium onion, sliced
1 tablespoon olive oil
2 tablespoons vinegar
1 tablespoon water

1 teaspoon garlic powder
Dash of sugar
Salt to taste
Sprinkle of lemon-pepper
   seasoning
¼ pound Feta cheese
Portuguese anchovies
Greek black olives

Mix first 12 ingredients together. Spread anchovies and olives on top. Serves 8.

Gus Frank

FREEZER RYE BREAD

9 cups all purpose flour
4½ cups rye flour
4 packages yeast
½ cup butter or margarine
2 tablespoons salt

3 tablespoons sugar
4 cups hot water
⅔ cup molasses
2 tablespoons caraway seeds

Combine all flours in large bowl. In another large bowl, combine two cups of flour mixture with yeast, butter or margarine, salt and sugar. With mixer at low speed, gradually add hot water, molasses, and caraway seeds until blended. Increase speed to medium, beat 2 minutes, occasionally scraping bowl with rubber spatula. Gradually beat in 2½ cups more of the flour mixture, or enough to make a thick batter, continue beating 2 minutes, occasionally scraping bowl with wooden spoon. Gradually stir in remaining flour mixture to make a soft dough (dough should be a little sticky). Turn dough onto lightly floured surface and knead until smooth and elastic, about 10 minutes. Add more all purpose flour while kneading, if necessary. Let dough rest 15 minutes. Cut dough into four pieces, shape each piece into a smooth round ball and place on two large greased cookie sheets. Or, with lightly floured rolling pin, roll each into a 12 x 8-inch rectangle. Starting at 8″ end, tightly roll dough jelly-roll fashion. Pinch seams to seal, press ends and tuck under. Place roll, seam side down, in greased 9 x 5-inch loaf pan. To bake bread same day, cover loosely with towel and let rise in warm place until slightly more than doubled, about 1 hour. If not baking bread same day, cover with plastic wrap and freeze until firm. To thaw, remove from freezer and let stand at room temperature, about 2 hours. Then let rise until slightly more than doubled, about 2 hours. To bake, preheat oven to 375 degrees. Bake 35 minutes or until loaf sounds hollow when lightly tapped with fingers. Makes 4 loaves.

Stephen K. Marsh

GAZPACHO III

2 tablespoons wine vinegar
4 tablespoons olive oil
2 cloves garlic, pressed
1 teaspoon shallot, finely sliced
Salt and pepper
¼ teaspoon ground oregano
3-4 cups ice water, divided

2 tomatoes, peeled, seeded and
   diced
1 cucumber, peeled and thinly
   sliced
1 bell pepper, diced
Ice cubes
1 cup croutons

Mix vinegar and oil in bowl. Add garlic, shallots, salt, pepper and oregano. Pour 1 cup ice water into bowl and add all remaining vegetables. Mix and let stand for 20-30 minutes in refrigerator. Stir in remaining ice water and ice cubes. Just before serving, remove ice cubes and add croutons.

Archie Hooton

CORN CHOWDER

5 slices raw bacon
3 tablespoons bacon drippings
1 medium onion, separated
     into rings and sliced
2 medium potatoes, pared and
     diced

½ cup water
1 17-ounce can cream style corn
2 cups milk
1 teaspoon salt
Dash of white pepper
Pat of butter for each bowl

In large saucepan cook bacon until crisp. Remove bacon; crumble and set aside. Reserve 3 tablespoons bacon drippings in saucepan; discard remainder. Add onion slices to saucepan and cook until lightly browned. Add potato and water; cook over medium heat until potato is tender, about 10-15 minutes. Add corn, milk, salt and pepper; cook until heated through. Pour into warm soup bowls. Top each serving with a pat of butter and crumbled bacon. Serve with crackers. Serves 4-5.

E. J. Blanchard

TURKEY BONE GUMBO

Turkey bones
Water
½ cup bacon drippings
1 cup flour
2 onions, chopped
3 cloves garlic, crushed
1 bell pepper, chopped
2 stalks celery, chopped
Approximately 2 quarts turkey
     broth
Salt and pepper
Tabasco

2 bay leaves
1 teaspoon basil
2 tablespoons chopped fresh
     parsley
2 cups turkey, chopped (more if
     you have it)
1 pound smoked sausage, cut into
     bite size pieces
Green onion tops, minced as
     garnish
Cooked rice

After turkey is carved, put bones into water and boil about 1½ hours until meat falls off bones. Make a roux of bacon drippings and flour. Add onions, garlic, celery, and bell pepper and cook until wilted. Add hot broth, salt, pepper, Tabasco, bay leaves, basil and parsley. Simmer one hour. Add turkey and sausage and cook 15 more minutes. Serve over rice and put a few minced green onion tops over each serving. Freezes well.

B. L. Credle

SWEDISH COFFEECAKE

¼ cup butter
1 cup sugar
1¼ cups flour
2 teaspoons baking powder

½ teaspoon salt
2 egg yolks
½ cup milk
2 egg whites

Cream butter and sugar. Sift together the flour, baking powder and salt. Beat egg yolks and combine with milk. Add this mixture alternately with the dry ingredients to the creamed butter and sugar. Beat egg whites until they are stiff but not dry. Fold them into the batter. Pour the batter into a 9 x 9 well-buttered pan. Sprinkle the cake with a mixture of sugar, cinnamon and nuts. Bake 30 minutes (or until it tests done) in a 350 degree oven.

TOPPING:
½ cup sugar
½ teaspoon cinnamon

¼ cup pecans, almonds or walnuts, chopped

Mix well.

Gunnar J. Erickson

HUSH PUPPIES

½ cup stone ground corn meal
½ cup flour
2 tablespoons onion, minced
½ teaspoon salt and pepper
½ teaspoon baking powder

½ teaspoon soda
¼ cup buttermilk
1 8¾-ounce can whole kernel corn
    with half the juice
Hot oil

Mix meal, flour, onion, salt, pepper and baking powder. Dissolve soda in milk and add to meal mixture. Add corn and juice. Beat well and drop from spoon into hot oil. Brown on both sides. These are good and fool proof. Yields 20 to 24.

Charles E. Friedman

YANKEE PEACH PIE

1 9-inch deep dish pie shell,
    partially baked
¾ cup sugar
¼ cup flour

Pinch of salt
8 peaches, peeled and halved
½ pint heavy cream

Mix sugar, flour and salt. Sprinkle half of mixture on pie shell. Place peaches on next. Sprinkle rest of the mixture over peaches. Pour heavy cream over peaches until they are covered. Bake 45 minutes in 350 degree oven. Serves 6 to 8.

Russell Hyman

STROM THURMOND'S PECAN PIE

3 eggs
1 cup dark brown sugar
1 cup light corn syrup
1 tablespoon butter or
    margarine, melted

⅛ teaspoon salt
1 teaspoon vanilla
1 cup pecans, chopped
9 inch pastry shell, uncooked

Beat eggs, adding sugar gradually; add syrup, butter, salt, vanilla and pecans. Pour into pastry shell. Bake at 350 degrees for 1 hour.

Strom Thurmond

PEANUT BRITTLE

1 cup white corn syrup
2 cups sugar
½ cup water
2 cups raw Spanish peanuts
    with red skins

1½ tablespoons butter
1½ teaspoons vanilla
2 teaspoons soda
¾ teaspoon salt

Cook in a heavy iron skillet the corn syrup, sugar and water until it reaches the soft ball stage (approximately 230 degrees). Test by dripping from a spoon until this forms the very finest of threads. At this point add the raw peanuts and continue cooking and stirring until the peanuts crack open (about 302 degrees). Turn off heat and stir in until blended, butter, vanilla, soda, and salt. Quickly pour brittle onto a surface lightly greased with butter, preferably marble but a cookie sheet will suffice, and then spread thin with a spoon. When cold, break into pieces.

John H. Masters

Index

TABLE OF EQUIVALENTS

FOOD EQUIVALENTS

Apples	3 pounds	= about 2 quarts, sliced
Baking Powder	1 t. single-acting	= ¾ t. double-acting
Cheese	1 pound	= 4½ cups
Cottage Cheese	1 pound	= 2 cups
Chocolate, unsweetened	1 square (1 oz.)	= 3-4 T. grated chocolate
Cornstarch	1 T.	= 2 T. flour
Crackers, graham	3 cups crumbs	= 30-36 crackers
Crackers, salted	1 cup fine crumbs	= 20 crackers
Dates, pitted	1 pound	= 2 cups
Eggs		
Whole	1 egg	= about 3 T.
	1 cup	= 5-6 eggs
Whites	1 white	= about 2 T.
	1 cup	= 8-10 whites
Yolks	1 yolk	= about 1 T.
	1 cup	= 14-16 yolks
Figs, chopped	1 pound	= 3 cups
Flour, unsifted	1 pound	= 3 cups
All-purpose, sifted once	1 pound	= 3¾ cups
Cake, sifted once	1 pound	= 2 cups
Gelatin, unflavored	1 envelope (Knox)	= 1 T.
Lemon	1 average size	= 2-3 T. juice, 3 T. rind
Lentils	1 cup dry	= 2 cups cooked
Macaroni	1-1¼ cups dry (4 oz.)	= 2¼ cups cooked
Marshmallows	½ pound	= 30 standard size
	1 standard size	= 10 miniature
Noodles	1½-2 cups dry (4 oz.)	= 2¼ cups cooked
Prunes, dried	1 pound, dried	= 2½ cups
	1 pound, cooked	= 4 cups
Punch	1 gallon	= serves approx. 20
	12 quarts	= 96 punch glasses
Raisins	1 pound seeded	= 2½ cups
	1 pound seedless	= 3 cups
Rice	1 cup raw	= 3-3½ cups cooked
	1 cup pre-cooked	= 2 cups
Shortening, Butter	1 pound	= 2 cups
	½ pound	= 2 sticks
	1 stick	= ½ cup or 8 T.
Spaghetti	1-1¼ cups raw (4 oz.)	= 2½ cups cooked
Sugar		
Brown, sieved and packed	1 pound	= 2⅛ cups
Confectioners' sifted	1 pound	= about 4 cups
Granulated	1 pound	= 2⅛ cups
Yeast	1 cake yeast	= 1 level T. active dry
	1 pkg. dry yeast	= 1 level T. active dry
Vanilla Wafers	1 cup crumbs	= about 22 wafers
Zweiback	1 cup crumbs	= 8-9 slices

SEA ISLAND SEASONS
Post Office Box 75
Beaufort, South Carolina 29901

Please send me _____ copies of SEA ISLAND SEASONS at $15.95
plus $3.50 handling. S.C. residents add 5% sales tax.
Enclosed is my check or money order for $_____ .

Name _____

Address _____

City_____ State____ Zip_____

SEA ISLAND SEASONS
Post Office Box 75
Beaufort, South Carolina 29901

Please send me _____ copies of SEA ISLAND SEASONS at $15.95
plus $3.50 handling. S.C. residents add 5% sales tax.
Enclosed is my check or money order for $_____ .

Name _____

Address _____

City_____ State____ Zip_____

SEA ISLAND SEASONS
Post Office Box 75
Beaufort, South Carolina 29901

Please send me _____ copies of SEA ISLAND SEASONS at $15.95
plus $3.50 handling. S.C. residents add 5% sales tax.
Enclosed is my check or money order for $_____ .

Name _____

Address _____

City_____ State____ Zip_____

Re-Order Additional Copies